Minding Spirituality

RELATIONAL PERSPECTIVES BOOK SERIES

LEWIS ARON AND ADRIENNE HARRIS
Series Editors

Minding Spirituality

Randall Lehmann Sorenson

THE ANALYTIC PRESS
2004   Hillsdale, NJ   London

Published by
The Analytic Press, Inc., Publishers
Editorial Offices:
101 West Street
Hillsdale, NJ 07642

www.analyticpress.com

Text design and composition by EvS Communication Networx, Pt. Pleasant, NJ

Earlier versions of chapters 2, 4, and 6 appeared in *Psychoanalytic Dialogues* and *Soul on
the Couch* (edited by Charles Spezzano and Gerald Gargiulo, TAP, 1997).

Library of Congress Cataloging-in-Publication Data

Sorenson, Randall Lehmann
    Minding spirituality / Randall Lehmann Sorenson.
        p. cm. – (Relational perspectives book series ; v. 24)
    Includes bibliographical references and index.
    ISBN 0-88163-344-5
    1. Psychoanalysis and religion. 2. Spirituality–Psychology. I. Title. II. Series.

BF175.4.R44S67 2004
200'1'9–dc22   2004063594

Printed in the United States of America
10 9 8 7 6 5 4 3 2

For Anita

About the Author

Randall Lehmann Sorenson, Ph.D. (1954-2005) was a Professor of Psychology at Rosemead School of Psychology in La Mirada, CA and Training and Supervising Analyst at the Institute of Contemporary Psychoanalysis in Los Angeles.

Contents

Acknowledgments

I am grateful for audience and panelist critiques during presentations of this book's chapters at annual conventions of the American Psychological Association (APA) or the APA Division 39 (Psychoanalysis) spring meetings in New York City, Los Angeles, Boston, Denver, Washington DC, Minneapolis, Santa Monica, and Santa Fe. Stimulating discussions over the years with my colleagues James Jones, Jeffrey Rubin, Steve Sandage, Michael Mangis, and Terri and Bob Watson have influenced my thinking, as have interactions with students and my fellow faculty members at the Rosemead School of Psychology and the Institute of Contemporary Psychoanalysis, where I have taught part time for 20 years and 10 years, respectively.

Over the past 25 years, the patients with whom I have worked have led me to mind spirituality in ways this book details. I am indebted also to the teachers and clinicians who have shaped me, especially Judith Broder, Joe Elmore, Richard Gorsuch, Victoria Hamilton, Stephen Mitchell, and Judith Vida. Carl and Paul Sorenson offered expert help with SAS statistical programming, and a Los Angeles study group on Relational psychoanalysis provided a context for invaluable feedback, especially from long-time members Sue Mendenhall, Helen Ziskind, and Elaine Bridge.

The Analytic Press has been all I could ask for as an author, including Stephen Mitchell's welcoming of this project, Paul Stepansky's support for an interdisciplinary volume, and timely and discerning guidance from Relational Perspectives Book Series editors Lewis Aron and Adrienne Harris. I am grateful for editorial assistance from Nancy Liguori and expert copy editing by Cynthia McLoughlin.

Anita Lehmann Sorenson's love, support, and challenge have sustained all of my work, and without her I could not have written this book.

Introduction

Throughout this book I use multiple methods to examine my topic. At times I interpret religious or spiritual experience using psychoanalytic theory. At other times I interpret the behavior of psychoanalytic groups using the sociology of religion. And at still other times I speak from personal experience or use quantitative empirical analyses. In the midst of these varying methods, however, one aspect abides: I am a clinical psychoanalyst. I believe this book is appropriate for a wide array of mental health practitioners, including psychodynamic or psychoanalytically oriented psychotherapists, students, pastoral counselors, and interested lay people, but this does not diminish that I write as a clinical psychoanalyst to clinical psychoanalysts. I invite us to take an interest in our patients' spirituality that is respectful but not diffident, curious but not reductionistic, welcoming but not indoctrinating. Another way of saying this, of course, is that all I want is what good psychoanalysis has always been. The problem with putting it this way is that it understates not only how what constitutes our ideal of "good analysis" is something of a moving target—and rightly so for any discipline that continues to evolve and change—but also how religion or spirituality has historically received problematic treatment from analysts as have few other expressions of cultural diversity, including socioeconomic status, race, ethnicity, gender, or sexual orientation. If my invitation is to what good psychoanalysis has always been, this doesn't mean it is what all psychoanalysts have always done. This book is a modest proposal to accept this inevitable discrepancy, to acknowledge the progressive changes in psychoanalytic treatment of spirituality that have evolved across the past several decades, and to outline possibilities for ongoing dialogue in the future.

In chapter 1, I introduce how psychoanalysis can mind spirituality in the threefold sense of legitimately being bothered by it, attending to it,

1

and even exercising stewardship or husbandry over it. I then place this thesis in a historical context in chapter 2. I argue that psychoanalytic theory has continued to shift and transform across the past 100 years, and that these shifts and transformations have radically different implications for the analysis of religious and spiritual experience. Chapter 3 puts the changes detailed in chapter 2 to an empirical test. My colleague Christine Benson and I analyzed nearly 7000 occurrences of the word *religious* in the first 75 years of psychoanalytic journals in order to see if how analysts addressed the topic was consistent with ongoing change in psychoanalytic theory. Our answer is a qualified Yes. The proportion of wholesale pathologizing of religion in psychoanalytic journals decreased significantly following Freud's death, compared to more nuanced and balanced accounts of religion that have appeared in the years since, although opportunity for more sophisticated and progressive treatment of the topic remains. Chapter 4 examines what such progressive treatment would look like in terms of clinical technique, and chapter 5 illustrates this with a clinical case presentation. Chapter 6 asks how to train future generations of psychoanalysts who are sensitized to the clinical considerations this book highlights. I argue that, as counterintuitive as it might seem, psychoanalytic education could benefit from exploring models of theological education. Chapter 7 concludes by posing a question that more traditional psychoanalytic formulations might reflexively reject as preposterous: Are psychoanalysis and religion in the same business? My answer is No, but I argue that the reasons for saying so are not what they once were, and that the new criteria for demarcation offer rich opportunities for interdisciplinary dialogue between psychoanalysis and spirituality.

The painting on this book's dust jacket is by Albert Bierstadt, a European-born New Englander and artist who visited the American West before it was widely populated. Bierstadt was well received for a time in his day, although, as is typical of nineteenth-century Romanticism, his critics faulted him for being overly subjective if his scenes did not correspond point for point with known geographic features. As I see it, another word for Bierstadt's sensibilities is *mythic*. Myths, it has been said, are things that never happened but always occur. The painting is titled *Merced River, Yosemite Valley* (1866). Whether there is such a view along that river I do not know, but I do know that for me Bierstadt powerfully depicts a sense of human finitude, at once frail and precious, before the enormity and grandeur of nature, and ultimately the cosmos, that can occasion spirituality; at first glance it is possible not to notice the people on the rock jetty, even though they are in the center foreground of the composition. In any case, Bierstadt's depiction is consistent with this book's treatment of spirituality as not something other-worldly or merely intangible, but as human experience that is embodied and situated.

Mapping Psychoanalytic Scholarship

Bierstadt traveled west with a team whose tasks included cartography, and one of my goals in this Introduction is to offer a provisional map of psychoanalytic scholarship. Victoria Hamilton (1996) interviewed prominent psychoanalysts in North America and Europe about their views on analytic theory and technique. She found that Kleinians and self psychologists, despite being mirror opposites of each other on many substantive points, were remarkably similar sociologically. Both groups tended to stick to themselves, quoted heavily from their own traditions, and rarely mentioned psychoanalytic scholarship outside their own clans. Empirical analysis revealed a third group of North American analysts that read widely in psychoanalytic literature and was conversant with multiple points of view (including Kleinian, self psychological, and others)—a group I believe has become the American Relational analysts. I describe Hamilton's research in more detail in chapter 6, but for my present Introduction I extended her work using multidimensional scaling, and instead of asking analysts in a two-hour interview to *say* who had influenced them, I decided to check to see *whom they actually cited* in their published articles over a 10-year period.

To assess Relational psychoanalysis, I used *Psychoanalytic Dialogues* from 1991 through 2000.[1] For Kleinian psychoanalysis across the same years I used *Melanie Klein and Object Relations*,[2] and for self psychology I

---

[1] Relational psychoanalysis has emerged as a tradition with two distinct meanings: (1) a broad scope that includes all of object relations, self psychology, intersubjectivity theory, infant research, and interpersonal psychoanalysis; and (2) a more narrow focus on those analysts who are selectively appropriating these sources to create a new psychoanalytic movement. To distinguish these two uses of the word relational throughout this book, the latter group of analysts is capitalized as Relational and the former is not. For further definition of Relational psychoanalysis, see chapter 1.

[2] With Vol. 14, No. 2 in 1996 it was retitled the *Journal of Melanie Klein and Object Relations*, which ended with Vol. 17, No. 2 in 1999. In order to sample Kleinian journals across the same 10-year period, I needed one more year, so I used Vol. 1 of the *Kleinian Studies Electronic Journal*, an Internet-based journal that began in 2000, just after the conclusion of the previous Kleinian journal. In what follows I refer to this sequence of three Kleinian journals by the shorthand *Melanie Klein and Object Relations*.

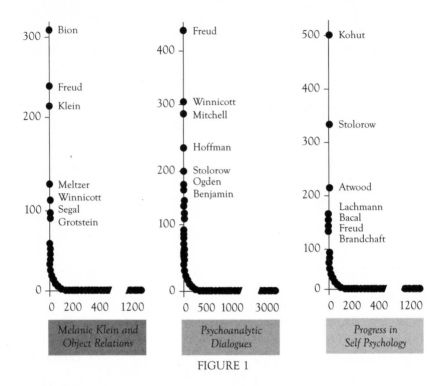

FIGURE 1

used *Progress in Self Psychology*.[3] While these three publications are not, of course, the only venues for Relational, Kleinian, and self-psychological perspectives, each is a significant representative of, and forum for, the advancement of its theoretical traditions. Tallies of the names that appeared in the references for articles in each publication across the decade are summarized in Figure 1. The horizontal axes list the unique names found,[4] which are sorted by how many times each name appeared, as plotted on the graphs' vertical axes.

Two things are immediately apparent from the graphs. First, as the long and contiguous series of dots to the right on each graph depicts,

[3]Self psychologists often entertained the possibility of producing a quarterly or semiannual journal, a project of which Kohut himself approved, but financing such a project proved daunting. Not long after Kohut's death, a group of self psychologists decided instead to combine the most prominent papers in self psychology from the previous 12 months into a recurring annual volume whose length and quality would be comparable to a quarterly journal, thus generating the serial publication *Progress in Self Psychology* (Goldberg, 1985, pp. vii–viii).

[4]There were 1244 in *Melanie Klein and Object Relations*, 3057 in *Psychoanalytic Dialogues*, and 1154 in *Progress in Self Psychology*.

most authors were cited once in the journal and then never appeared again throughout the decade. The next most common frequency was to be cited just twice. In fact, 90% of authors were cited three times or fewer for each journal's entire decade. The other result that is immediately apparent is depicted in the vertical ascent of the most frequently cited authors on the left side of the graphs. If most authors are cited rarely, a handful of other authors are cited frequently, and, among these, who is cited varies according to the journal's psychoanalytic tradition. All three traditions cite Freud frequently, although his relative ranking varies and is supplemented by other voices. For Kleinians, Bion and Klein are also central; Relationalists add Mitchell and Winnicott; and self psychologists focus on Kohut and Stolorow.[5] For all three publications, there was a gap below the seventh most frequently cited author, after which there was a contiguous slope that turned into the long stream of less often cited authors to the right on each graph. I used this break as a naturally occurring threshold and submitted the seven most frequently cited authors above it in each tradition to multidimensional scaling.

A good way to explain multidimensional scaling is that it works a lot like finding the distance between any two cities on a map, only in reverse. On a map, you find the distance by measuring with a ruler and converting the measurement to miles using the map's scale. Multidimensional scaling works the other way around: give it all the pairwise distances between cities and it creates the map. The difference is that, in social science, the space is perceptual, not geographic, with perceptual space defined in this instance by the co-occurrence of cited names in the list of references. The more often two cited names both appear in articles' reference lists, the more proximal these names are in conceptual space. By contrast, names that rarely co-occur in articles' references are mapped as more distal to one another. I had a computer count every pairwise occurrence of the seven most cited authors in *Melanie Klein and Object Relations*, *Psychoanalytic Dialogues*, and *Progress in Self Psychology* from

---

[5] I am well aware that Wilfred Bion was an original theorist in his own right, not classifiable simply as "Kleinian," and that Kleinian theory itself values critical thinking such that to categorize even those often regarded as "Kleinian" is something of a misnomer. I also affirm that Robert Stolorow and other Intersubjectivists are meaningfully distinct from self psychology, and that self psychology has by now gone through multiple generations, including classical and more contemporary psychologies of the self. In the research summary that follows, for purposes of parsimony I acknowledge these richly varied traditions by the shorthand of "Kleinian" or "self-psychological"; a basic point of the research is that there are important differences between analysts, even among those perceived as belonging to a common tradition.

Multidimensional Scaling of
Most Frequently Cited Authors 1991–2000 in

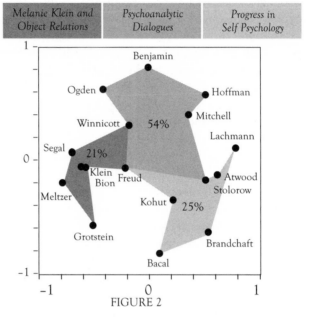

FIGURE 2

1991 through 2000. A total of 899 articles generated 22,721 instances of a name that appeared in the reference section. Because some of the top seven authors in one journal were also among the most cited in one or both of the other journals, there were 17 unique names: George Atwood, Howard Bacal, Jessica Benjamin, Wilfred Bion, Bernard Brandchaft, Sigmund Freud, James Grotstein, Irwin Z. Hoffman, Melanie Klein, Heinz Kohut, Frank Lachmann, Donald Meltzer, Stephen Mitchell, Thomas Ogden, Hannah Segal, Robert Stolorow, and Donald Winnicott. The resulting similarity matrix was analyzed by multidimensional scaling, which produced the map shown in Figure 2.[6]

As is evident from the map, self psychologists occupy a narrow band extending diagonally from Bacal to Lachmann, with a slender peninsula to Freud accessed via the group's primary interpreters, Kohut and Stolorow. Kleinians occupy a narrow crescent whose center hinges on

---

[6]A convention for determining the number of dimensions to use in multidimensional scaling is to accept models with Stress values less than .200; a two-dimensional model yielding a Stress value of .194 and accounting for .924 of the dispersion in the present data was therefore suitable. For this research, I did not attempt to interpret the two dimensions.

Bion and Klein, extending in one direction toward Meltzer and Grotstein, and in another toward Freud and Winnicott. It is important to note that, substantively, the self psychologists and Kleinians have no point in common other than Freud—and what they do with him goes in opposite directions. According to authors in all three journals, the most prominent self psychologist who is perceived as having the greatest affinities for object relations theory is Bacal, and the Kleinian seen as having the most interest in self psychology is Grotstein. Even so, the perceptual space between Grotstein and Bacal is greater than, for example, Grotstein and Bion or Bacal and Kohut.

Multidimensional scaling shows that authors who cite Klein are also very likely to cite Bion; authors who cite Kohut also tend to cite Stolorow. Freud and Winnicott, who are the most cited authors in the Relational literature, are less tightly associated than Bion and Klein, or Kohut and Stolorow, in the Kleinian and self-psychological literature, respectively. Some Relationalists are perceived to be closer to the Kleinians—especially Ogden, and to a lesser degree Benjamin—although for both this occurs via their more immediate proximity to Winnicott. Other Relational authors, like Stolorow, overlap more with the self psychologists and are quite distal from Relationalists with Kleinian or other object relational sensibilities. Given their respective distances on this map produced by multidimensional scaling, it would seem that Stolorow's version of "intersubjectivity" is not interchangeable with Benjamin's, or, for that matter, with Ogden's (1989) concept of a "psychoanalytic third," even though all three authors are influential sources for Relational psychoanalysis. The third most often cited author in the Relational literature, Mitchell, is perceived as somewhere between the Kleinians and self psychologists, although he is also situated in Relational territory for which Hoffman is an exemplar.

I offer this research in my Introduction not only to locate Relational psychoanalysis (a move worth making since, to the best of my knowledge, this is the first book by a clinical psychoanalyst that addresses spirituality from explicitly Relational psychoanalytic perspectives) but also to illustrate what I mean by multiple methods, in this case quantitative empirical analysis and how the sociology of religion can illuminate the behavior of psychoanalytic groups. Recall from the map that whereas the Kleinians and self psychologists have almost nothing in common substantively, the Relationalists share common boundaries that extend with the Kleinians all the way from Freud to Winnicott, and with the self psychologists all the way from Freud to Stolorow. These common boundaries were not, however, something all groups used for mutual exploration. During the 10-year period I examined, articles in *Psychoanalytic Dialogues* cited Kleinians and self psychologists, but articles in neither *Melanie Klein and Object Relations* nor *Progress in Self Psychology* reciprocated by citing Relationalists at commensurate levels. The lack of reciprocity was so great that the likelihood of observing this result solely by chance is less than 1 in 1000.[7] Another way of saying this is that the Relationalists read and interacted with the Kleinian and self psychological literature, but there was not commensurate evidence that the Kleinians and self psychologists read the Relational literature—or, if they did read it, they did not interact with it as much as evidenced by their citations.

In Hamilton's (1996) research, the Kleinians and self psychologists were tightly knit groups, a finding that the present data replicate. Both Kleinian psychoanalysis and self psychology are strong traditions with a canon of core writings that are cited frequently by those working within either tradition. If authors are Kleinians or self psychologists, whom they cite relies on a list of names that are closely correlated. When considering the total area of each of three groups on the map, cited authors in *Progress in Self Psychology* and *Melanie Klein and Object Relations* were distributed in tightly associated conceptual space (accounting for just 21% and 25% of the mapped areas, respectively), whereas the Relationalists covered more than twice as much intellectual territory (54%). One way to understand high group cohesion sociologically is via fundamentalism, a term I address in chapters 1 and 6. For now I wish only to note that some analysts tend to assume that analytic groups that exhibit traits of fundamentalism have suddenly and inexplicably become "religious." Given the fractious history of psychoanalysis during the past 100 years or so,

---

[7]The most cited Kleinian authors unique to that tradition and not already among the most cited Relational authors (namely Bion, Grotstein, Klein, Meltzer, and Segal, excluding Freud and Winnicott, who were common to both traditions) were cited 232 times in 529 articles in *Psychoanalytic Dialogues*. The most cited Relational authors unique to that tradition and not already among the most cited Kleinian authors (Benjamin, Hoffman, Mitchell, Ogden, and Stolorow), however, were cited significantly less often, proportionally—50 times in 172 articles in *Melanie Klein and Object Relations* ($\chi^2 = 15.280$, 1 df, $p < .001$). In similar fashion, the most cited self-psychological authors unique to that tradition and not already among the most cited Relational authors (Atwood, Bacal, Brandchaft, Kohut, and Lachmann, excluding Freud and Stolorow, who were common to both traditions) were cited 494 times in 529 articles in *Psychoanalytic Dialogues*. By contrast, the cited Relational authors unique to that tradition and not already among the most cited self-psychological authors (Benjamin, Hoffman, Mitchell, Ogden, and Winnicott) were cited significantly less often, proportionately—155 times in 198 articles in *Progress in Self Psychology* ($\chi^2 = 173.014$, 1 df, $p < .001$).

this assumption makes about as much sense as if religious groups, when encountering fundamentalism, accused one another of becoming suddenly and inexplicably "psychoanalytic." Groups behave in fundamentalistic ways not because they are religious or psychoanalytic but because they are anxious over knowledge that is necessarily partial, provisional, incomplete, a construction. In the face of uncertainty, one recourse is toward certitude, to know beyond doubt, to be a part of a group that knows, for which outsiders are in error and need not be read except as illustrations of false steps. Religion and spirituality certainly can be used for defensive purposes to justify xenophobia and marginalize outsiders, but this is not its only possible effect. It also can generate increased respect for diversity and a genuine openness for dialogue with those outside one's own tradition. The same obtains in our use of psychoanalytic theory.[8]

Four clarifications may be helpful. First, the map produced by multidimensional scaling is not a depiction of where the various theorists actually are with respect to one another's theories, nor is it where the various theorists would necessarily locate themselves in relation to each other. It is a map of where they are *perceived to be* according to more than 900 authors who cited them over a 10-year period.[9] Second, I do not view quantitative research as something that trumps all other possible conversations, as though it accounts for "what really happened" and banishes

---

[8]We could also extend this and say the same applies to fundamentalism's influence on terrorism. Philip Ringstrom (2002) perceptively noted that fundamentalism has both religious and secular forms. Ruth Stein (2002), in a thoughtful analysis of the 9/11/01 terrorist attacks, pondered why so few analysts have written on the conjunction of religiosity and evil. From the perspective of social psychology, James Waller (2002) offers at least the beginning of an answer to Stein's question. Waller studied not the principal architects of terror or their midlevel bureaucrats, but rather the (otherwise) ordinary people who actually pulled the trigger, released the poison gas, or bulldozed mass graves. Waller's historical examples are as chilling as they are gripping, and if the psychological model he advances to explain terrorism is true, it also accounts for a dearth of writing on the conjunction of religiosity and evil. In Waller's multifactorial model, it is the social death of the Other that promotes and permits terrorism, something for which religion and spirituality certainly *can* be used, but not necessarily or invariably so. If all terrorists are fundamentalists, not all fundamentalism is religious, and not all religion is fundamentalistic.

[9]Although some of the 17 most cited authors had their *own* articles published in the journals and time period under examination, thus making the resulting map partially a reflection of these authors' perceptions of themselves and each other as well, such occurrences were a distinct minority; of the 819 articles in the three journals between 1991 and 2000 that cited one or more references, 737 (90%) were written by authors *other* than the 17 on the map.

all else as mere opinion or speculation. Some who will laud the original research I offer throughout this book (including, in later chapters, time series analysis and structural equation modeling) may also deem this research incompatible with my interest in hermeneutics, just as those who share my interest in narrative constructions may assume that this obviates the need for empirical scrutiny. I do not see it this way. I think familiarity with philosophical hermeneutics makes for more interesting original research and I think interesting original research makes for richer dialogue within broader cultural horizons. Third, it is important to note that people can switch group memberships, although if they came from a group with strong cohesion, they often gravitate to a new group that is similar sociologically. A child raised in a Baptist household may become a self psychologist as an adult; Pentecostals or Calvinists may become Kleinians; analysts who no longer are Kleinian often become self psychologists. When this switch occurs, adherents typically view their previous group membership with embarrassment and sheepishness and tend to distance themselves from their previous commitments, even though their new group has similar characteristics sociologically. Fourth, the boundaries on the map I have produced are not static or permanent. Just as geopolitical boundaries change periodically, often dramatically so, so does any map of psychoanalytic scholarship. Were this research to be replicated for subsequent decades, I would not be surprised if the resulting map were profoundly different. After all, Kleinian and self psychological views are dynamic, vibrant traditions that continue to grow and change in ways that those outside the tradition are prone to underestimate. As for Relational theory, the decade I examined was the first for *Psychoanalytic Dialogues* and it is possible the journal's openness to dialogue with other traditions may be an artifact of its initial stages. As Relational psychoanalysis matures and progresses, it may begin to cite authors primarily from within its own tradition and to show less interest in outsiders, as is the case for Kleinian and self-psychological views, which are psychoanalytic orientations with more established traditions. In any case, I do not view high group cohesion as an unalloyed liability; as I argue in chapter 6, it also can promote a shared language that supports theoretical refinement in successive generations of practitioners.

The most common way of imagining a relationship between psychoanalysis and spirituality is to envision spirituality as something like a dependent variable. According to this arrangement, spirituality is the product of psychoanalysis, the independent variable, which explains spirituality through various psychological processes. This strategy has been a fruitful one, although, as I detail in chapters 2, 4, and 5, it also suffers from certain conceptual and clinical liabilities. A less common yet no less fruitful strategy is one that imagines neither psychoanalysis nor spirituality as the cause of the other, and instead sees both as parallel and complementary approaches to problems in living, an option I take up in chapter 7. A third and rarely entertained possibility reverses the usual arrangement and considers how spirituality might influence our own psychology and how we work clinically. I turn to this third possibility as a way of concluding my Introduction, using notions of kenosis and alterity in Christian spirituality to describe my abiding interest as a clinical psychoanalyst.

Kenosis and Alterity in Christian Spirituality

Kenosis is a word that means "self-emptying" and it appears in a hymn that was sung in the first century of the Christian church. A stanza in the hymn affirms that Jesus, who though God, emptied himself of a demand for power (Phil. 2), an ideal that Christians are challenged to approximate in their own lives. I don't think Christianity is unique in affirming this virtue of self-emptying. The concept of *sunyata* in Buddhism seems similar, for example, and in any case, kenosis, or what Thomas Moore (2002) calls being empty of ego, is central to human flourishing: "Jealousy empty of ego is passion. Inferiority empty of ego is humility. Narcissism empty of ego is love of one's soul" (pp. 13–14).

In my clinical work, a patient will occasionally lose track of his or her thought. When that happens, sometimes we will just wait and see what happens next. Other times we may explore what possible conflict interfered with his or her thought. And at still other times, I will propose that I say something and then see where that takes us. In those moments, if I offer some dynamic formulation that has been germinating in me, possibly a construction that connects the transference with genetic conflicts from the patient's family of origin, when I finish, it is not uncommon for the patient to smile and volunteer with renewed enthusiasm, "I remembered what I wanted to say!" When moments like that first occurred, I began to wonder if my comments were merely ill-timed or if I was something like a therapeutic white noise machine—random background noise that masks other sounds—but I don't think that is quite right. That metaphor is too impersonal and it de-emphasizes the human quality of my presence. I have things to say. Some of them I believe are important and I want others to view them as important, too. And it is certainly possible that patients may thwart my interpretations or want to avoid them. But I also am not transfixed with the prospect of my patients having to pay attention to me, whether they have lost their thought or otherwise.

Recently I offered what I thought was useful insight for a patient. When I had finished speaking, she paused, looked off to the side with a thoughtful look in her eye, and confessed, "All kinds of interesting things occurred to me while you were talking." I hear this sort of comment all the time. In her case I, too, found what she had to say really interesting, although it was only obliquely related to what I had said. I sometimes bemusedly tell myself that my patients seem to do some of their best work while I am talking because, in these moments, they are often only half listening to me. It is much the same thing for me as a teacher. If I peer at students' (to me) upside-down notepads and spy that, after an hour or more of class time that seems to have gone by quickly, all they have written is the class name and date at the top of the page and nothing more, I often suspect it has been a good class. Their empty page of notes does not necessarily mean that they did not learn anything; sometimes they may have found the discussion, along with their own thoughts, interesting or engrossing enough that they didn't want to interrupt themselves by writing any of it down. An acquaintance who is a playwright once remarked to me that the role of the artist is to give words to something that the rest of us cannot articulate, a task that was, my acquaintance suggested, analogous to my own role as a psychoanalyst. I replied that, for me, it was as much the other way around, that my job was to be the appreciative and willing audience to my patient's artistry. I am reluctant to play the part of the analyst as bard, the oracle who divines and interprets for the benefit of an appreciatively mute patient. For all I know, that may be the role of great art as well—that its function is not simply to speak for us, but to call forth from us the claiming of our own convictions, many of which we may not even have known were ours until we heard ourselves say so.

In these examples I am not suggesting at all that I set out self-consciously to be kenotic, or that all Christians (or only Christians) are. I also suspect that my being an analyst influences what kind of Christian I am. But—and this is my point—I also suspect that my being Christian influences what kind of analyst I am. It is my impression that years of participation in communal spiritual practices (liturgy, meditation on sacred texts, social service, etc.) partially shape and influence my character. And my character, for better or worse, impacts the work I do. The spiritual communities of which I have been a part value and model kenosis, so much so that I even hope those who turn the pages of this book will find the thoughts that are occurring to them while reading are as interesting as anything I have written.

Alterity, a word that is based on the Latin *alter* (other), simply means "otherness" and the most prominent Christian text about otherness is Jesus' parable of the Good Samaritan. Clarence Jordan, founder of Koinonia Farms, a pioneering interracial farming community in Georgia, translated the Greek New Testament into what he called *The Cotton Patch Version* because, in his view, "The Scriptures should be taken out of the classroom and stained-glass sanctuary and put out under God's skies where people are toiling and crying and wondering, where the mighty events of the good news first happened and where alone they feel at home" (Jordan, 1968, p. 7). Here is Jordan's (1969) updated version of the dialogue with Jesus about the good Samaritan, recast as mid-twentieth century figures in the deep South (and with Jordan's footnotes inserted parenthetically):

> One day a teacher of an adult Bible class got up and tested him with this question: "Doctor, what does one do to be saved?" Jesus replied, "What does the Bible say? How do you interpret it?" The teacher answered, "Love the Lord your God with all your heart and with all your soul and with all your physical strength and with all your mind; and love your neighbor as yourself." "That is correct," answered Jesus. "Make a habit of this and you'll be saved." But the Sunday school teacher, trying to save face, asked, "But . . . er . . . but just who *is* my neighbor?"
>
> Then Jesus laid into him and said, "A man was going from Atlanta to Albany and some gangsters held him up. When they had robbed him of his wallet and his brand new suit, they beat him up and drove off in his brand new car, leaving him unconscious on the shoulder of the highway. Now it just so happened that a white preacher was going down that same highway. When he saw the fellow he stepped on the gas and went scooting by." (His homiletical mind probably made the following outline: 1. I do not know the man. 2. I do not wish to get involved in any court proceedings. 3. I don't want to get blood on my new upholstering. 4. The man's lack of proper clothing would embarrass me upon my arrival in town. 5. And finally, brethren, a minister must never be late for worship services.) "Shortly afterwards, a white Gospel song leader came down the road, and when he saw what had happened, he too stepped on the gas." (What his thoughts were we'll never know, but as he whizzed past, he may have

been whistling, "Brighten the corner where you are.") Then a black man traveling that way came upon the fellow, and what he saw moved him to tears. He stopped and bound up his wounds as best he could, drew some water from his water-jug to wipe away the blood, and then laid him on the back seat." (All the while his thoughts may have been along this line: "Somebody's robbed you; yeah, I know about that, I been robbed, too. And they done beat you up bad; I know, I been beat up, too. And everybody just go right on by and leave you laying here hurting. Yeah, I know. They pass me by, too.") "He drove on into Albany and took him to the hospital and said to the nurse, 'You all take good care of this white man I found on the highway. Here's the only two dollars I got, but you all keep account of what he owes, and if he can't pay it, I'll settle up with you when I make a pay-day.' Now if you had been the man held up by the gangsters, which of these three—the white preacher, the white song leader, or the black man—would you consider to have been your neighbor?"

The teacher of the adult Bible class said, "Why, of course, the nig-, I mean, er . . . well, er . . . the one who treated me kindly."

Jesus said, "Well, then, *you* get going and start living like that!" [Luke 10:25–37].

Jesus redefined neighbor in terms of praxis, not propinquity. Jesus' interrogator was asking, At what point does sufficient interpersonal distance make someone no longer my neighbor? Jesus reframed the question to make it be about how decently we treat one another, rather than the ideologies to which we give intellectual assent (although the two may be related). Neighbor is determined by what we *do*, and not by the relative absence of alterity. Clinically, of course, we experience alterity even within ourselves, and not just between us and other people. I view one measure of how successful analysis has been that patients come to view themselves with loving curiosity—even about things in themselves that they hate or abhor—and to view their own minds as objects of potentially endless fascination. As I see it, the challenge is to extend neighbor love to disowned or distal regions of ourselves, as well as to others. Ironically, if we are to love our neighbors the way we love ourselves, sometimes that is just the problem: we can be as brutally dismissive or mindless of aspects in ourselves that are robbed, beaten and, as Jordan says, "unconscious," as we are of these in other people.

At the same time, I do not wish to minimize the very real impact of meaningfully different cultures and traditions, and I keenly appreciate that many of the sensibilities that I express throughout this book will necessarily strike some readers as foreign or alien. A different way of saying this is that I freely recognize that for some readers I will be the Other, and my hope is that when that happens neither of us will, to use Jordan's language, step on the gas and scoot past the other. I have deep admiration for Yossi Halevi (2002) who, as a religious Israeli Jew, sought to encounter the devotions of what he called "my Christian and Muslim neighbors" (p. xiii). Halevi spent time in prayer with Christian monastics and Islamic mystics, and participated in the holiday cycles of mosques and monasteries. After two years of frank conversation and open dialogue, he concluded with these words: "The one enduring transformation that I carry with me from my journey is that I learned to venerate—to love—Christianity and Islam. I learned to feel at home in a church, even on Good Friday, and in a mosque, even in Nuseirat. The cross and the minaret have become for me cherished symbols of God's presence, reminders that He speaks to us in multiple languages—that He speaks to us at all" (p. 314).

What I admire about Halevi's journey is that contact did not require capitulation. He was able to retain his own distinctiveness and yet was also open to being transformed through dialogue, much like the Relationalists' engagement with alterity in rival psychoanalytic traditions that my previous map surveyed. My own tradition is Protestant Christianity, and it is that tradition from which I have written this book. Some may see this as bias on my part that distorts my perception, especially of spirituality or religion that is non-Western. I think anxiety about bias arises from values related to the modern project of the Enlightenment which, as I discuss in chapter 7, was dominant from about 1650 to 1950. The project of modernity hoped to locate truth claims that were independent of historical context or cultural circumstance, a move that has become increasingly dubious to postcritical theorists, as I detail in chapters 1 and 4. I write from my own tradition because it's who I am and it's what I know. But more importantly, I also believe that belonging to a tradition does not necessarily *preclude* dialogue and may well be a *precondition* for it. As for Christianity being primarily a Western religion, demographers forecast that by the year 2050 the axis of Christendom will have shifted from Europe and North America to Africa, South America and Asia (Jenkins, 2002). If in 1950 a list of the most populous Christian countries would have included Britain, France, Spain and Italy, none of these will appear on a comparable list of countries by the middle of the twenty-first century. African theologian John Mbiti has argued the centers of Christendom are no longer in Geneva, Rome, Athens, Paris,

London, and New York, but instead are now becoming Kinshasa, Buenos Aires, Addis Ababa, and Manila; Kwame Bediako, another African theologian, subtitled his work on Christianity in Africa "The Renewal of a Non-Western Religion" (Bediako, 1995; Mbiti quoted in Bediako, 1995, p. 154). A case could be made that Christianity never was Western in its origins and is rapidly shifting to a predominantly non-Western future.

As for me, I most certainly am biased, but if the critics of modernity are right, so are we all. As I argue in chapter 4, situated subjectivity is the only option we have, and even the Enlightenment project arose out of particular circumstances that account for its values (Toulmin, 1990). In my case, the tradition out of which I write may well have pragmatic value for clinicians. Religious diversity is a rich resource in American experience (Eck, 2001), a diversity that is not contingent upon demographic prevalence. The National Opinion Research Center at the University of Chicago conducted well-designed research to assess religious diversity in America and found that Judaism and Christianity make up about 97.5% of Americans' religious affiliations. Of the remaining 2.5% that follow other religions, about half are represented by the combined numbers of Buddhists, Hindus, and Muslims. Of these, among adults in the United States, Buddhists constitute between .2% and .6% of the population, Hindus .1% to .4%, and Muslims less than .5%. Other Eastern religions, including Jainism, Sikhism, and Taoism, along with Native American religions, witches and Wiccans, or those with "personal" religions, each represent about .1% of the American population. The National Opinion Research Center concluded that "non-Judeo-Christian religions are much smaller than frequently cited high-end estimates and have hardly transformed the religious landscape as much as often portrayed" (Smith, 2001, p. 4). I suspect that the tradition out of which I write is one that most clinicians will encounter if our practices are at all representative of the North American population, although it is a tradition with which most clinicians are not personally conversant, as all seven of the following chapters detail.[10]

Kenosis means self-emptying, but it is not exactly the same thing as emotional absence. It is a sort of emptying that paradoxically permits a

---

[10]Useful books have already been written to address in psychotherapy the content of specific religious traditions like African American churches, members of Latino/Latina spiritual traditions, Asian spiritualities, and Native American spiritualities (Richards and Bergin, 2000), or to situate religion within the context of clinical psychology more broadly (Shafranske, 1996a). The best general purpose book for modeling interventions to access patients' spirituality in psychotherapy is by Griffith and Griffith (2002).

different kind of fullness, much like the passion, humility, and love of one's soul that Thomas Moore mentioned. Perceptive readers will note that Jesus, for Christians the exemplar of one who embraced and welcomed alterity, was also the one who, in Jordan's account, really "laid into" the Sunday school teacher. Kenosis is not synonymous with spinelessness, but it has a way of enfolding alterity: the "me" and the "not-me" end up being more related than I first guess. When I buy a book, on the inside front page I sign and date when I read it and make comments with that pen throughout the book's margins. If I reread a book some years later, I'll note the new date on the front page again with whatever I'm using to mark new comments in the margins. To my consternation, throughout the book I routinely find comments I had previously made with which I no longer agree, especially if it has been five or ten years, let alone twenty, since my last reading. In the spirit of perhaps both kenosis and alterity, sometimes I wonder whether, if I live long enough, I'll eventually disagree with everything I've ever thought. Maybe that way lets us have ever-fresh ways of minding spirituality.

Chapter 1

Minding Spirituality

As the French and English workers, using massive tunnel-boring machines, drilled out from the shores of their respective homelands and toward each other midway beneath the English Channel, they chiseled the last few feet with a much smaller probe, hoping for a point of contact. Through the resulting small opening, the first thing the lead French worker heard was a voice addressing him from the other side with a greeting of "Bonjour!" Chuckling, the Frenchman replied, "Hello." At this, the English tunnelers heard shouts coming to them from the other side of the portal exclaiming "God save the Queen!" to which the English workers answered with cries of "Vive la France!" (Associated Press, 1990).

There is much at which to marvel in the completion of the English Channel Tunnel (or "Chunnel" as it has been nicknamed) not least of which is that the two drilling teams managed to meet at all. It would have been a difficult enough feat to accomplish had the Chunnel been simply a straight line, since in that case either crew's initial misalignment by as little as an inch would have made the tunnels miss each other and, to make matters worse, the boring machines were incapable of backing up. Although citizens of Dover with a telescope on a clear day could claim to read the hands of the clock on the Calais town hall, tunneling under the seabed required the workers to stay within a narrow band of geologic chalk that was impervious to water, structurally stable, and relatively easy to mine. The problem was not only that deviation from this chalk stratum meant encountering unstable and porous rock that would cause the tunnel to collapse and fill with water, but also the chalk stratum itself wasn't straight or level. The narrow band pitched and dipped, angled one way and then another. Global positioning satellites gave the miners who were navigating several hundred feet beneath the water's surface an estimate of latitude and longitude, but equipment used at the time could not give reliable information about their vertical location. Local measurements relative to the surface were equally unworkable because the earth's rotation and wind patterns actually make sea level different on the English and French sides of the Channel. Line-of-sight measurements were tricky for surveyors because air near tunnel walls is warmer than air a few feet away from the walls, causing refraction much like how a stick appears to bend where it enters water. Some of the most helpful information came from geologists, who determined the tunnelers' relative depths according to fossil evidence obtained at the leading edge of the tunnel's face. In the end, the two crews proved to be out of line horizontally by a mere 20 inches, which caused one engineer to remark, "It was like throwing out a line to the moon and getting within a 10-foot circle" (Redman, 1990, p. 49).

Another marvel beyond the fact that the two groups managed to meet at all is the way they greeted one another once they met. Their greetings, in addition to the Chunnel project overall, serve as a useful metaphor for imagining constructive relations between psychoanalysis and spirituality. Two groups who had been episodic enemies across centuries, who appreciated the respective benefits of their separation from each other, and who had developed completely different cultures, now managed to acknowledge each other's legitimacy, at least momentarily, and to greet one another not only in the other's native tongue (Bonjour, Hello) but also within the other's indigenous values (God save the Queen, Vive la France). This didn't mean, of course, that the French had suddenly become English, or vice versa, but the Chunnel can be seen as an expression of a desire to make contact, along with a belief that making such contact could offer something beneficial to both sides.

That said, the French and the English had distinctly different attitudes toward the prospect of any link between their countries. Fetherston (1997) compared the two:

> As in the past, the groups that opposed the tunnel drew their energy
> from a vast seething pool of antitunnel feeling that lay close beneath
> the calm, often cool surface of British society. That society—riven
> though it might be by divisions of class, geography, education, wealth,
> color and accent—wished, on balance, that the whole idea of a tunnel
> would simply go away. In France, there were islands of doubt among
> the sailors and dockworkers of Calais and shoals of Anglophobic

resistance, but these were scattered in an ocean of enthusiasm. The French loved great projects, and a Channel tunnel, though it did not strike the eye as handsomely as would a grand bridge across the strait, was surely a *grand projet*. To appreciate it was to show intelligence and good taste. In Britain, enthusiasm for the tunnel marked one as a crank [p. 84].

The English preference for insularity was observed as long ago as William Shakespeare, who called England "this precious stone set in the silver sea" for which the Channel served "as a moat defensive . . . against the envy of less happier lands" (*King Richard the Second*), and as recently as the *Sun*, London's leading tabloid, which warned, "It won't be long before the garlic-breathed bastilles will be here in droves once the Channel Tunnel is open" (Redman, 1990, p. 49). The English were wary of the Chunnel serving as a conduit for contamination from foreigners, including their animals, whether pets or wild beasts roaming the Continent. The English have a profound fear of rabies, a disease that, although eradicated in Britain in 1902 by the slaughtering of all suspected dogs, British immigration posters continue to emphasize today even more than the threat of terrorist bombs. At the behest of English citizens, a boundary fence with mesh fine enough to stop small animals and even rodents from entering (in France) and exiting (in England) was erected at both ends of the tunnel, with the fence extending down into the ground to block burrowing creatures as well. Roving patrol dogs and in-tunnel closed circuit television cameras supplement police encouragement for the public to report any animal, or anyone seen with an animal, near the tunnel. Electrified grids near the entrances pulse with 150,000 volts and extend 10 feet back into the tunnels so that no animal could leap across. A worker commented wryly that, if a person accidentally stepped on the grid, "[He'd] never have to worry about getting rabies" (Fetherston, 1997, p. 364).

A case could be made that, when it comes to spirituality, psychoanalysis historically has behaved like the English toward the prospect of a tunnel to France, and when it comes to psychoanalysis, religion or spirituality has behaved more like the French. It is not just that Freud's (1914) reveling in his "years of splendid isolation" (p. 22) is similar to the English preference for insularity, or that the number of people worldwide with various sorts of religious involvements far surpasses the number of people with experience in analysis, much as the population of a continent outnumbers the population of an island. It is also that psychoanalysis and spirituality have had distinctly different levels of interest in making contact with each other. For many religious leaders, to appreciate psycho-analysis has been evidence of intelligence and good taste; by contrast, for many psychoanalysts, at least historically, to appreciate spirituality or reli-gion marked one as a crank. Whereas Freud thought psychoanalysis pre-cluded the possibility of its practitioners being religious leaders, throughout the first 100 years of psychoanalysis, religious leaders such as Freud's contemporary, the Swiss Lutheran pastor, Oskar Pfister (1928), and later Anton Boisen (1936), the founder of the pastoral counseling movement in North America and Europe, have argued for the benefits of cross-cultural contact more in the spirit of Bonjour/Hello and God save the Queen/Vive la France. Whereas Freud imagined psychoanalysis as a profession in which practitioners need not be physicians and should not be priests (Meng and Freud, 1965, p. 126), Alan Jones (1985), himself an Episcopal priest, described psychoanalysis and contemplative spirituality as twins separated at birth and raised independently without either be-ing aware of the other's existence.

Jones may have a point. Cynics who cast aspersions on the value and legitimacy of a connection between England and France (or, for that matter, between psychoanalysis and spirituality) because such a link is deemed artificial, and thus inappropriate, may be shortsighted. Geolo-gists tell us that England and France have been linked by naturally occur-ring land bridges many times, the most recent appearing about 8300 years ago. What is more, the waters that now divide England and France, however choppy and inclement, are shallow: if Westminster Cathedral were placed on the floor at the deepest part of the Channel, its top would rise well above the water's surface, and the Eiffel Tower would likewise stand nearly three-quarters above water. Across even longer stretches of geologic time, if the pangaea hypothesis about plate tectonics is correct, England and France were indeed, as Jones' metaphor suggests, once joined in a common ancestry.

Defining Spirituality and Religion

The *Second Edition of the Oxford English Dictionary* (OED2) defines spiritu-ality as "attachment to or regard for things of the spirit as opposed to material or worldly interests," and throughout its definitions it is impor-tant to add that the OED2 consistently links spirituality with ecclesiasti-cal pursuits. This link between spirituality and religion may perplex those who presume antithetical relations, particularly in the sense of being "spiritual but not religious." Presuming such a dichotomy, however, has proven problematic in at least three ways. First, it is not the only logical possibility, as even those authors who are sympathetic to a distinction between spirituality and religion are quick to point out (Roof, 1999, p. 178; Fuller, 2001). If some people describe themselves as "spiritual but not religious," others are "religious but not spiritual," "both spiritual and religious," or "neither religious nor spiritual." To limit investigation to only the first group excludes vast portions of the American population who are in one of the other logical categories, and is therefore a second way that requiring spirituality to exclude religion is problematic. Sociologist Robert Wuthnow (1998) argues that a society's experience of spirituality parallels its sense of the social order. Times of relative tranquility and stability promote what Wuthnow calls "a spirituality of dwelling" whose archetype is the cathedral; times of social ferment and transition, by contrast, foster a much more provisional and nomadic sensibility that he calls a "spirituality of seeking" that is better symbolized by a tent. It might be tempting to see the former as religion and the latter as spirituality but to do so according to Wuthnow's typology is a mistake because a spirituality of dwelling, although different than a spirituality of seeking, is an expression of *spirituality* nevertheless. And sociologists Hout and Fischer (2002) caution that, even among the small but growing number of Americans who claim no religious preference, and who therefore could be candidates for the "spiritual but not religious" category, the majority continue to hold conventionally religious beliefs. A third limitation is clinical. Some of the most difficult patients for many analysts to reach are those who describe themselves as "spiritual and religious," or even "religious but not spiritual." To exclude these patients a priori is to forego understanding the patient populations for whom many analysts often admit they most need help. This book, therefore, treats religion as one possible expression of spirituality that, while not synonymous with it, is also not necessarily inimical to it.

There are two predominant approaches to defining religion: substantive and functional. Substantive approaches emphasize specific beliefs or practices as the hallmark of religion (examples are prayer and belief in God or a Higher Power), but these founder when confronted with major world religions like Buddhism that are not necessarily theistic and thus do not fit the substantive criteria. Functional approaches to religion attempt to avoid the limitations of substantive definitions by focusing on what religions do and how they function in the lives of participants rather than on specific beliefs or practices. One example of a functional approach is Paul Tillich's (1958) definition that a person's religion is whatever he or she holds as his or her ultimate concern. If substantive definitions stumble by not being inclusive enough, functional definitions of religion falter by being overly inclusive (depending on the person, ultimate concerns could be anything from a walk on the beach to a good game of golf). The result is that no one can be excluded, even those who do not identify themselves as religious.

The etymology of the word religion is typically associated with *legere* (to gather together) or *ligare* (to bind or tie together, from which we get the English word ligament), although another possible root is *alego* (to care for or have regard for), which suggests that religion is about what we hold dear (Saler, 1993, p. 65; Schlauch, 1999). Whatever its etymological roots, it is also worth noting that the word religion invokes the language of an outsider and is experience-distant from the perspective of adherents of many historic traditions of spirituality, including Judaism, Christianity, and Islam, among others (Smith, 1963, pp. 125–126). For an observant Jew, for example, Judaism isn't religion per se; it is a way of life. The same applies for a Christian or a Muslim. As Smith (1963) observes:

> So for the Hindu, the Buddhist, the Tierra del Fuegan. If we would comprehend these we must look not at their religion but at the universe, so far as possible through their eyes. It is what the Hindu is able to see, by being Hindu, that is significant. Until we can see it too, we have not come to grips with the religious quality of his life. And we may be sure that as he looks around him, he does not see "Hinduism." Like the rest of us, he sees his wife's death, his child's minor and major aspirations, his money-lender's mercilessness, the calm of a starlit evening, his own mortality [p. 138].

How well psychoanalysis learns to see things like the man's experience of his wife's death, his children's aspirations, or the calm of a starlit evening is the focus of this book. The relationship between psychoanalysis and spirituality is legitimately complex, which is what makes it so rewarding to examine.

Three Ways of "Minding" Spirituality

One way psychoanalysis has minded spirituality is in the sense of being bothered by it, much as the English feared contamination that might spread to them through the Chunnel. Only instead of electrified grids, fine mesh extending well below ground level, surveillance cameras and patrol dogs, psychoanalysis has kept spirituality and religious experience at bay by interpreting it as psychopathology and nothing more. This interpretation has a point. Religion and spirituality certainly have been used for pathological purposes throughout human history and have been a source of intolerance, bigotry, and xenophobia. But a case could be made that the very values of tolerance, respect for individual difference, and the free pursuit of knowledge that pathological manifestations of religion oppose also stem from various theological traditions (Marsden, 1994; Cahill, 1998, 1999), which highlights a beneficial role of religion. One of the themes of this book is a call for a more nuanced psychoanalytic appreciation for religion and spirituality as something more than simply wholesale psychopathology. Such appreciation is more complicated than psychoanalytic splitting that simplifies religion or spirituality as either "all good" or "all bad," (or, for that matter, regards religion as "all bad" and spirituality as "all good").

Freud objected to priests as analysts because he thought the resulting transference would be contaminated by the sort of credulity and rank capitulation to authority that he took to be religion's core. He sought a professional class that did not yet exist—secular caretakers of the soul (*Seelensorger*). So when Pfister reminded Freud that Protestantism had been a movement to abolish differences between laity and clergy, he asked if Freud really wished to exclude from analytic work a "priesthood" understood in this secularized sense. Freud replied that his opinion about priests as analysts hadn't been very tolerant and then conceded with a verbal shrug: "For the present I put up with doctors, so why not priests too?" (Meng and Freud, 1963, pp. 128–129). Another theme of this book is that psychoanalytic theory, as well as philosophies of science more broadly, has continued to evolve and change in the years since Freud's death, and that many of these changes have implications for the analysis of religious experience that are very different from what analysts once assumed. Contemporary psychoanalytic epistemologies support fewer reductionistic and dismissive interpretations of religious experience, and contemporary philosophies of science no longer sustain the dichotomy that Freud imagined between scientific skepticism and religious credulity. In one sense, these changes actually make religion and spirituality even more bothersome for psychoanalysis today than they were for Freud, since it is much more difficult to dismiss them now as having no legitimate commonality with psychoanalytic pursuits. Psychoanalysis is right to continue minding spirituality in the sense of being bothered by it because the two are not in the same business, although the lines of demarcation are no longer what Freud once envisioned. The goal is not to spiritualize psychoanalysis, to psychoanalyze spirituality, or to harmonize or minimize differences by subsuming one discipline into the other, but rather to let each stand in genuine conversation with the other and to welcome ongoing difference.

A word of warning: this stance of dialogue is particularly difficult for fundamentalists, be they religious or psychoanalytic. Martin Marty, in his five volume treatment of fundamentalism (Marty and Appleby, 1991–1995), reminds us that there are many kinds of fundamentalists, including Christian, Jewish, Islamic, and Buddhist, to name just a few. Paul Williamson (Hood, Hill, and Williamson, in press) argues that fundamentalism is best defined not by any particular religious beliefs, or even by a style of cognitive rigidity, but by a commitment to *intra*textuality that privileges a revered text (and traditions associated with it) above all other sources of knowledge. Fundamentalists dismiss outsiders as unbelievers (in God; in psychoanalysis) and therefore persons to be kept at a distance and to be viewed as a threat to the purity and security of the fundamentalist worldview (a liability I take up in more detail in chapter 6). In Williamson's view, nonfundamentalists tend to be characterized by what he calls *inter*textuality: a willingness to engage alterity, to listen to outsiders, and not only to have a community's sacred texts interpret current experience, but also to have that experience shape or inform the community's understanding of its texts. I have found that fundamentalists, whether religious or psychoanalytic, tend to reject the sort of conversation this book proposes, as though dialogue were superfluous and all further thought on the matter foregone and foreclosed. Even so, I believe fundamentalists have something important to contribute, and in my view genuine conversation requires neither fundamentalists' capitulation nor the minimizing of difference or disagreement. Greeting one another in the other's language and idiom did not mean that the French and English tunnelers forfeited their national identities.

A second way that psychoanalysis can mind spirituality is to be alert to its presence and attending to moments of transition between various levels of experience, much as signs on the British underground transit warn travelers exiting subway cars to "mind the gap" when stepping out onto the platform, and other British signage alerts pedestrians to "mind the step," if there is movement proceeding up or down. Just as the British hoped that the whole idea of a Chunnel would simply go away if they ignored it, there is evidence that psychoanalysis, when not pathologizing

TABLE 1. Number of Books with the Word "Spirituality"

Years	In the Title	Anywhere as Key Word
1950–1959	42	48
1960–1969	87	110
1970–1979	142	180
1980–1989	430	564
1990–1999	873	1166

spirituality, has tended to ignore it. For example, I searched the catalog of the Library of Congress for books published in English during the past 50 years that either had the word "spirituality" in the title or, for more relaxed search criteria, had it as a key word anywhere within the entry. As shown in Table 1, I found that, on average across the previous half-century, the number of books on spirituality doubled every decade.

I then searched the Library of Congress for books that had "Spirituality" and "Psychoanalysis" as key words anywhere within the records. As shown in Table 2, I found that, on average across the past 50 years, for every 1000 titles in psychoanalysis, just three address spirituality. To be fair, psychoanalysis has historically addressed the topic not in terms of spirituality but "religion." Even then, according to the Library of Congress, 95 out of every 100 psychoanalytic titles published during this same 50-year period don't address religion either. When they do, it is in one of four ways: sectarian treatments, psychohistories, edited volumes, or nonsectarian book-length treatments by solo authors.

Examples of sectarian treatments are books that address Buddhism (Epstein, 1995; Rubin, 1996), Judaism (Spero, 1992), or Roman Catholicism (Wolman, 1995). The strength of these approaches is that they delve deeply into a specific religious tradition, but this may restrict their findings to a fairly narrow population. Psychohistories either study a prominent

TABLE 2. Number of Books on Psychoanalysis and Spirituality

Years	As Key Words
1950–1959	0
1960–1969	0
1970–1979	0
1980–1989	1
1990–1999	12

religious figure via a psychoanalytic interpretation, such as Erikson's (1962) analysis of Martin Luther or Meissner's analysis of Ignatius of Loyola (1992), or they examine a prominent psychoanalytic figure through a developmentally informed religious interpretation, such as the volumes by Vitz (1993) or Rizzuto (1998) on Freud. Such case studies are often fascinating but they cannot escape the limitations inherent in any psychohistory: it is hard enough to analyze someone we see in person in our office; it is much more difficult to analyze someone we have never met, using only what they have written or what other people have said about them—and this decades or centuries after the fact.

The most common strategy for a psychoanalytic book on religion is an edited volume with contributors who are typically one of two types: academics who do not work as full-time psychoanalytic practitioners (see some chapter entries in Capps and Jacobs [1997] or Smith and Handelman [1990]), or practicing psychoanalysts who have not pursued full-time graduate study of religion or other theological education (see some chapter entries in Finn and Gartner [1992], Randour [1993], or Spezzano and Gargiulo [1997]). In edited volumes on psychoanalysis and religion, readers typically get to see an author's first thoughts on the topic, which could be an advantage, but a disadvantage is that, in most cases, they're seeing the author's last thoughts on the topic as well, since most never address it again. A welcome exception is Safran (2003).

In my view, the most influential books in the field of psychoanalysis and religion have all been book-length, nonsectarian treatments by a solo author (Rizzuto, 1979; Leavy, 1980, 1988; McDargh, 1983; Meissner, 1984; Jones, 1991, 1996, 2002; Eigen, 1998; Rubin, 1998). The increasing number of psychoanalytic books addressing spirituality in the past decade underscores another theme of the present volume: not only has psychoanalytic theory changed across recent decades, but so has the way analysts have treated the topic of spirituality and religion in psychoanalytic publications. Psychoanalysts have been among the vanguard who defended others' rights for individual difference with regard to sexual orientation, ethnicity, and race, and this book presents quantitative evidence that analysts across the twentieth century began also to respect religion as an aspect of cultural diversity.

A common objection to minding spirituality in the sense of attending to it is that analysts do not see much of it in their clinical work and that the topic just does not come up. When it does, some analysts feel a certain amount of discomfort either because they do not relate to the topic personally or they are afraid of offending or alienating the patient by exposing differences between them. These concerns are not without merit. This book addresses the sociology of religion, including the work of Peter Berger, who once quipped that, if India is the most religious country in the world and Sweden is the least, the United States is a country of Indians ruled by Swedes. The point I add is that in America the typical analyst is a Swede who is analyzing Indians. National surveys have repeatedly shown that psychotherapists are much less religious personally than is the North American population (Lehman and Shriver, 1968; Bergin, 1980; Regan, Malony, and Beit-Hallahmi, 1980; Bergin and Jensen, 1990; Shafranske and Malony, 1990; Kosmin and Lachman, 1993; Gallup, 1994; Hoge, 1996a; Shafranske, 1996b), and this is not simply a result of a commitment to scientific skepticism. My own discipline of clinical psychology shows the lowest level of involvement with religion even when compared to all other scientists (Leuba, 1950; Shafranske, 1996b), so much so that one proposal is that psychologists gravitate to the field as a compensation to replace earlier involvement with religion in the psychologist's family of origin (Beit-Hallahmi, 1992).

Bernard Brandchaft has written about pathological accommodation and how seamlessly it occurs, often outside conscious awareness of either analyst or analysand (Stolorow, Brandchaft, and Atwood, 1987). Patients learn what interests their analyst and begin to tailor their presentations of themselves in a way that they suspect conforms to their analyst's views. Religion is personally meaningful for the vast majority of the American population. According to recent data available from the Gallup organization (Gallup and Lindsay, 1999), 96% of Americans believe in God, 90% say they pray, and—no less striking—these data are remarkably consistent over time: in national surveys from 1947, for example, 95% of Americans believed in God, and 90% said they prayed. Today, 87% of Americans say that religion is important in their life, 71% report an interest in developing their relationship with God, and 82% feel a need to experience spiritual growth. Faith-based small groups involve "a staggering number of Americans—100 million and growing" (p. 82), and, of these, the majority include prayer (69%) and Bible study (56%). Eighty-nine percent would want a child of theirs to receive religious education, and when accessing resources to face a crisis, American adults value prayer (80%) and Bible reading (64%), and are less inclined to seek a secular psychotherapist (31%) than one with religious affiliations (40%) (Gallup and Lindsay, 1999). Given these numbers, one explanation for why some analysts don't hear much about their patients' religion or spirituality in treatment is that their patients are accommodating to them, in Brandchaft's sense of the term. A theme of this book is that we can benefit from minding spirituality not only by paying attention to it, but also by being suspicious of the ways we subtly transmit and sustain a taboo about exploring religious experience and spirituality clinically.

A third and final way of minding spirituality is in the sense of "minding the store," a kind of minding that the *OED2* defines as "to remember, regard, or care for." Minding in this sense has to do with husbandry, a cultivation of resources, or, to use a more religious word, stewardship. Religious groups often inappropriately de-emphasize how profoundly human relationships color and structure theological insights, something to which psychoanalysis rightly directs us. As just one example, I think of Karl Barth, arguably the most influential Protestant theologian in the twentieth century. Recent scholarship has highlighted the significance of his 35-year relationship with his personal secretary, Charlotte von Kirschbaum (Köbler, 1989; Selinger, 1998). They met when Barth was 38 and she was 25. When Barth's wife refused a divorce, he arranged for von Kirschbaum to live as a permanent resident in the Barth household, giving her a bedroom that was accessible only through his private study. She stayed with him in a remote mountain cottage for months at a time while he wrote his theology, and she accompanied him whenever he traveled to lecture elsewhere. Most tellingly, first-time visitors to the Barth household often mistook Frau Barth, who would answer the door, for a household servant, and when they first encountered von Kirschbaum they would typically greet her in a manner that assumed she was Barth's wife. The point I want to emphasize is that Barth's theology of *Mitmenschlikeit* (cohumanity) and his profound theology of male and female, for which he is justly famous, seem to have been profoundly shaped by his passionate and lifelong relationship with von Kirschbaum. As psychoanalysis would teach us, theology and experience co-inform each other (McClendon, 1990). Many religious traditions are uncomfortable with this possibility and want to locate theology as something found, not made. Even among those religious traditions that recognize God as Wholly Other, however, there is often a reception of revelation as something occurring within the boundary conditions of the receiver. Revelation is confessionally acknowledged as being shaped by individual and communal subjectivities, which is why there are theologies. Within these traditions, religion becomes a very human enterprise, even if divinely initiated; revelation and construction are seen as complementary and not mutually exclusive.

The reverse is no less the case: spirituality and world religious traditions have something of potential value to offer psychoanalysis, which can become unwittingly and uncritically accommodated to the very societal structures it purports to challenge (Fromm, 1970; Cushman, 1995). When Richardson, Fowers, and Guignon (1999) ask if the modern therapy enterprise "to some extent subtly reinforces a shallow, one-sided individualism in our kind of society," one that helps to perpetuate "such modern social ills as the loss of community, the decay of any sense of individual purpose beyond shallow and self-serving ends in living, emotional isolation, alienation, and emptiness" (p. 4), their book-length answer is Yes. Psychoanalytic theories cannot avoid reckoning with inherently moral dimensions for what constitutes a good life, a life well lived, as defined by various psychoanalytic ideals that function much like articles of faith—and I believe this psychoanalytic faith is impoverished if it ignores the millennia of religious faiths that preceded it and form its context. When cultural historian Philip Rieff (1966) spoke of "the triumph of the therapeutic," in his judgment the victory was pyrrhic because the language of the therapeutic is comparatively thinner and lacks the social cohesion that religious narratives provided (see also Rieff, 1959).

Perhaps the most important theme of this book is that analysts can mind their patients' spirituality by offering husbandry or cultivation, and that doing so does *not* require analysts to become any more (or less) religious or spiritual than whatever they already happen to be. Contrary to various theoretical speculations that in order to understand their patients' religion or spirituality, analysts must (or must not) be religious or spiritual themselves, the present volume offers quantitative evidence that what matters is how analysts behave in session and the attitudes they convey. Incredible as this may sound, analysts (whether secular or religious) have a greater impact on patients' spirituality and religious formulations than do even the patients' parents in the family of origin or the patients' religious authorities (rabbis, priests, pastors, imams, etc.) from whatever religious tradition in which the patient was raised. (See chapter 4.) Systematic avoidance or indiscriminate pathologizing of the patient's religious or spiritual life has a toxic effect on the analysand's spirituality, whereas friendly interest has the opposite effect. Sustained empathic inquiry into the patient's world of meaning—which many would argue is no different than what good analysis has always entailed—is what I advocate, although I contend that psychoanalysis has not always been as consistent as it could be when applying this to religious or spiritual experience. I do so from a perspective as a relational psychoanalyst and a Protestant Christian—aspects to which I now turn.

Relational Psychoanalysis

One way to understand relational psychoanalysis is that it says psycho-analysis is the product of multiple authors, whose very diversity fostered schisms and strife within the field that have led to the understatement of agreement and points of concordance among rival traditions. Saying this in no way detracts from Freud's seminal contributions, to which all forms of psychoanalysis today are indebted. But as L. L. White (1960) has chronicled, concepts of the unconscious—including disowned dynamic forces, slips of the tongue, and hidden or asocial motivation—existed for more than 2000 years before Freud, and reached a fever-pitch crescendo in the eighteenth and nineteenth centuries just prior to Freud's writings. As Goethe, one of Freud's favorite writers, once warned: "No one can take from us the joy of the first becoming aware of something, the so-called discovery. But if we also demand the honor, it can be utterly spoiled for us, for we are usually not the first. What does discovery mean, and who can say that he has discovered this or that? After all, it's pure idiocy to brag about priority; for it's simply unconscious conceit, not to admit frankly that one is a plagiarist" (cited in White, 1960, p. v).

If Freud wasn't actually the first person to discover the unconscious, he was its mighty explorer and chronicler. He taught us that there is more to us than we know. Sándor Ferenczi taught us that it is affective engagement more than rationalistic explanation that shapes the form of psychoanalytic cure. Melanie Klein taught us that the capacity for thought is not something to be taken for granted and is in fact a dyadic achieve-ment: it takes two to know one. Similarly, Donald Winnicott, in declar-ing that there is no such thing as a baby, taught us that all experience is systemic and ecological. Harry Stack Sullivan, in paying attention to the question What's going on around here? taught us how dramatic themes are sustained not just from the distant past but from habitual, reciprocal interactions in the present. And Stephen Mitchell, a quintessentially postclassical and relational psychoanalyst, taught us that the unconscious can be recast not as a seething cauldron of putatively asocial drives, but rather as a source for appreciating the human mind as infinitely com-plex, a source of potentially endless fascination and richly rewarding ex-ploration. In this sense, there is more to us than we can ever know.

Relational psychoanalysis, as I understand it, says not only that there was more than one contributor to the origins of psychoanalysis but that many of these contributors were women. A case could well be made that psychoanalysis was as much the creation of incredibly perceptive female patients as it was their (usually) male analysts (Appignanesi and Forrester, 1992). Emmy von N was unresponsive to suggestion, and insisted that her doctors be quiet and let *her* do the talking. Lucy R could not be hypnotized, and suggested instead that it would work better to just let her free associate to whatever came next. Elisabeth von R demanded that *all* of her symptoms be analyzed. And Lou Andreas-Salomé, who proposed alternative explanations for women's psychology and a less reductionistic approach to interpretations, was described by Karl Abraham to Freud in these words: "I have never met anyone with so deep and subtle an understanding of psychoanalysis" (p. 241).

The multiplicity of authentic contributors to the development of psychoanalysis is, I think, crucial to understanding the distinctiveness of relational psychoanalysis. In a very real sense, relational psychoanalysis, which began to coalesce in the early 1980s through the work of Stephen Mitchell, Jay Greenberg, and Merton Gill, arose out of an appreciation for there having been "many Freuds," whose many backgrounds and particular psychoanalytic cultures caused commonalties to be obscured. In the opening editorial of the first issue of *Psychoanalytic Dialogues*, Mitchell (1991) offered the following comments about how psychoanalysts from rival traditions tend to talk past each other:

> Each tradition has a standard formula for what is missing in rival theories, and the key phrases are intoned with a kind of resonance that dismisses, sadly but knowingly, cardboard versions of alternative approaches. Non-Freudians live in a world without "drives," disembodied, air-brushed and pollyannaish; noninterpersonalists live in a fantastic world, without an awareness of "real" transactions between "real" people; non-self psychologists perpetually miss, coldly and insensitively, the key importance of "empathic" connections, developmental "strivings," and "selfobject" needs; and non-object relations analysts live innocently and ignorantly on the surface of experience, unaware of the inner world of internal object relations that guides and shapes life from within. Concepts are reified, spoken of as if they really exist in the world in the way physical objects do; theories are elevated into Truth; alternative frameworks, if read at all, are read for the purpose of demonstrating shortcomings, to be dismissed as self-deception or ignorance, usually both [p. 2].

The term "relational" exists as a link to both object relations and interpersonal relations within psychoanalytic theory and history. A central conviction that animates relational psychoanalysis is that it is relationship, both intrapsychic and interpersonal, that structures and sustains all psychological health and psychopathology. Relational psychoanalysis emphatically rejects both a dithering of theoretical differences between the many psychoanalytic traditions and any attempt simply to seek some least common denominator. Instead, it seeks to hold each tradition in tension with its competitors, honoring and safeguarding points of disagreement while being open to whatever is useful clinically.

A Brief Interlude: My Own Journey

Because contexts are also personal, and not just theoretical or conceptual, I also thought to include some of my own journey concerning spirituality and psychoanalysis. I venture to include this not because I fancy my own narrative as somehow normative but rather because I want to be as explicit as I can be about my biases and idiosyncrasies. I grew up in the religious tradition of liberal Protestantism, and when going off to college I wanted to study human subjectivity, which I thought would be the province of psychology. As a psychology major, I soon discovered that psychologists had words for everything, although the subjectivities this psychology addressed weren't quite what I was looking for. For example, I remember learning that psychologists had a term for how, when you have been wearing a hat for a while and then take it off, it can feel like the hat is still on your head. Psychologists called this the "hat effect." I remember taking my yellow highlighter and solemnly marking the phrase in my undergraduate textbook: *hat effect.* I also learned that the retina of the frog's eye was hard wired to detect small black moving objects. Psychologists had a term for this too. It was called the "bug detector." I remember taking my yellow highlighter and solemnly marking that phrase in my textbook as well: *bug detector.* The hat effect and the bug detector, along with Ebbinghaus's nonsense syllables and the rest of general psychology, was interesting but not particularly focused on the kind of human subjectivity I sought, so I switched majors to English because I found more of the psychology I was looking for in Shakespeare, Dostoyevsky, or twentieth-century playwrights than I had ever found in psychology. I studied abroad, dropped out of school and traveled internationally, and then transferred to a small Quaker college from which I graduated with a degree in psychology, although in this school's theological context psychology was at once more humanistic and more linked to global awareness of human rights and social justice. My major professor there, Joe Elmore, was an ordained Methodist minister who had trained at the Menninger Institute. He taught courses on psychology and religion in which we studied Carl Jung's (1963) psychospiritual integration, Philip Rieff's (1959, 1966) critique of Freud from the perspective of moral theory, and Paul Tillich's (1952) theology of correlation that tacks dialectically between psychology and faith. Paul Pruyser (1974), a psychoanalyst on staff at the Menninger Institute, came to our class and challenged us to think psychoanalytically about both belief and unbelief.

Upon graduation, I thought about being either a psychologist or a pastor, and since there seemed to be many more pastors who went on for training in psychology than there were psychologists who went on for theological training, I figured I had better pursue seminary education first. While at seminary I interned at a church and soon discovered that religious leadership involved a fair amount of budgetary and fund-raising considerations, committee meetings, and other administrative concerns—none of which I was particularly good at. By contrast, there was another element to pastoral care in which I felt completely at home. Meeting with couples who were celebrating the beginning of a marriage or confronting the pain of divorce, parents who were bringing a child into the world or mourning a loss due to Sudden Infant Death Syndrome, young adults addressing questions of sexual orientation—any circumstances where persons were wrestling with questions of meaning at the boundary conditions of life—I found compelling, even though other people told me they experienced these moments as noxious or aversive.

After earning my M.A. in theology, I considered a Ph.D. either in pastoral counseling from a university or in clinical psychology from a seminary, and opted for the latter. The APA-accredited seminary program in clinical psychology that I attended was based on the Boulder model of scientist-practitioner, and from it I gained good competence in research. I also had an interest in psychoanalysis, so I pursued training at an institute at which I now am faculty member, as well as a training and supervising analyst. In addition to full-time practice in psychoanalysis and psychoanalytic psychotherapy, for the past 20 years I have also taught part-time at another APA-accredited clinical psychology doctoral program that is affiliated with Protestant Christianity and is based on the tripartite institute model of personal analysis, supervision, and coursework.

As a member of multiple communities, occasionally I encounter some curiosity about my various allegiances. Colleagues in university settings appreciate my research and publications, but challenge me to drop my involvement not just with psychoanalysis, which they say lacks empirical support, but also with clinical practice generally, so that I can have greater impact on people through teaching which, they say, offers the equivalent interpersonal satisfaction of clinical work. Colleagues in clinical settings recognize me as a clinician and urge me to not waste my time in academia with people who do not believe in psychotherapy, have never really benefited from it personally, do not understand how it works, and generally discourage others from pursuing it. Instead, they say, I should concentrate on helping patients in clinical practice who not only appreciate the work but also are transformed by it personally on levels that academic instruction rarely touches. Colleagues in religious settings recognize me as a person of authentic faith, but wonder about my involvements with psychoanalysis, which has had a reputation, historically at least, of being evangelistically atheistic. Secular colleagues in psychoanalysis tend to regard me as a competent psychoanalyst but will ask occasionally, with some tentativeness, "Are you somehow religious?"

I do not experience myself as particularly contrarian, and, if anything, have come to appreciate that *any pronouncement on the inherent incompatibility of psychoanalysis and spirituality is necessarily community-dependent.* If I am creating the impression that few people relate to my interests, the opposite is actually the case. I relay these details of my personal history to underscore that for nearly 30 years I've been a part of diverse communities throughout the world for whom interdisciplinary dialogue between psychology and faith is welcomed and considered natural. I recognize that everyone's background is different, but this means some backgrounds are much less inimical to cross-cultural contact than others. I also recognize that my background colors how I see things (how could this be otherwise?), and that things I take for granted will stand out as peculiar and not-taken-for-granted by those from other backgrounds. (As just one example, I have already acknowledged how my interest in making contact with those outside my tradition is itself an aspect of my own tradition, and not a value that all traditions share.) While doing the research and writing for this book across the past decade, I met with a study group hosted by Marilyn Saur and John McDargh that gathered for a couple of days just prior to the annual convention of the American Psychological Association in whatever city the convention was that year. The group was comprised of psychologists with an interest in psychoanalysis who also were practicing Catholics, observant Jews, born again Evangelicals, charismatic Episcopalians, dedicated Buddhists, devout Mormons, and others committed to various spiritual paths unassociated with any world religion. There was no mistaking that we were all very different from each other, and getting to know one another better did not dispel this awareness. And yet I suspect I was not alone in my impression that our differences were not a threat, keen though they were. They were interesting. They were compelling. They seemed valuable—to ourselves and to others. There also was a quiet commonality among us in how we each were authentically wrestling with the ways our respective traditions of spirituality stood in dialogue with our own identities as analysts. I hope what I have written here invites something similar.

A Concluding Clinical Illustration

A patient I saw some years ago often chronicled his sadomasochistic involvement with women in which he preferred his partners to be bound, spanked, and otherwise dominated. In more metaphorical terms, his preference for dominance and hierarchical control also applied to his work relations, his social relations and, not surprisingly, his transference with me. I found that I had to sit silently for long stretches of time, speak when spoken to, interact with him according to his dictates, and generally play the game his way. Although I experienced myself as more constrained and restricted than I generally am with others, I also found him to be very bright, sensitive, and somehow courageous in what he was willing to face in himself, so long as his conditions were met. I could use the word "captivating" to describe him, only in this instance my description was more than merely metaphoric. Nonetheless, my experience was not altogether onerous; if I had to be someone's captive, I didn't mind that it was his. He spoke once in elaborate detail about how it took him up to half an hour to swallow a pill—how he positioned it on the back of his tongue and tried to flip his head backward to trick himself into ingesting anything.

One particular day while he was speaking, I found my mind wandering to an experience I'd had with my children at an ice skating rink. The older one zipped off confidently on her own but the younger one, an early elementary student at the time, was quite wobbly on her skates. She wanted me to hold her hand, but we found if I pulled her at all, she just tipped forward at her waist and was uncomfortable. We found a way that I could skate behind her with my arms grasping the backs of her legs in such a way that her body rested upright along the length of my arms. After a few laps like this at a very slow rate, when we encountered an opening on the ice I ventured to push off with my skates and generate a little more speed, enough so that the wind we encountered in the indoor rink blew more loudly in our ears—almost like a feeling of flight—at which point she blurted out spontaneously, "Ooooh, this is wonderful!" I realized once she had said it that the moment was indeed wonderful, only I had not known it was until I heard her say so. I mused about how many moments like that must go by in my life that I never even notice, about how her own mode of self-expression seemed so much less inhibited and unselfconscious than anything I ever remembered of my own experience when I was her age, and about how, with her, I experience—at least vicariously and perhaps even directly—another chance at being fully alive, at living. Although I was ostensibly the one helping her learn to skate, it occurred to me, Who is the student and who is the teacher?

I flashed back to my patient, and wondered about the daydream I had just had. Was I feeling buoyant through my surrender to his dominance? Could I be tapping into my own delight in some sadistic thrill of dominating him, or perhaps experiencing the emancipation he experiences through domination? Perhaps all of these are at play in some way or another, but I also was experiencing the conversation with him in a way that reminded me of skating with my daughter. I am not sure whether he was leading me or I was leading him, but it seemed as though he and I had stumbled onto a new experience, an extended moment of indeterminate hierarchy in which the question of who was master and who was slave did not seem to apply. I like relational psychoanalysis because it gives me room to explore multiplicity of experience—my own and my patients'—in ways that do not force me to prematurely adjudicate whose is whose or to enforce static hierarchies of power or domination.

There is something similar in how the French and English tunnelers greeted one another when they finally met beneath the Channel, and the Chunnel project can be a metaphor for possible relations between psychoanalysis and spirituality, although, if the metaphor applies, it also suggests that any linkage between the two is not without risks. One critic warned that the Chunnel could be an attractive target for terrorism, and if a fire ever spread it would quickly become the world's longest crematorium. As with the English and French tunnelers, any navigation between psychoanalysis and spirituality can turn to no global positioning satellites in geosynchronous orbits, no laser-guided surveying, because the optimal material to support the tunnel pitches one way and then dips another, angles this way and then that. Like the geologists who determined the workers' relative depths by paying close attention to the fossil evidence obtained at the leading edge of the tunnel's face, we clinical psychoanalysts may have reason to suspect that we have drifted off course if the clinical material with our patients becomes consistently and utterly devoid of any wrestling with questions of personal meaning in the face of mortality. At their best, psychoanalysis and spirituality have a chance to meet in a profound space in which neither is statically master or slave, neither annexes or subsumes the other, thus opening quiet opportunities for "Bonjour/Hello" or even, "Ooooh, this is wonderful!"

Chapter 2

Ongoing Change In Psychoanalytic Theory

Implications for Analysis
Of Religious Experience

"Ascience that hesitates to forget its founders is lost." This famous dictum and admonition by Alfred North Whitehead (cited in Kuhn, 1962, p. 138) is especially intriguing for the double meaning of the word "lost," with both meanings having implication for ongoing change in psychoanalytic theory in general and for the analysis of religious experience in particular.

One meaning of the word "lost" is doomed, forfeited, or foreclosed. Thomas Kuhn (1962), in his now classic study on the sociology of knowledge in science, would characterize this interpretation as prototypic of what he termed "normal science," a view of science that de-emphasizes distant events in history and promotes the priority of data and method over the personality of the founder. From this viewpoint, for science to be truly scientific it must not hesitate to forget its founders. Forgetting founders and being scientific are synonymous. Anything less is to elevate and enshrine incidental personalities with a kind of cultic allegiance that is unbecoming and the very antithesis of true science, whose sole legitimate concern is replicability of results and the public domain of data and method.

A second meaning of the word "lost," however, has to do with having an unknown location, or of losing one's sense of direction. Kuhn's whole thesis was that the process of scientific knowing is an inherently social enterprise, and deceptively so if viewed only from the ahistorical, apersonal perspective of normal science. Science needs its heroes, not merely for reasons of personal solace that are otherwise extraneous to the scientific method, but as exemplars of the fullest embodiment of science itself. Forgetting becomes imperative once again, only now what is needed is not to forget the founders as persons, but to forget or modify their works (Kuhn, 1962, p. 139). It is the perseverative loyalty to conventional ways—not only of how problems are analyzed, but even of which questions are asked—that perpetuates normal science. The capacity to make a profound paradigm shift calls for the courage and independence of thought that characterized the visionary pioneers. In this second sense of the word, then, science is indeed lost—at an unknown address—when disconnected from the intent or vision of its founders.

With these differing perspectives on the history of change in science in general as a backdrop, several questions emerge for the enterprise of psychoanalysis in particular. What, then, is the place of Freud in the science of psychoanalysis he founded? How is change to occur in psychoanalytic theory? And what import does this have for the analysis of religious experience? I am aware that by questioning Freud's status as psychoanalysis' creator *ex nihilo*, I will be regarded by some as being not properly "analytic" (disloyal), as having issues with authority, as having been incompletely analyzed, and so on. Still others would say the reverse— that not to subject Freud to critique is obsequious and sycophantic. The irony is that Freud the iconoclast has now become Freud the icon. What are orthodoxies, after all, but successful heresies? Through appreciation of the interdependence of heresy and orthodoxy I am seeking to play with dialectically a respect for methods and founders. Such respect is, I believe, the most dynamic and ultimately useful. My desire is neither to be a Freud idolater nor a Freud demonizer, except as these polarities may commingle and create new thought.

Freud as Founder: Haunting Ghost or Formative Forefather?

Harry Guntrip (1971) once said that Freud's place as the founder of psychoanalysis was as secure as Newton's was to the founding of physics. Both men were authentic pioneers and, of the many different leads their work suggested, some will prove fruitful and others not, but all will have to be explored and investigated. As pioneers their task, like that of all founders, was to have the first word, not the last word.

Freud (1923) himself was clear that psychoanalysis was something incomplete and necessarily open to modification. The problem arises, however, in determining just how exactly this modification is to occur. During one period of theoretical ferment in psychoanalysis—the infamous "Controversial Discussions" in Great Britain between Melanie Klein and Anna Freud—James Strachey addressed this quandary: "Who is to decide whether a particular extension [of psychoanalytic theory] is justifiable or a particular correction necessary? Only if we had an omniscient leader who could impose his opinion on us, or if by some miracle we all of us always arrived at the same conclusion could this difficulty be avoided." Strachey added wryly, "And neither of these ways out seems likely to be offered to us" (quoted in King and Steiner, 1990, p. 604).

More than any other modern discipline, psychoanalysis is portrayed as the product of a singular genius, Sigmund Freud. An advantage to having a singular genius for a founder is that not only can "defectors" be clearly identified and controlled, but also radical change in fundamental theory can occur readily. All Freud had to do was change his mind. One need only recall the switch from the seduction theory to the theory of infantile sexuality as one example, or the switch from the topographic model to the tripartite theory of ego psychology as another, or the addition of a new drive, the death instinct: the list is long. All this is a tribute to Freud's genius—that he was able to amend and alter his theories continually in the light of new thoughts or ongoing clinical experience right up to his death.

What if, as argued in chapter 1, there had been ten Freuds instead of just one? What if psychoanalysis had been the product of not one but several persons? James Strachey (quoted in King and Steiner, 1990) proposed exactly this as a thought experiment:

> We may find it instructive if, for a moment, we try to picture what would have happened if the whole chain of Freud's discoveries and theories had been made, not by a single man in the course of one lifetime, but by a succession of men over a longer period of years. What would have been the attitude of analysts who had been brought up in the straightforward theory of the neuroses to the man who first adumbrated the concept of narcissism? In what terms . . . would [other analysts] be inclined to characterize the treatments carried out in the old days when everything had by hook or by crook to be accounted for in terms of the direct Oedipus complex? It is not very fantastic to

suppose that every one of such modifications as these would have provoked crises exactly comparable to our present one and to the many others which may be ahead [pp. 606–607].

Freud's enduring presence in the lives of his followers has been, depending on one's perspective, either stifling or steadying. Chronicling both effects, Robert Wallerstein (1988), in an analysis of unity and pluralism in contemporary psychoanalytic theory, observed that psychoanalysts have yet to come to terms fully with Freud's death, even though he died over half a century ago. Hans Loewald (1980) noted that Freud likened the indestructibility of the unconscious to the ghosts of the Odyssey's underworld—"ghosts which awoke to new life as soon as they tasted blood" (p. 248). Loewald continued: "Those who know ghosts tell us that they long to be released from their ghost life and led to rest as ancestors. As *ancestors* they live forth in the present generation, while as *ghosts* they are compelled to haunt the present generation with their shadow life" (p. 249, italics added). One way that change occurs, whether in science in general or psychoanalysis in particular, is simple: people die. An oligarchical gerontocracy yields its power only at the point of death. In psychoanalysis, however, sometimes this is not true even then. Freud's power over the minds of present-generation analysts is arguably even greater from the grave than it was over the minds of his contemporaries during his lifetime. Employing Loewald's helpful metaphor, Stephen Mitchell (1993) noted that the intellectual integrity and vitality of psychoanalysis depends on shifting our view of Freud "from an improperly buried ghost who haunts us to a beloved and revered ancestor" (p. 176).

Nowhere is Freud's enduring presence greater than in psychoanalytic perspectives on religion, and, lamentably, it is often as an unburied ghost. Evolving changes in psychoanalytic theory over the last few decades, however, permit respectful revision and amendment to his work in a way that allows Freud to be a dearly honored ancestor from whom we are all psychoanalytic descendants. In particular, three areas of change in psychoanalytic theory have special implication for the analysis of religious experience: illusion, narrative, and constructivism.

Illusion

Freud's views on religion were complex and yet unambiguous. In his justifiably most famous essay on religion, "The Future of an Illusion," he offered this summary: "I have tried to show that religious ideas have arisen from the same need as have all other achievements of civilization: from the necessity of defending oneself against the crushingly superior force of nature" (Freud, 1927, p. 21). All aspects of religious life were, for Freud, "illusions, fulfillments of the oldest, strongest and most urgent wishes of mankind"—to have the illusion of safety amidst feelings of helplessness when confronted with the cruel indifference of nature (p. 30). The renunciation of such wishes and the eventual disavowal of these infantile illusions were for Freud the very badge of emotional maturity.

More recent psychoanalytic theorists, however, have recast their understanding of the developmental utility of illusion. Rather than viewing it as a flight *from* reality, for example, Donald Winnicott (1971) saw the child's capacity for illusion as one type of transitional phenomenon that is prerequisite for increasing relatedness *toward* reality. This capacity for illusion, moreover, is not something that is ever outgrown or renounced in the name of emotional maturity. The teddy bear's passing from significance for the toddler is not mourned, argued Winnicott (1975), precisely because its meaning becomes gradually diffused over all of culture, into areas that include "play, and of artistic creativity and appreciation, and of religious feeling" (p. 233).

Freud himself made it clear that he saw no necessary correlation between an atheistic statement of faith and psychoanalytic competence. To his lifelong correspondent and friend, Oskar Pfister, Freud wrote: "Let us be quite clear on the point that the views expressed in my book [*The Future of an Illusion*] form no part of analytic theory. They are my personal views, which coincide with those of many non-analysts and pre-analysts, but there are certainly many excellent analysts who do not share them" (Meng and Freud, 1963, p. 117). It is striking that, unlike such other early analysts as Adler, Rank, and Jung, who had fallings-out with Freud, Pfister was able to maintain close family ties with Freud while also being ruthlessly blunt about their differences over the issue of religion. I think the published correspondence of letters between the two is a good example of wise, deep, and mature object relations.

Pfister was the exception rather than the rule, however, when it came to psychoanalytic perspectives and religion. In a ground-breaking study on object relations and God representations, for example, Ana-María Rizzuto (1979) lamented the normative influence Freud's atheism had had on future generations of analysts, an effect more like that of an unburied ghost than of a beloved forefather:

Throughout his long life, Freud was preoccupied with the question of religion and most specifically with the psychological origins of God. He made a strong case for a direct correlation between the individual's relation to the father, especially with regard to resolution of the Oedipus complex, and the elaboration of the idea of God. After Freud, however, nobody undertook a study of that correlation or its implications. Freud himself—contradicting his own finding about the life-long importance of the father—insisted that people should not need religion, called it a cultural neurosis, and set himself up as an example of those who could do without it. Intentionally or unintentionally, he gave the world several generations of psychoanalysts who, coming to him from all walks of life, dropped whatever religion they had at the doors of their institutes. If they refused to do so, they managed to dissociate their beliefs from their analytic training and practice, with the sad effect of having an important area of their own lives untouched by their training. If they dealt with religion during their own analyses, that was the beginning and end of it [p. 4].

Peter Cohen's (1994) study of psychoanalysts who had religious commitments in their developmental histories provides clinical and empirical support for Rizzuto's allegations (see also Sorenson, 1994a). Odilon De Mello Franco (1998) likewise questions the presumed priority of atheism for analysis: "If religious feelings are approached not as symptoms but as configurations as basic as those of sexuality, there is no reason to insist that an analyst should be an atheist or agnostic in order to analyze. This would be just as absurd as maintaining that, in order to interpret his patients' sexuality 'impartially,' the analyst should not himself have a sex" (p. 120).

W. W. Meissner (1984, 1990), a Jesuit and psychoanalyst, has taken Winnicott's work on the value of the capacity for illusion and applied it directly to psychoanalysis and religious experience, with particular attention within a developmental context to the dimensions of faith, God representation, use of symbols, and experience of prayer. I think Meissner's analysis shows seasoned judgment and thoughtful familiarity with the issues. His theological and psychoanalytic sophistication is evident, to cite just one example, in that he does not revert to psychological reductionism, and yet neither does he place any aspect of religious experience outside the domain of legitimate psychological inquiry. The thrust of Meissner's work is to locate different experiences of faith along a developmental continuum, with psychopathology on one end and maturity on the other. Meissner (1984) writes:

There is, however, a world of psychological difference between religious faith seen as an obsessive expression of repressed infantile wishes and religious faith seen as a restitutive inspiration of man's creative resources. It is the difference between a conception of man as neurotically captive to his infantile needs and wishes and a conception of man as capable of autonomous and genuine creativity in achieving mastery, competence, and integrity in the vicissitudes of tragedy and life [p. 70].

Meissner's language of ego psychology is reminiscent of that of another scholar who wrote a couple of decades earlier on the value of religion. Erik Erikson, in his psychosocial analysis of human development across the life span, agreed with Freud about the origin and function of religion, except that Erikson saw it not as a necessary indicator of manifest or latent psychopathology but as a prerequisite for health. Like Freud, for example, Erikson believed religious sentiment is informed by early life experience between infant and caregiver. "In that first relationship man learns something which most individuals who survive and remain sane can take for granted most of the time," wrote Erikson (1962). "Only psychiatrists, priests, and born philosophers know how sorely that something can be missed." Also like Freud, Erikson believed that the desire is for security at a profound and basic level. "I have called this early treasure 'basic trust'; it is the first psychosocial trait and the fundament of all others." Unlike Freud, however, Erikson viewed this trust as a legitimate wish for individuals. "Basic trust in mutuality is that original 'optimism,' that assumption that 'somebody is there,' without which we cannot live." And also unlike Freud, Erikson viewed this trust as a legitimate expression of religion culturally: "One basic task of all religions is to reaffirm that first relationship" (pp. 118-119).

Freud's positivistic beliefs have not escaped scrutiny, both by his historical contemporaries and by modern revisionists. As a historical contemporary and loyal biographer, Ernest Jones (1953) observed that Freud from his youth felt a need to believe in something, and in Freud's case it was Science with a capital "S" (p. 40). Freud's solemn oath of allegiance to a Helmholtzian reductionism of chemistry and physics, like all faith commitments, helped him see certain things and obscured others. One such hazard was Freud's (1927) bifurcation of reason and intuition, with a deification of the former and a dismissal of the latter.

The riddles of the universe reveal themselves only slowly to our investigations; there are many questions to which science today can give no answer. But scientific work is the only road which can lead us to a knowledge of reality outside ourselves. It is once again merely an illusion to expect anything from intuition and introspection; they can give us nothing but particulars about our mental life, which are hard to interpret, never any information about the questions religious doctrine finds it so easy to answer [pp. 31–32].

A contemporary theorist who has continued to modify psychoanalytic perspectives according to ongoing infant research, Joseph Lichtenberg has written of his discomfort with Freud's agenda for procuring knowledge of the so-called real world outside ourselves, the polemical antipathy between "slow" science and "easy" religion, and the pejorative treatment afforded intuition and introspection. Displaying sophistication in contemporary epistemology, Lichtenberg (1985) avers: "I would argue that introspection, empathy, and intuition are not only indispensable tools of the science of psychoanalysis (giving us particulars about our mental life), but of all scientific (and aesthetic) creativity as well" (p. 346). He also wonders why Freud espoused a philosophy of science that was so cold, rationalistic, and positivistic, when his clinical method was so experiential. One answer Lichtenberg gives for this riddle is that Freud's imagination seemed inexorably drawn to opposing pairs, warring factions.

Another contemporary revisionist of psychoanalytic theory, Charles Rycroft, notes this same point, and expands upon it further. Rycroft wonders why there had to be two drives. Why not three, or one, or four, or five? And why for Freud must they be in perennial opposition and not complementary? For Rycroft the answer lies in the Teutonic formation of Freud's intellectual heritage, something that made certain observations self-evident to those who shared this lineage and arbitrary to those who did not. "Was it really because the clinical facts compelled him to make these assumptions," Rycroft (1985) muses, "or was it perhaps because linguistic habits of thought impelled him to follow Hegel and Marx and to construct a dialectical theory which came naturally to him but which seems alien to those who have been nurtured on the English language and English empiricism?" An Oxford-educated Englishman, Rycroft once muttered, "Hegel and Nietzsche are not in my bones" (p. 5).

What is not in the bones of contemporary psychoanalysts is a necessary antipathy between the capacity for illusion and emotional maturity. Contemporary psychoanalytic scholarship is replete with examples of this point. Reminiscent of Michael Balint's (1968) concept of "the area of creation," an area of the mind inscrutable to the observer but pivotal for the subject's mental health, Michael Eigen (1981) has written of what he has called "the area of faith" in the work of Winnicott, Bion, and Lacan. Offering a feminist critique of Freud and faith, Judith Van Herik (1982) has made the case that Freud's theory of religion can be profitably interpreted as a special but integral case of his broader theory of gender, in whose moral economy the renunciation of wishes is tied to masculinity and cultural achievements, and the fulfillment of wishes to cultural regression, religious illusion, and femininity.

Another example is the work of Emmanuel Ghent (1990), who has developed the thesis that masochism and submission are a perversion of what in its pristine state is a desire for surrender—a fundamental yearning for the unmasking of defensive barriers and the uncovering, discovering, and expansion of one's true self by a facilitating and responsive other. The function of this "other" that Ghent writes about strikes me as not unlike what Erik Erikson meant by that special "'somebody' who is there," without which life ceases to be life. Surrender, as Ghent develops the term, has less to do with notions of defeat than it does transcendence (p. 111). Philip Bromberg (1998) notes that it is incumbent upon the analyst not merely to grudgingly permit illusory enactments in the transference, but to engagingly participate in them, and to do so implicitly through the courtship of experience, rather than explicitly through language. Regarding the patient's capacity for illusory space, the analyst's "job is not to correct it, but to know it with the patient so that the patient can make the most use of it creatively and imaginatively" (pp. 170–171). Contemporary psychoanalytic theorists argue that, rather than illusions being necessarily inimical to maturity, imaginative capacities can contribute positively to empathic introspection, nuanced ethical sensitivities, and the progressive articulation of authentic experiences of self.

Anita Sorenson (1990) summarized these contemporary trends in the psychoanalytic study of illusion as they are transposed to religious experience in particular: "Rather than every religious illusion dying of disenchantment as a person's mind matures, one's religious beliefs undergo continuous transformation and revision, simultaneous with other developmental progress." God representations change likewise. "One's image of God as an object, then, bears the imprint of the person's evolving, developmental experience. In the ever-expanding development of the human being, the illusion has a future" (p. 216).

Narrative

In his instructions to patients about psychoanalysis' basic rule—free association—Freud (1913b) likened the patient's task to that of passenger on a train looking out the window at the passing scenery (pp. 134-135). The patient's job is to report out loud to the analyst whatever changing thoughts occur in the patient's mental "scenery." Donald Spence (1982) represents a development in contemporary psychoanalysis that challenges the possibility of such naïve perception, and that mistrusts the seeming accuracy of memory or self-report, whether from the patient or the analyst. From this new perspective, what matters more—and what is closer to what analyst and patient actually do in analysis—is a quest for not a positivistic historical truth but a hermeneutical construction of narrative truth (p. 82).

In what sense, however, is this shift from historical truth to narrative truth any different from Freud's original vision of psychoanalysis? After all, the real birth of psychoanalysis, the discovery of the dynamic unconscious, occurred with Freud's shift from the seduction theory to the theory of infantile sexuality, crystallized in Freud's famous letter to Wilhelm Fliess of September 21, 1897 (Masson, 1985). The birthright of psychoanalysis therefore involves a reckoning with an intrapsychic reality, not merely a kind of sociology that chronicles the effects of events between people, such as the actual trauma of sexual abuse. Besides, as Frank Kermode (1985) has shown, Freud himself was well aware of the narrative quality of his work. "In my mind I always construct novels," Freud confessed to Stekel. His paper on Leonardo da Vinci he called "partly fiction." And "Moses and Monotheism" had the working title "The Man Moses: An Historical Novel" (p. 4).

I think the problem with Freud for modern narrative revisionists of psychoanalysis like Spence is not that Freud's accounts of others have a narrative appeal, but that Freud in his positivism downplays the narrative contribution he himself makes to the process. The problem is not that Freud's presence as observer of the observed makes a contribution — something as desirable as it is necessary—but rather that he is unaware of this contribution. Thus Freud's hypothetical construction about a case, which he presents to himself and to his audience as initially provisional and tentative, can become a convincing brute fact to Freud in his own mind through the process of his hearing himself tell the story, as happened with the Wolf Man (Spence, 1982, pp. 116-119). This led Spence to lament the dearth of accumulative, archival observations that could falsify or validate psychoanalytic principles. "Instead of an archive, we have a literature of anecdotes, a dumping ground of observations which have little more evidential value than a 30-year-old collection of flying saucer reports" (Spence, 1987, p. 80).

Seen from this narrative perspective, as George Howard (1991) has argued, psychopathology becomes "stories gone mad," and psychotherapy entails "exercises in story repair." As the title of Marie Cardinal's (1983) lyrical autobiography of her experience in psychoanalysis suggests, *The Words to Say It*, the task of healing involves claiming our own authentic language of experience. To my mind, this has import for contemporary psychoanalytic perspectives on religious experience. Religion, particularly in the Jewish and Christian traditions, is primarily a story. It is, for religious believers, the story of God with his people. It is thus a particular kind of story—a religious story—with both special significance for people of religious faith and special opportunity for those who would work with this population therapeutically (Vitz, 1990, 1992a, b). Expanding on an idea from Anton Boisen, Charles Gerkin (1984) has suggested that clinicians bring to the therapeutic setting the same skills required of hermeneutical exposition of biblical texts, only the text in question is a living human document.

Contemporary psychoanalysis seems to me to be about half a century behind similar developments in theology. The concern for narrative truth versus historical truth, for example, is reminiscent of Protestant neo-orthodoxy's debate mid-twentieth-century between *Historie* (a theological term that means objective verification independent of human subjectivity) and *Geschichte* (a subjective rendering of events' personal meaning). Just as the concern at the time was about the challenge of theologian Rudolph Bultmann and the seeming impossibility of ever "getting behind the Easter faith," namely, the *Geschichte* of theological meaning that the early communities of faith confessed, to *Historie*, the positivistic recording of external events, so now the lament in psychoanalysis about ever getting past psychic reality to external reality. In some sense, with the head start that theology has had this century, it may have something to teach the discipline of psychoanalysis: as elusive as reconstruction of past events may be, the difficulty of the task does not justify abandoning the quest, and narrative coherence alone in psychoanalysis is not enough (Strenger, 1991, pp. 186–194; for contrasting views see Geha, 1993; Sass, 1993; Spezzano, 1993a). Historicity matters. Jeffrey Masson (1990) made exactly this point when he investigated Freud's cryptic remark, never further elaborated, that Freud had "heard things in the Paris morgue of which medical science preferred not to know." Masson said he went to the Paris morgue, examined the records of the day that Freud had visited, and discovered that the forensic psychiatrist Paul Brouard had presented a case to Freud and the audience that day of "the corpse of a child who had been raped and murdered by her father" (p. 26). Masson's argument is not only that children's reports of abuse were true, rather than products of their imaginations, but also that Freud knew they were true and shrank back from this realization in horror, revising his whole edifice of psychoanalysis as a defense against this awareness. One problem with historicity, of course, is that it demands corroboration and is thus open to subsequent critique. Masson also wrote a book in which he asserted that morgues in nineteenth-century France never kept records at all, thus undercutting his own claim to evidence (Davis, 1994, p. 645).

Another problem with historicity is that although obtaining corroboration is difficult, it is what survivors of trauma want. It is often said, among relational analysts, that patients come into analysis thinking they will find out what really happened and get to the bottom of things in their pasts, and that what patients gradually come to recognize across the course of their analyses is that there is no end to the possibilities of how their pasts can be productively and convincingly construed. Just as soon as they think they have got their past understood from one vantage point, something new will occur—in the analysis, or in the patient's constructed memory, or perhaps an event in the patient's present life outside the analytic consulting room—and it casts everything that has been understood up to that point in a new and totally different light.

Critics of relational psychoanalysis complain that if our patients really knew what we had to offer, many of them would not want what we're selling, and I think such critics have a point we need to reckon with, at least when it comes to trauma. If the tension regarding trauma for classical analysis involved drive theory, for contemporary relational analysis it involves our narrative epistemologies. Once we posit that all human knowledge is a human narrative, something made, not found, and that we have no unmediated access to knowledge apart from interpretation, this means everything we know is continuously reconstituted and co-constituted through reciprocal interactions in which each of us as humans is inextricably embedded. This makes "history" something forever malleable and, in my own experience with patients, it is this very malleability to which survivors of trauma typically object. For them, the trauma happened. *It happened.* And the historicity of the trauma happening is not something they want open to subsequent amendment if this means it might no longer have happened, or that it wouldn't be so traumatic if only they thought about it more charitably. If anything, survivors of trauma have typically been around figures who wanted to dismiss or ignore the reality of the trauma, and for the survivor to acquiesce to this dismissal invites a retraumatization in the present. Although they do not say so in exactly these words, in clinical work survivors of trauma often seem to want to point to the trauma in ways that make ontological claims—it is *there* in a way that antedates any human construction and is not properly open to interpretive revision if this effectively undoes trauma's ugly reality. The kinds of questions with which theology has been wrestling for 50 years suggest that there is something about trauma that is by definition unintegratable. It has a stubborn otherness to it, a horrible alterity that periodically forces itself upon us from without in a way that seems much more found than made, a brutality that is not of our own making, something it would be wrong of us to try to magically undo through imaginative conjury or inventive reinterpretation.

Constructivism

As psychoanalysis begins its second century, it finds itself in the midst of a radical paradigm shift, one as dramatic and far reaching for psychoanalysis as the Copernican revolution was over the Ptolemaic astronomy of the sixteenth century. During any such periods of profound change and ferment, now as then, description of the old order is easy. Description of the new-order-in-formation is not. Edward Glover, for instance, in his attempt to describe the British Independent Group of object relations while it was still in formation during the 1940s in London, knew that these analysts had varying sympathies both for certain aspects of Melanie Klein's work and for the general teaching of Freud and his daughter, Anna. But he didn't know what to call this new group. As chairman of the Training Committee he knew what to call the "Vienna Group," and the "Klein Group," but I think it is wonderfully illuminating how he referred to the third group: "The (?middle, ?moderate, Compromise, Composite, Remaining) Group (title uncertain)" (memorandum of September 21, 1942, cited in King and Steiner, 1990, p. 599).

It is no easier today to give the present movement a precise name, but one aspect of it involves a shift from a one-person psychology to what has been called a two-person psychology, although it now might better be called an N-person psychology, using the symbol N from statistics to represent any number, thereby emphasizing that a two-person psychology is really a systems psychology. Michael Balint (1968), in his description of an equally historic switch from a triadic, three-person constellation of oedipal rivalry and neurotic guilt to a two-person object relations psychology of oneness and separateness, complained that to call this domain "preoedipal" is misleading because the characterization is incomplete. To call it preoedipal defines it only by what it comes before; it does not describe it for what it is on its own terms, which Balint termed "the Basic Fault." Calling it preoedipal makes about as much sense as calling oedipal issues "post-Basic Fault." In the same fashion, it is easier to describe what this new, evolving two-person perspective is not: not hierarchical, not positivistic, not authoritarian. The task of psychoanalysis during this paradigm shift is to learn to articulate what it is, not just what it is not, and one of the best terms to date is "constructivism" (Berger and Luckmann, 1966; Von Glaserfeld, 1984; Watzlawick, 1984, 1990; Anderson, 1990; Mitchell, 1992; Stern, 1997; Hoffman, 1998). This term is elegant, nuanced, and complex, entailing not only a relational shift from a one- to a two-person psychology, but also an epistemological shift from a positivistic to a constructivist stance. These shifts, often assumed to be synonymous, are actually not and should be appreciated as distinctive and complementary elements to this alternative psychoanalytic paradigm.

Even though Freud's theory centered on the neuroses, or three-person oedipal conflicts involving, for example, a son's competition with father for mother's love, a prominent and enduring aspect of Freud's basic vision was essentially a one-person psychology of energic discharge. This is so because Freud viewed relations with other people merely as a means to this end of drive satisfaction—a kind of endogenous torpor—a view generally unsupported by empirical research. As Morris Eagle (1984) has reminded us, Harry Harlow's historic studies in the 1950s with primates were fundamentally an empirical test of drive theory versus object relations, something we would now, nearly five decades later, characterize as the relational shift that is so prominent in contemporary psychoanalysis. Infant primates taken from their mothers and raised in cages with artificial figures as surrogate mothers, one a wire-surface figure that had milk-dispensing nipples and another figure that was supple and covered in a soft terrycloth but that dispensed no food, had strikingly different patterns of attachment. According to drive theory, the infants should have preferred the drive-reducing pleasure of the nipple-bearing wire mother and made it their primary attachment figure. In a series of varied experiments, however, the infants consistently chose the terrycloth mother, who offered what Harlow termed "contact comfort" over the milk-dispensing figure. Moreover, it was not that the terrycloth mothers dispensed "contact comfort" analogous to the milk dispensing of the wire figure; infants showed a greater pattern of generalized attachment to the soft-surface mother and clung to it in situations of perceived danger or uncertainty (p. 11; see also Harlow [1986]).

Also in support of the concept that persons are not primarily pleasure seeking but object seeking was Ronald Fairbairn. In the preface to Fairbairn's (1952) *Psychoanalytic Studies of the Personality*, Ernest Jones offered a succinct summary of this beginning shift to a two-person, relational psychology:

> If it were possible to condense Dr. Fairbairn's new ideas into one sentence, it might run somewhat as follows. Instead of starting, as Freud did, from stimulation of the nervous system proceeding from excitation of various erotogenous zones and internal tension arising from gonadic activity, Dr. Fairbairn starts at the centre of the personality, the ego, and depicts its strivings and difficulties in its endeavour to reach an object where it may find support [p. v].

This ongoing shift in contemporary psychoanalysis is difficult to isolate and identify, despite its long history and numerous proponents, perhaps because of the many different theoretical advocates it has had. Each relational theorist speaks in a slightly different psychoanalytic dialect, and most of them rarely acknowledge the contributions of others, with the unfortunate effect that, as Mitchell (1988) has observed, "it is often not appreciated how different from Freud's initial vision psychoanalysis has become" (p. 2). Reminiscent of Strachey's musings about what if there had been ten Freuds, in this shift from a drive theory to a relational model there have been dozens of "Freuds," each eager to differentiate his or her contributions from those of others, thereby obscuring frequent and fundamental points of intersource agreement.

It is not enough, however, to say that this paradigm shift in contemporary psychoanalysis is merely one from a drive structure model to a relational structure model. For the second aspect of the change at hand, as mentioned earlier, really amounts to *a revised psychoanalytic epistemology*, and one that is not strictly equivalent to the drive versus relational model. The reason for this lack of equivalence is that all contemporary psychoanalytic theories, whether ego psychological, object relational, self psychological, or interpersonal, usually contain latent elements of unacknowledged positivism. These elements surface in the adjudication of others' "realistic" perceptions, "irrational" ideas, or "actual meanings." Irwin Hoffman (1991) has characterized this shift from positivism toward social constructivism as endorsing the conviction that "the personal participation of the analyst in the process is considered to have a continuous effect on what he or she understands about himself or herself and about the patient in the interaction. The general assumption in this model is that the analyst's understanding is always a function of his or her perspective at the moment" (p. 77).

Gone with this perspective is the notion that there is a single correct and complete way to describe experience. Freud's vision was that there is a necessary, singular solution to the problem that the "data" demand, something Spence (1987) describes in psychoanalysis as "The Sherlock Holmes Tradition":

> The genre is familiar to us all. It features a master sleuth (therapist) who is confronted by a series of bizarre and disconnected events (symptoms) reported by a somewhat desperate and disorganized client (patient). . . . In the typical Sherlock Holmes adventure, the eccentric client makes a dramatic appearance, often arriving on a dark and stormy night, and presents an account which seems partly fantastic and somehow familiar. The events seem to have no logical connection with one another or with pieces of his past; frequently he seems close to despair and may have come to Holmes only as a last resort. Holmes, by contrast, listens calmly and dispassionately, serene in the knowledge that the patient sifting of all the evidence will always yield the *singular solution*. And it does [p. 114; emphasis added].

Another variant of this idea of the singular solution is the metaphor of the blind men feeling different parts of the elephant: if there are different perspectives, they are just different vantage points on different parts of the animal—head, ears, trunk, legs, tail. The various perspectives may be manifold, but they all ultimately lead to the same singular solution. Mitchell (1988) expresses an aspect of the constructivist's epistemology with this warning:

> This outlook can be very misleading. Reality is not simply discovered, but is partially created by theoretical presuppositions. There are lots of blind men out there, but they are not all operating on the same premises, within the same reality; they are not all exploring

elephants. Some may be grappling with giraffes. To try to contain all reports within the same framework may lead to strange hybrids: four stout legs, a long graceful neck; four thin legs, a long trunk, and so on [p. viii].

The problem with the epistemology of the singular solution is that it de-emphasizes the contribution of the knower to what is known, making disconfirmation of beliefs difficult. As Paul Wachtel (1981) has suggested, the interpersonal world does not "hold still" and allow or require us to accommodate to it in the way the physical world does. Instead, the interpersonal world accommodates to us. "Our suspicions, and the actions they motivate, lead others to in fact be hostile; our expectations of seductive behavior lead to eroticized interactions with others; our submissive behavior, based on past experiences as well as defensive needs, induces others to expect more compliance from us than they do from others" (p. 70).

This lack of a singular solution is worrisome for some religiously committed persons who fear the only alternative is an abject relativism—a concern not unique to persons of faith. Allan Bloom (1987), for example, excoriates American university students who, in the name of limitless openness, lack the courage of their convictions.

Relativism is necessary to openness; and this is the virtue, the only virtue, which all primary education for more than fifty years has dedicated itself to inculcating. Openness—and the relativism that makes it the only plausible stance in the face of various claims to truth and various ways of life and kinds of human beings—is the great insight of our times. The true believer is the real danger. The study of history and of culture teaches that all the world was mad in the past; men always thought they were right, and that led to wars, persecutions, slavery, xenophobia, racism, and chauvinism. The point is not to correct the mistakes and really be right; rather it is not to think you are right at all. . . .

What right, they ask, do I or anyone else have to say one [culture] is better than the others? If I pose the routine questions designed to confute them and make them think, such as, "If you had been a British administrator in India, would you have let the natives under your governance burn the widow at the funeral of the man who had died?" they either remain silent or reply that the British should never have been there in the first place. It is not that they know very much about other nations, or about their own. The purpose of their education is not to make them scholars but to provide them with a moral virtue—openness [pp. 25–26].

Epistemological nihilism is not a necessary consequence of constructivism. As Donnel Stern (1992) avers:

> As constructivist psychoanalysts we remain passionate in our search for what is true, and we have the strongest feelings that one thing is more true than another. Giving choice and conviction their due in the process of thought is not at all the same thing as saying that we can conclude anything we please and still claim to be carrying out our work responsibly. We still have to choose the point of view that works the best, that is most complete and satisfying in its account of the phenomena in question. We certainly do not have to accept that reality itself has no structure apart from that which we impose upon it [p. 333].

Constructivism means that there is more to knowing than knowing will ever know. For example, in his book *Personal Knowledge*, which drove the final nail in the coffin of positivism as an intellectually defensible position, the philosopher of science Michael Polanyi (1958) noted that persons most familiar with a district are the worst at giving a stranger directions. "They tell you, 'Just keep going straight on,' forgetting the forks at which you will have to decide which way to go. They cannot realize that their indications are altogether ambiguous, because to them they are not. They say confidently, 'You can't miss it'" (p. 170n).

I believe that all these changes in psychoanalytic epistemology have implications for the analysis of religious experience. If, indeed, there is more to knowing than knowing will ever know, then there also is more to faith than can ever be explicitly specified. Moreover, from this perspective, there is an element of faith in all human knowing. As Polanyi wrote, "into every act of knowing, there enters a passionate contribution of the person knowing what is being known, and this coefficient is no mere imperfection but a vital component of his knowledge" (p. viii).

Further Considerations for Future Studies

My argument has not been to try to prove that psychoanalytic theory has changed, using conceptions of religion as ancillary illustrations. My argument is the other way around. It is, rather, that because theory has continued to evolve and change—often radically from Freud's original conception—we should not forget to apply these changes to how we conceptualize and interpret religious experience in our patients. Or perhaps I should say, in the spirit of my interpretation of Whitehead's admonition, we must not forget and we must forget—in the dual meanings I first detailed. This kind of creative flexibility and freedom is especially difficult, however, if Freud is more our ghost than our ancestor. And when it comes to addressing issues pertaining to religion where Freud serves as our ghost, psychoanalytic authors who are otherwise lyrical, sensitive, and poetic can take on a kind of theoretical clunkiness.

Perhaps even that clunkiness is no inherent liability any more than Freud's ghostliness is. Conceivably, in cultures other than our own the distinction between ghosts and ancestors is blurred. Could Freud, like Casper, ever be a friendly ghost? Is the distinction between ghosts and ancestors that the latter are happy or good objects, whereas the former are objects that are experienced as unhappy or persecutory? If Vamik Volkan (1988) is right that the need to have enemies and allies serves vital developmental functions, then the persecutory and the inelegant are no less valuable than the benignly lyrical. Clunkiness, to paraphrase the compulsive's credo, is no less next to godliness. The liability is not in the occurrence of one side of a polarity or the other (elegance-clunkiness, reductionism-transcendence, ghosts-ancestors), but rather in the failure to allow for the creative interplay of both. Seen in this light, for example, the space for destruction is as vital as the capacity to survive aggressive hating and destruction.

In the hope of offering constructive alternatives that support such dialectical play, I would like to develop seven points for further consideration in future study of the analysis of religious experience.

First, these modern trends in psychoanalytic theory no more "validate" religion than Freud's classical position in earlier times "refuted" it. The author C. S. Lewis (1970) once threatened to write a story about a fictional character, Ezekiel Bulver, who at the age of five heard his mother arguing with his father over whether the sum of the length of two sides of a triangle was greater than the third. The mother believed this was not so, and, unable to convince the father otherwise, she finally exclaimed, "Oh, you believe that because you are a man!" This moment was an epiphany for young Bulver, who realized that instead of showing that a person is wrong and then explaining why, you begin by presupposing—as an act of faith—that he is wrong and then explain how he ever came to be so silly (p. 273).

In "The Future of an Illusion" (1927) Freud Bulverized religion. As he confessed, "To assess the truth value of religious doctrines does not lie within the scope of the present enquiry. It is enough for us that we have recognized them as being, in their psychological nature, illusions" (Freud,

1927, p. 33). It would also be possible to Bulverize Freud by interpreting his own motivations for his opinions about religion. As Meissner (1984) has written, for example, "Behind the Freudian argument about religion stands Freud the man, and behind Freud the man, with his prejudices, beliefs, and convictions, lurks the shadow of Freud the child" (p. vii; see also Sorenson, 1990, pp. 211–212, for a summary of others' critiques of Freud). But interpreting a person's motives, valuable as this may be in its own right, can make no ultimate comment about the truth of the person's beliefs. John McDargh (1983, p. 69ff) has understood this and proposed a constructive model of interdisciplinary study between psychoanalysis and theology in which neither discipline discredits—or as Lewis might say, "Bulverizes"—the other, and yet each also has the capacity to criticize and instruct the other. Armand Nicholi (2002) likewise offers a fair-minded and thoughtful comparison of Lewis and Freud.

Second, I view ongoing change in psychoanalytic perspectives on illusion and narrative as special cases or subsets of a larger constructivist paradigm shift in contemporary psychoanalysis; the implications for analysis of religious experience, while significant clinically, are incidental to the main points of the shift. Bruno Bettelheim (1977) has written on the meaning and importance of fairy tales for children's healthy development. Ellen Handler Spitz (1988) has likewise provided a provocative and thoughtful analysis of the dialectic between image and word in Maurice Sendak's (1963) illustrated children's book, *Where the Wild Things Are.* And Ann and Barry Ulanov (1983) have offered an extensive theological and psychological analysis of envy in the story of Cinderella from a Jungian perspective. The shift in contemporary psychoanalysis is about the value of illusion and intersubjectivity in general, not religious illusion in any particular sense.

Third, I think it is useful to beware of possible colorations and distortions of Freud's attitude toward the life of the soul that are artifacts of our English translation of Freud's native German. Neville Symington (1986) placed Freud not only in the Darwinian and physicalist traditions that were prevalent in nineteenth-century Vienna (pp. 51–61), for example, but also argued that Freud's theorizing was profoundly rooted in the late eighteenth-century Romanticism (pp. 72–83). Bettelheim's (1982) real criticism was not of James Strachey's English translation per se, but more fundamentally of the philosophy of science that lay behind it, namely Strachey's positivism which, for Bettelheim, obscured what Symington termed "Freud the Romantic." Strachey's Freud is not the Freud Bettelheim knew from reading the text in his native German tongue.

Efforts to integrate, say, Freud and religion, according to Bettelheim, would really be efforts to integrate religion with the Freud of Strachey's translation—a solely positivistic Freud of positively no soul.

Fourth, I think the recent shifts in psychoanalytic theory have profound implications for the analysis of religion and convey a view quite foreign to Freud's original inchoate and unreflective positivism. About the child's transitional object, for example; Winnicott (1975) stressed:

> The parents get to know its value and carry it round when traveling. The mother lets it get dirty and even smelly, knowing that by washing it she introduces a break in continuity in the infant's experience, a break that may destroy the meaning and value to the infant [p. 232].
>
> *Of the transitional object it can be said that it is a matter of agreement between us and the baby that we will never ask the question, "Did you conceive of this or was it presented to you from without?" The important point is that no decision on this point is expected. The question is not to be formulated* [pp. 239–240].

These perspectives are a long way from Freud's view that illusion is a departure from reality, rather than a facilitator of it. Meissner (1984) understands well the shift in more modern philosophy of science when he writes about the potential value of sustained empathic immersion in the religious patient's point of view.

> While an insistence on psychological and methodological purity has its place, science, it turns out, is not always scientific. A case can and should be made for the usefulness of empathic observation or even participation in the psychological approach to religious phenomena. Freud's limitation was that he was not a believer, and that he held fixed and prejudicial ideas about the role of religion in human life, so that he could not be an objective or perceptive observer of it. There is much in his life history that gave rise to this posture, but here it is sufficient to note that such influences do play a significant role. We might argue, then, that the psychologist who sets out to study religious experience must possess an empathic openness to and respect for the meaning and relevance of the phenomena he studies [p. 7].

Meissner's comments bring to mind William James, a contemporary of Freud, who articulated a perspective nearly 100 years ago that has come to represent, oddly enough, contemporary extensions of Freud's thought. On the value of what we now would call sustained empathic inquiry and the necessity of transitional phenomena for psychological integrity, James

(1902) wrote, "One must have musical ears to know the value of a symphony; one must have been in love one's self to understand a lover's state of mind. Lacking the heart or the ear, we cannot interpret the musician or the lover justly, and we are even likely to consider him weak-minded or absurd." James saved his punch line for last: "The mystic finds that most of us accord to his expectations an equally incompetent treatment" (p. 300).

Fifth, I think there are probably limits to how far even this revised psychoanalytic epistemology can go in being empathically attuned to the lived experience of the religious believer. The psychoanalyst Stanley Leavy (1990) has argued that to avoid analyzing religious material makes the analysis less than complete, and to analyze religious material as wholly illusory is an experience-distant posture from the perspective of the analysand. "When the analyst analyzes religious beliefs as illusions, the process is to that extent external to the patient, however satisfying it may be to the analyst" (p. 50). Besides, external confirmation is normally neither required nor desired to explicate the patient's experience. Leavy reasons, "A carefully preserved letter to the patient from an angry parent, written many years ago, has nothing to offer beyond what the memory of the letter can provide. Descriptions of the beauty of a lover require no photographs to be convincing" (p. 50). Why, then, do we demand more, or something else, Leavy asked, when the patient's relationship with God is the focus of psychoanalytic study? Leavy offers an answer to his own question:

> The answer is obvious enough: parents and lovers and all the others with whom people exist in relationship are external "objects," whose reality is open to consensual validation. God is not such an object; God is the reality, according to believers, who transcends external objectivity. God is a class of one. It is there that the skeptical psychoanalyst, like other skeptics, is likely to hold that the patient talking about God is in a dreamworld, from which a successful analysis will awaken him or her. So Otto Fenichel, with monumental confidence, assured us that as his patients progressed in their analyses they became gradually liberated from their religion. And Helene Deutsch had to conclude regretfully that the Catholic teacher she had treated so effectively for her obsessional neurosis was unable to accomplish a real cure since she remained within her religious order as a nun [p. 50].

Leavy's objection is that the experience of the believer, although it never goes beyond the domain of appropriate psychological analysis, does go beyond the purview of psychological reductionism.

> For all the increased generosity and vision in the later views [of contemporary psychoanalysis], they do not succeed, cannot succeed, in representing religion as it appears to believers. The *anthropological* grasp that these authors present is no small thing itself, but it is one that holds at a distance the idea of the transcendent reality, God. I call it "anthropological" because it can include the idea of God only as a man-made symbol. Contrariwise, at the heart of religion is the conviction that the symbol is not totally man-made, not a golden calf, not just the product of the yearning but is a point in which the encounter with a self-revealing transcendent Other is made concrete [p. 55].

James Jones (1991) makes a similar point about the priority of transcendence versus psychological analysis.

> One of the major methodological conflicts between religious studies and psychoanalysis as they have developed in the twentieth century involves precisely this issue. A rejuvenation of theology in the West took place in midcentury around this assertion that reflection on religion must begin with God rather than with human experience as had been the case in the mainstream of nineteenth-century European theology; in contrast, psychoanalysis continued Freud's trajectory of reducing religious concepts to intrapsychic dynamics [pp. 7–8].

Sixth, introduction of this revised psychoanalytic epistemology into the curriculum of psychoanalytic training programs might actually be assisted by following the lead of contemporary models for theological education today, a possibility that I take up in more detail in chapter 6. This is an especially difficult point for some psychoanalysts to imagine, as if it meant that psychoanalytic education should somehow be "religious." Otto Kernberg (1986), in a description of the varieties of psychoanalytic training, has outlined four models: those of the trade school, the art institute, the university, and what he views unfavorably as the theological seminary. He claims that current approaches today are some combination of the seminary and trade schools, whereas the ideal would be a merging of the art institute and university models. Douglas Kirsner (1990) has underscored the irony that the organization of professional psychoanalysis in North America has taken on the very characteristic that Freud criticized organized religion—that of a universal obsessional neurosis. The task of psychoanalysis, according to Kirsner, is to organize itself as a group while also allowing for the disturbing presence of creative reformers, critics with a different viewpoint—what Wilfred Bion (1970) called Mystics.

Contemporary theological education in North America often exposes students to courses on intellectual history, the nature and science of hermeneutics, cross-cultural anthropology, and the formation of meaning through the use of symbolic ritual in community and personal reflection in dialogue. If anything, the complaint of most mainline Protestant denominations is that seminaries take conservative students and turn them into critically thinking liberals. Would that this were the typical problem of organized psychoanalytic education!

Seventh, Thomas Kuhn gave a panel presentation in July 1961 at Oxford University just months before his now classic book on the structure of scientific revolutions was first released in 1962. The title of his talk at Oxford was "The Function of Dogma in Scientific Research." Contrary to the typical attitude that dogma has no place in science, Kuhn maintained that its place in science is as essential as it is ubiquitous. Kuhn's (1963) argument was that "though a quasi-dogmatic commitment is, on the one hand, a source of resistance and controversy, it is also instrumental in making the sciences the most consistently revolutionary of all human activities." He concluded, "One need make neither resistance nor dogma a virtue to recognize that no mature science could exist without them" (p. 349). As a panel respondent to Kuhn, Polanyi (in Kuhn, 1963) was most sympathetic:

> The paper by Mr. Thomas Kuhn may arouse opposition from various quarters, but not from me. At the end of it he says that the dependence of research upon a deep commitment to established beliefs receives the very minimum attention today. I could not agree more; I have tried in vain to call attention to this commitment for many years. I hope that if I join forces with Mr. Kuhn we may both do better. His mastery of the history of science should help to establish this fact so firmly that its vast implications will have to be faced by all [p. 375].

Polanyi's (1958) point was to show that complete objectivity, usually lauded in science, is a misleading and false ideal, not just for the social sciences but for the physical sciences themselves (p. 18). Personal conviction and involvement are essential for all genuine knowledge, even though this involvement necessitates an epistemology predicated on the belief that there is more to knowing than knowing will ever know.

Seen in this light, dogma per se is not inherent liability. Much as Gadamer (1975) describes prejudice as that which paradoxically limits and allows new thought, dogma is the tradition that revolutions need to push against (Steiner, 1985). Loewald (1988) took such dichotomies (dogma-revolution, subjectivity-objectivity, unconscious-conscious) and, through an extension of Winnicott's notion of transitional phenomena, recast them as fertile antinomies.

> The journey does not start from the subjective; it is a journey from a state *prior* to the differentiation of subjectivity and objectivity to a state when subjectivity and objectivity *come into being.* Transitional objects and phenomena are transitional not by virtue of being in transit from subjectivity to objectivity, but insofar as they represent *way stations* from *indeterminacy* to *determinacy* or from the *ineffable* to the *effable* [p. 72; emphasis added].

In this sense, dogma or prejudice might be not an enemy of rationality and progress as much as it might be the midwife who assists in the birth of meaning, from indeterminacy to determinacy, from the ineffable to the effable. And this midwifery casts new light on the original question about any science that hesitates to forget its founders becoming lost. Loewald filed a protest about the increasing hegemony of the ego over the id. The rallying cry, "Where id was shall ego be," is too linear, too unidirectional, and ultimately stultifying. More satisfying is to permit a circularity, something like intrapsychic composting: the appropriation of unconscious material into consciousness, but also the relinquishing of certain conscious mentation into the domain of unconscious mental activity—and then back again. This permits a reversal, a delightful heresy: "Where ego was shall id be." Loewald (1978) reasoned, "The richer a person's mental life is, the more he experiences on several levels of mentation, the more translation occurs back and forth between unconscious and conscious experience. To make the unconscious conscious is onesided. It is the transference between them that makes life a human life, that makes life human" (p. 31).

If this be so, then it is as inevitable as it is essential that psychoanalysis as a science become "lost," and to do so in the alternating meanings of both senses described at the beginning of this chapter—a dialectical forgetting of methods and founders. It could indeed be that it is the transference between them that makes both psychoanalysis in general, and the analysis of religious experience in particular, a divinely human science.

Chapter 3

How Being "Religious" Was Treated in Psychoanalytic Journals from 1920 to 1994

with Christine Hebert Benson

The past 100 years of research in the psychology of religion has established one finding if nothing else: religion is multifactorial. It is complex. It is not just one thing. A recent compendium of psychological measures of religion (Hill and Hood, 1999), for example, contains over 70 instruments, most of which are multidimensional. Factor analyses of items on religious measures invariably produce multiple dimensions, as typified by a classic study (Glock and Stark, 1965) that found five factors: ideological (religious belief), ritualistic (religious practice), experiential (religious feeling), intellectual (religious knowledge), and consequential (religious effects).

More recent reviews of empirical studies on religion also highlight a second trend in the literature: a positive relationship between religion and mental health. In their analysis of 30 empirical articles published between 1984 and 1992, for example, Worthington et al. (1996) found generally consistent results that "religion does not affect mental health negatively" and, on the contrary, appears to have a positive relationship with mental well-being overall (p. 451). Another extensive literature review by Gartner, Larson, and Allen (1991) found that religion is positively associated with increased physical health, greater longevity, decreased juvenile delinquency, lower divorce rates, higher marital satisfaction, greater general well-being, lower psychological distress, and lower levels of depression. Pargament (1997, 2002), Koenig (1998), Powell, Shahabi, and Thorsen (2003), and Seeman, Dubin, and Seeman (2003) reported similar findings.

Despite a century of research indicating that religion is multidimensional and has a complex impact on mental health (including both positive and negative effects), psychoanalysis has tended to pathologize or ignore religion (chapter 1) by making Freud a ghost instead of an ancestor (chapter 2). Stanley Leavy (1990) reasoned that "while no analyst would infer from the fantasies of a patient about Antarctica that there is no such continent because neither the patient nor the analyst had ever been there, the nonexistence of God may be built into the analyst's deepest convictions," so much so that analytic writers "make their points on matters of religion as if the nonexistence or at least the irrelevance of God, and the illusory nature of belief, had been sufficiently demonstrated to them and to their readers and required no further argument" (p. 49). The result of this presumption on the part of analytic authors is the systematic de-emphasis of religion in psychoanalytic publications. LaMothe, Arnold, and Crane (1998) examined articles between 1990 and 1994 in six psychoanalytic journals to determine how often authors mentioned religion as a cultural variable of diversity in psychoanalytic case presentations. They found that only one in 10 case studies ever mentioned religion, and of those that did, only one in 11 actually explored the patient's religious experience. Thus, in the years that LaMothe et al. examined, fewer than 1% of published psychoanalytic case studies considered religion a topic that merited empathic exploration. "The inference is that analysts start from a preconceived, a priori notion that religious behavior necessarily implies a primitive, neurotic content to be decoded and eliminated through interpretation, and that the nonreligious condition should not interest the psychoanalyst because it already represents liberation from 'infantile illusions,'" declared De Mello Franco (1998, pp. 113–114). This "turns the analyst's function into that of an 'exorcist,' who is supposed, through his interpretations, to free the analysand from the trammels of his belief" (p. 114).

In contrast to LaMothe et al. (1998), who limited their study to a five-year period and, within that, only to clinical case presentations, my colleague Christine Hebert Benson and I examined every occurrence of the word "religious" throughout psychoanalytic journals, cover to cover, that were published over a 75-year period. We used the first volume of the Psychoanalytic Electronic Publishing (PEP) CD ROM, which contains a computer search engine and word-for-word transcriptions of the following publications: the International Journal of Psycho-Analysis, volumes

1-75 (1920-1994); the *Bulletin of the International Psycho-Analytic Association*, volumes 4-75 (1923-1994); the *Psychoanalytic Quarterly*, volumes 1-63 (1932-1994); the *Psychoanalytic Study of the Child*, volumes 1-48 (1945-1993); the *Bulletin of the American Psychoanalytic Association*, volumes 9-43 (1953-1987); the *Journal of the American Psychoanalytic Association*, volumes 1-42 (1953-1994); *Contemporary Psychoanalysis*, volumes 1-30 (1964-1994); and the *International Review of Psycho-Analysis*, volumes 1-19 (1974-1992). We examined each occurrence of the word "religious" within its textual context and rated it as falling into one of three categories: *descriptive, pathological,* or *integrative* (Benson, 2000).

A *descriptive* coding was defined by use of the word religious in a strictly nonevaluative context, one that was purely descriptive and did not locate the word in a context of either pathology or health. An example of a descriptive use comes from John Bowlby (1940), who used the word "religious" in a list of demographic characteristics that included "economic conditions, housing conditions, the school situation, diet and religious teaching" (p. 154). In a similar manner, Harold Borris (1994) noted how some analysts "tell their patients even before the work starts that they take regular summer or winter vacations or attend specified meetings or will be off during Federal or religious holidays" (p. 312). Sándor Radó (1932) likewise provides a purely descriptive reference in his allusion to "religious and scientific conceptions of the universe" (p. 693). In each of these instances, the word religious is a purely descriptive term that excludes evaluative appraisal, whether positive or negative.

A *pathological* coding of the word religious was defined as a contextual association of the word as all-bad and associated solely with psychopathology. In his description of Freud's view of religion, Nathaniel Laor (1989) referred to "religious experience as illusory and . . . regressive" and equated it with "psychosis" (p. 217). In the same reference to Freud by Laor, religion is depicted as "a major hindrance to personal growth" and that with which the "mature adult" must dispense (p. 217). Another example of a pathological coding of the word religious is seen in a reference by Otto Fenichel (1932) that describes a "religious person" as being similar to "a compulsive neurotic" (p. 642). In a discussion of group functioning, Phyllis Greenacre (1960) included "riots and states of religious excitement" as examples of "group irrationalities" (p. 583). In each of these examples, being religious is located within a context of immaturity or severe psychopathology.

An *integrative* coding of the word religious was defined as a contextual association that recognized religion as a possible resource for health.

It is important to add that occurrences coded as integrative did *not* have to depict religion as all-good, and only had to distinguish it from indiscriminate pathology. One example of an integrative use is Anna Freud's (1929) description of religious affects and ideas as performing "a unifying function within the psychic life" and contributing "to a greater unity in the character and conduct of the personality" (p. 503). Another example is T. L. Dorpat's (1975) clarification that "religious-like feelings which occur in the transitional mode" belong to the "illusory" realm, "but not delusional [experience]" (p. 237). Nathaniel Ross (1958) suggests that one not "consider religious experience per se as pathological," for it "appears to be entirely compatible with high degrees of emotional maturity" (p. 526). These integrative coding examples include a capacity for ambivalence regarding religion, as well as more nuanced presentations of religiousness that allow for potential health.

My colleague and I independently rated occurrences of the word religious over the period during which we coded the PEP CD ROM entries. We assessed how well we agreed on our coding (known in statistics as "inter-rater reliability") for 75 occurrences during the initial phase, 50 occurrences during the middle phase, and 75 occurrences during the final phase of our work, and demonstrated good agreement.[1]

We found 6916 occurrences of the word "religious" across the 75 years of psychoanalytic journals, and, of these, 5214 occurrences were descriptive, 1302 pathological, and 376 integrative. Thus the majority of occurrences were purely descriptive and nonevaluative, but when the word "religious" did occur in evaluative contexts, 77% of the time it was pathologized. A Chi-square analysis examined the observed frequencies of pathological versus integrative coding categories and compared these against what would be expected if these two categories occurred with equal frequency. Results indicated that the disproportionate amount of pathologizing associated with being religious was not attributable to chance.[2] As depicted in Figure 3, the total number of articles in the PEP CD ROM database varied from year to year, with some years having a lot more publications than other years. Therefore, before graphing the yearly tallies of the coding categories, we divided each by the total number of articles that were published that year. Without this adjustment, an apparent change in the tally of coding categories could simply be a function of there being more (or fewer) articles published in a given year.

---

[1] r = .84, .94, and .86 for coding phases one through three, respectively, $p < .01$ for all.
[2] $\chi^2 (1, N = 1678) = 511.01, p < .0001$.

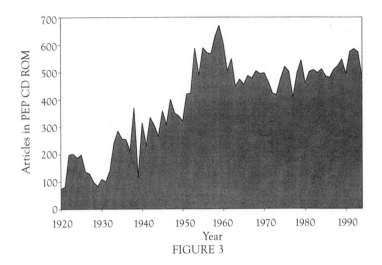

FIGURE 3

Figure 4 shows the occurrences of the word religious in each of the two evaluative coding categories (pathological or integrative), divided by the total number of articles in the database for each year. Figure 4 is a stacked area chart; the integrative occurrences are stacked "on top of" the pathological occurrences on the graph.

As a check against the possibility that the preponderance of pathological portrayals of being religious was an artifact of inclusion in clinical journals—which by definition are skewed toward addressing issues of

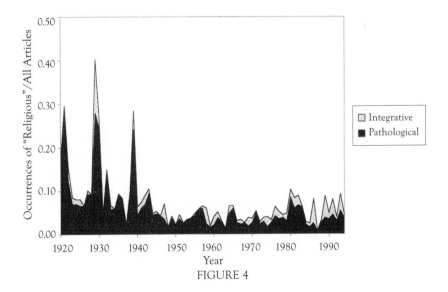

FIGURE 4

TABLE 3

Coding Category	"Religious" (N = 6916)	"Secular" (N = 279)	Total Frequency	Total Percent
Pathological	1302	30	1322	18.5%
Descriptive	5238	217	5455	75.8%
Integrative	376	32	408	5.7%
Total Frequency	6916	279	7195	
Total Percent	96.1%	3.9%		100.0%

χ^2 (2) = 26.80, p < .0001.

psychopathology—an analysis was performed for the word "secular," using the same three coding categories (descriptive, pathological, or integrative). An example of a descriptive coding of the word "secular" is Brill's (1922) comment about tobacco being originally used in "religious or secular ceremonies" (p. 433). Evans's (1949) remark about the "secular achievements of imperialism in its wealth, dominion, and power" (p. 39) highlights a more pathological aspect to secularism. And Bergmann's (1993) characterization of secular Jews as being "well educated and articulate" (p. 32) uses the word "secular" in a more favorably evaluative context, and is thus an example of the integrative category.

As shown in Table 3, being secular was treated in an even-handed way in psychoanalytic journals, with a balanced presentation of integrative and pathological appraisals, unlike being religious, which was so lopsidedly pathologized that the likelihood of these results occurring by chance was less than one in 10,000. This means the pathologizing of being religious was not simply a function of being in clinical journals, since occurrences of being secular in the same journals were not similarly pathologized.

When we looked at the timeline, it seemed as though there were fewer pathological portrayals of religion after 1939, so we decided to test this impression empirically by submitting the data to an interrupted time series analysis.[3] Results showed that after 1939 there was indeed a 59% decrease in the proportion of journal articles that pathologized being religious (p < .05). Why might this be so? Any possible answers are speculative at best, but one hypothesis is that Freud's own views on religion

---

[3]Specifically, a Box-Jenkins Auto Regressive Integrated Moving Average (ARIMA) model ([1,1,0], log10, differencing = 1). Statistical tests normally require uncorrelated error terms, but ARIMA models are a very sophisticated class of procedures that allow for correlated residuals, which tend to occur in time series analyses.

held sway over other analysts during Freud's lifetime. Freud was certainly the most influential figure in psychoanalysis while he was alive, and after his death (in 1939) other analysts may have felt more freedom to develop less pejorative portrayals of religion and spirituality. Further support for this hypothesis is found through closer inspection of the spikes on the timeline, which correspond closely with the publication of Freud's major polemics against religion. For example, after Freud's release of "The Future of an Illusion" in 1927, a frenzy of antireligious sentiment is echoed in psychoanalytic journals in 1928 and 1929. Similarly, Freud's publication of "Moses and Monotheism" in 1939 corresponds with another outbreak of religious pathologizing that year. And although Freud's first major treatise on the topic of religion, "Totem and Taboo," was published in 1912, psychoanalytic journals did not begin until 1920, thereby creating a backlog of pent-up psychoanalytic prejudice toward religion that could be vented once the journals were inaugurated.

Having Freud as a ghost has made the exploration of spirituality in psychoanalysis a taboo topic for generations of analysts, although this chapter presents evidence that the circumstances have begun to change. Gil Noam and Maryanne Wolf (1993) locate the source of this taboo in therapists' personal analyses.

> For most therapists it is far easier to discuss the joys and aberrations of sexual life, the honest and deceptive uses of money, the creative and petty elaborations of intimate love than it is to explore the role of prayer, meditation, and the discovery of meaning in the face of mortality. This difficulty in most clinical encounters can without exaggeration be called a taboo, first introduced during the training of the therapist and then transmitted in the clinical encounter with the patient [p. 197].

Ironically, this blind spot in analysts' training is not completely undesirable, given many analysts' discomfort in addressing issues of spirituality in treatment. As Noam and Wolf observe wryly, "The taboo mentioned earlier serves an important function: it shields clients from the lack of capability most therapists have in this area. Although the taboo is waning, a spiritual knowledge base for most therapists has not increased" (p. 203).

What Noam and Wolf highlight as an intergenerational link between the unexamined habits of student-therapists-in-training and their therapist-teachers is what Daniel Wile (1985) terms "psychotherapy by precedent": the bequeathing of an unwittingly superstitious legacy from one generation of clinicians to the next. If uninterrupted, this legacy continues in perpetuity. Elaborating on Wile's term, Paul Wachtel (1993) reflects that:

> Many of the features that give the therapeutic interaction its particu-
> lar relational structure and emotional shadings are conveyed from
> generation to generation of psychotherapists by a mode of transmis-
> sion that largely eludes reflective examination. The way one deals
> with patients' questions, whether and how one offers advice or opin-
> ions, how much or how little one reveals about oneself, and a host of
> other dimensions of the work that shape and influence the tone of
> the relationship are based very largely on an inner sense of what feels
> "right"—a feeling that derives significantly from the therapist's expe-
> rience in her own therapy. But *her* therapist's practices themselves
> were likely to have been influenced, in an equally unexamined way,
> by *her* experiences in *her* own therapy [p. 40].

This book is a call for further awareness and examination of possible expressions of spirituality in the consulting room, whether in the pa-tient, the analyst, or the unique combination of both. The process of change is already underway, and by welcoming it further, we interrupt the intergenerational transmission of a taboo that's an artifact of nine-teenth-century philosophy of science, a question I take up in more detail in this book's remaining chapters.

Chapter 2 addressed how psychoanalytic theory has changed in ways that have implication for understanding religious and spiritual experi-ence; this chapter tracked how these changes have played out historically in psychoanalytic publications. That psychoanalytic journal articles have changed their treatment of religion in the years since Freud's death is no small matter. Much progress has been made, and yet more remains to be realized. During Freud's lifetime, the number of pathological portrayals of being religious surpassed more integrative appraisals by a ratio of 9 to 1; after Freud's death this ratio has dropped to 3 to 1—an advance, to be sure, and yet still a preponderance of splitting when it comes to how analysts handle religion in print. In the next chapter, I examine how evolving changes in psychoanalytic theory impact clinical technique when analyzing spirituality.

Chapter 4

The Patient's Experience
Of the Analyst's Spirituality

W hen working with patients who are religious, does it make any difference if the analyst has some openness to the possibility of transcendence or experience of the sacred? Or, to put it in terms more narrow and stark, does it make any difference if the analyst believes in God? As addressed in chapter 1, some analysts may view participation in religious life as something totally separate from, if not actually inimical to, openness to the possibility of transcendence or experience of the sacred.[1] Psychoanalytic practice is rarely the unearthing of preexisting facts, however, and is more commonly the coconstruction of a particular analyst-patient dyad. In this chapter I present empirical evidence that the apparent foreclosure of mystery prevalent among religious analysands can be a coconstruction of patients' experience of analysts who view religion and spirituality as unrelated or even mutually exclusive. In any case, to focus on the patient's experience of the analyst's spirituality is, on the surface, an odd topic for psychoanalysis. Beyond the traditional antipathy between psychoanalysis and religion, which stems from the more circumstantial element of Freud's confession of atheism personally, there are three more substantial objections: one philosophical, another clinical, and the third pedagogical.

---

[1]See also Taylor (2002), who rejects any necessary dichotomy between religion and spirituality as spurious.

A PHILOSOPHICAL OBJECTION

Despite Freud's claims of ignorance about philosophy—or perhaps because of it—rank-and-file psychoanalytic clinicians, from Freud's day until recently, have been able to persevere in psychoanalytic practice in a manner largely uninformed by pertinent philosophical developments. This perseveration has yielded a double irony: not only could psychoanalysis be on the intellectual vanguard in some aspects of twentieth-century thought, while at the same time remaining on the trailing edge of other cultural developments, but also the discrepancy itself could occur through processes that function outside conscious awareness, the very domain to which analysts had laid special claim.

One such generally inexplicit philosophical strand in Freud's thought was a commitment to a positivistic epistemology, an orientation that was prevalent and convincing to many in early twentieth-century Vienna, but which has been generally discredited for more than half a century. Despite having fallen into disfavor in most other circles intellectually, Freud's legacy of positivism shows amazing persistence to this day in the practice of virtually all of us as psychoanalytic clinicians. Even in contemporary psychoanalytic discourse, it is not uncommon to hear appeals to "clinical facts" we are said to have in common and by which we are to adjudicate competing theories (Wallerstein, 1990), or, in psychoanalytic case conferences, to hear references made to the "clinical material," as though this were some kind of uninterpreted raw data or brute fact (Meehl, 1973). Another remnant of positivism in psychoanalysis is our continuing penchant for inanimate, impersonal metaphor which de-emphasizes a process of necessarily inextricable, highly personal, and intersubjective mutual influence. Whereas Freud spoke originally of a blank screen, fascination in subsequent decades has continued with notions of a container (Bion), a frame (Langs), and more recently still, a mirror (Kohut).

According to their Principle of Verification, positivists assigned all propositions to one of three categories: those that were empirically true, those that were empirically false, and the rest that were deemed "cognitively meaningless." A statement like "It is raining outside" fell into category one or two, whereas all reference to transcendence, such as "God is love," was relegated to category three. Although positivism did not last long as an intellectually viable position (some wag once pointed out that the positivists' Verification Principle was itself empirically unverifiable, and thus, by its own criteria, cognitively meaningless!), its vestiges in psychoanalysis may lead some contemporary analysts to believe that analysis of transcendent experience is necessarily wrongheaded and unscientific. By contrast, contemporary philosophers of science, to whom I suspect most of us practicing clinicians have not had much exposure, would warn us that criteria for distinguishing science from nonscience are more elusive than our positivistic heritage would lead us to believe (Laudan, 1983).

Given positivism's relatively brief flowering earlier this century, its long-term significance in the context of several millennia of intellectual history is uncertain. There is another movement of thought that has stood the test of time, however, and it makes a point somewhat similar to positivism with regard to transcendence. This much more substantial objection to the legitimacy of analysts addressing religious experience has its origins in the work, two centuries earlier, of Immanuel Kant. The genius of the philosopher from Königsberg was his creative synthesis between the earlier quest for certainty in Cartesian rationalism and the challenge of epistemological nihilism in Humean empiricism. In contrast to both, Kant argued that we could have true knowledge, but only through the sensory pathways by which our minds organize experience. We thus can never know a thing-in-itself (which he termed the "noumenal" realm); all our knowing is constrained by the imposition of our human mental channels of spatial-temporal organization (which he termed the "phenomenal" realm). On this point Kant (1787) was emphatically clear: "[T]he domain that lies out beyond the sphere of appearances is for us empty. That is to say, we have an understanding which problematically extends further, but we have no intuition, indeed not even the concept of a possible intuition, through which the objects outside the field of sensibility can be given" (p. 272).

Once we accept Kant's bifurcation as a satisfactory solution to the presumed dichotomy between objects-known and subjects-who-do-the-knowing, the conclusion is ineluctable: analysis of the noumenous is inherently out of the question. The legitimate purview of analysts cannot extend beyond the phenomenal realm. Noam and Wolf (1993), who teach at Harvard and Tufts Universities, respectively, describe an experience in New England that illustrates this Kantian approach to spirituality in psychoanalysis, an experience, I believe, that is indicative of a common psychoanalytic perspective on religion, regardless of geographic region.

At a recent meeting of psychoanalysts in Boston, a seasoned teacher reviewed the clinical work of a candidate whose patient was a deeply religious Catholic woman. The patient's psychological language incorporated many spiritual metaphors about the relationship between

God and guilt. Picking up on the insecurity of the analyst who mentioned that she had difficulties dealing with the religious experience of her patient, the consultant said with authority and conviction: "Why should you treat her religious concerns differently than you deal with any associations that emerge in psychoanalysis?" He meant his remarks to encourage the young analyst to enter all experiences of her patient and to try not to remain aloof from the religious ones. Although he sounded convincing, and had a positive impact on the treatment, the remark is troubling. Are spiritual associations really the same as any other associations? Should they be treated in the same way as other associations? [pp. 201–202].

John McDargh (1993), a theologian at Boston College who is involved in both clinical practice and the interdisciplinary conversation between psychology and religion, has raised a related question that, for psychoanalysts who endorse a Kantian epistemology, will also seem exceedingly odd. McDargh asks: "Is it *therapeutically* sufficient for a clinician to appreciate the psychological value of an individual's religion, or may it also be necessary for a clinician to take a position on the *ontological* status of the client's religious inner world?" (p. 173).

How we answer the questions by Noam, Wolf, and McDargh depends on the alternatives we perceive as available to us. If we endorse Kant's presentation of our options, then we have no other choice: we must say that spiritual associations are functionally the same as any others, and that it is indeed therapeutically sufficient to appreciate nothing beyond the psychological value of an individual's religion. For Kant, the idea of God can extend problematically beyond the phenomena; it's just that our knowledge is limited by the a priori categories. Or again: We can know things, including "God," but only through the categories. From this it follows that it simply will not do to try to smuggle transcendence through the portal of Kantian phenomena, if this invokes some sort of direct apprehension or unmediated access. Related to this impossibility, I find compelling the critique by philosopher and psychoanalyst Victoria Hamilton (1982) of Wilfred Bion, who, she argues, misunderstood Kant:

Bion blurs Kant's distinction between a priori and sensible knowledge when he proposes equivalence between the "things-in-themselves" and the "beta-elements"—that is, the raw, pure, discrete sense-impressions. Because both are ultimately unknowable, Bion states an incorrect equivalence. The chief characteristic of the "beta-element" is its corporeality and concreteness. It is "undigested"—that is, unworked over by mental functions. Inadvertently, Bion subsumes the noumenon under a corporeal conception. An elision occurs in his theory of thinking between the transcendental "thing-in-itself" and the psychotic "beta-element." In my view, this confusion arises because of Bion's misunderstanding of the problematical use of the concept of the noumenon. He fills up a concept which is "empty" (Kant) and gives it a positive employment [p. 251].

I understand Hamilton's point to be that there is no way to employ Kant's noumenal realm transcendentally, either by means of the ineffability of mysticism or the unspecifiability of intuition.

If Kant's thought is commonly regarded as the zenith of critical philosophy during the Enlightenment, ongoing intellectual history has continued to change in the centuries since, often in ways profoundly different from what those in the Enlightenment ever could have imagined. Even so, radical change often occurs in the name of non-change, through familiar and existing terms that disguise or simply do not convey the full extent of the revolution-in-process. Radio, in succeeding the telegraph, for example, was introduced as the "wireless"; the automobile was initially understood as a "horseless carriage." In neither case could anyone have envisioned the economic, ecological, and familial impact of the automobile on industrialized society, or the significance of radio signals in geosynchronous satellite transmission for an electronic global village. Kant's is termed "critical" philosophy; that a developing new constellation of thought is termed "postcritical" is similarly deceptive—much like the "wireless" or the "horseless carriage"—because this new term only describes what it comes after, and underemphasizes the radical transformation of epistemology it portends.

Throughout the twentieth century there have been multiple contributors to this emerging "postcritical" paradigm, and although these authors certainly would not agree with each other on every point, one vital thinker, already introduced in chapter 2, is Polanyi, whose 1958 book, *Personal Knowledge*, had as its apt subtitle *Towards a Post-Critical Philosophy*. Philosopher Ronald Hall (1993) contrasts critical and postcritical epistemology, arguing that, despite critical philosophy's attempt to oppose speculative ideals of objectivity, Kant's critique was not radical enough and falls short of what Polanyi offers. Hall (1973) explains:

> As I am reading it, objectivism presumes an ideal of objectivity according to which reality is defined as that which is completely independent

of a knowing subject. As objectivism has it, the embodied, situated, human knower inevitably contaminates this pure reality with subjective elements, that is, with evaluations, commitments, perspective, passion, and so forth. Consequently, the objectivist thinks that the ideal knower would be a disembodied god who passively comprehends, *sub specie aeternitatis,* the whole of reality as it is in and of itself [p. 73].

In Polanyi's work, Hall sees a new ideal of what comprises objectivity.

On this radically new ideal, we will not be inclined to say that as long as there is a subjective component in knowing, objectivity is an impossible dream. Rather, we will say that objectivity is obtainable because there is a subjective component in knowing. Post critical philosophy offers us the prospect of an access—a human access—to things-in-themselves; it tells us that we do not have to be gods to be objective knowers; it tells us, moreover, that human beings are not only not obstacles to objectivity, but the enabling means of its pursuit [p. 77].

From a slightly different vantage point, I view the work of Daniel Stern (1985) in infant observational research as also offering something like a neo-Kantian or even postcritical epistemology, especially in his work on affect attunement in infants. Like Kant, Stern posits modal sensory pathways through which infants (and all humans) know the world, including vision, audition, gustation, olfaction, and kinesthetic awareness, among others. Unlike Kant, however, Stern also posits an underlying capacity for amodal signal processing that is partially independent of, while also common to, all sensory input pathways. Also unlike Kant, for Stern the capacity for interaffectivity, rather than posing the skeptic's problem of how ever to know the existence of other minds, is what permits the psychological birth of human selfhood in the first place. Stern gives multiple examples of this phenomenon, of which I will mention just three.

A nine-month-old girl becomes very excited about a toy and reaches for it. As she grabs it, she lets out an exuberant "aaaah!" and looks at her mother. Her mother looks back, scrunches up her shoulders, and performs a terrific shimmy with her upper body, like a go-go dancer. The shimmy lasts only about as long as her daughter's "aaaah!" but is equally excited, joyful, and intense.

A nine-month-old boy bangs his hand on a soft toy, at first in some anger but gradually with pleasure, exuberance, and humor. He sets up a steady rhythm. Mother falls into his rhythm and says, "kaaaaa-bam, kaaaaa-bam," the "bam" falling on the stroke and the "kaaaaa" riding with the preparatory upswing and the suspenseful holding of his arm aloft before it falls.

An eight-and-one-half-month-old boy reaches for a toy just beyond reach. Silently he stretches toward it, leaning and extending arms and fingers out fully. Still short of the toy, he tenses his body to squeeze out the extra inch he needs to reach it. At that moment, his mother says, "uuuuuh . . . uuuuuh!" with a crescendo of vocal effort, the expiration of air pushing against her tensed torso. The mother's accelerating vocal-respiratory effort matches the infant's accelerating physical effort [p. 140].

In each of these episodes, *mere mimicry is not enough*. If the infant's voice rises and lowers in pitch, for example, and the mother merely does the same with hers, the infant experiences the mother as robotic, mechanical, and a less-than-fully human other, an outcome which engenders a similarly less vital sense of self in the baby. If, by contrast, the mother raises and lowers her eyebrows and facial expression, matched in time with the infant's vocalization, the baby has a sense of affective attunement, and self-enhancement ensues. It is as though the baby were saying, "I can see you get it—your response back to me shows me you aren't just mimicking me, you've taken it in, processed it, and sent it back to me in a way that shows you really understand!"

Stern's work on cross-modal perception and Polanyi's contributions toward a postcritical epistemology are but two instances among many that pose new possibilities for how psychoanalysts may think to work with all aspects of patients' experiences, including patients' religious experience—and these ways are very different from earlier perspectives steeped in critical philosophy and positivism. The point here is not that postcritical philosophers have supposedly had the final word and that no future conversations in philosophy will supervene; this is most certainly not the case. Besides, the unfolding trend-in-formation of what has been termed postcritical philosophy is a loosely organized, ramshackle structure at best, having no single spokesperson, no unified agenda, and an indeterminate future. The point, rather, is that intellectual history has continued to move on, not only from the positivism of Freud's day at the turn of the twentieth century, but also from the critical philosophy of the eighteenth-century Enlightenment. We psychoanalysts, however, to the degree that we imitate Freud's claim to ignorance about pertinent philosophical concerns, are at risk to persist in outmoded forms of empathic exploration of our patients' religious experience, as detailed in chapter 2.

A Clinical Objection

My question originally was, When working with patients who are religious, does it make any difference if the analyst has some openness to the possibility of transcendence or experience of the sacred? Or, more narrowly, does it make any difference if the analyst believes in God? Another objection is the clinical concern that it is the patient's reality alone that matters, and not the analyst's. Advocates of this perspective would express concern that it is the patient who is in analysis, not the analyst, and that ideally the analyst's contribution should be negligible, or at least so unobtrusive that the patient's experience is central and the analyst's idiosyncrasies and personal beliefs—regarding God or anything else, for that matter—are of no practical relevance.

Evelyne Schwaber (1986, 1990) is sometimes cited to this effect, as though her goal were total immersion in the patient's affective field so as to minimize the analyst's distinct presence. The way I read Schwaber, however, her interest is not that the analyst should try to disappear from the two-person intersubjective field, but rather the opposite. It is precisely because the goal of an invisible or noninteractive analyst is as impossible as it is misguided that it is essential to pay attention to the myriad ways in which the analyst impacts the patient—often without direct awareness of either analyst or patient. Lacking this awareness, the analyst then attributes the patient's motivation solely to intrapsychic processes within the patient.

Lewis Aron (1996) addresses this topic from a related and very creative perspective. The more customary approach for a psychoanalytic paper would be with a title something like "The Analyst's Experience of the Patient's Subjectivity," but Aron offers an insightful inversion. He writes on "The Patient's Experience of the Analyst's Subjectivity" (pp. 65–91). Aron avers that patients are motivated to probe beneath the analyst's professional façade much as children are motivated to penetrate beneath and to connect with their parents' core selves (p. 80). When thwarted in this regard, an experience of frustration may be mistaken as evidence of patients' innate aggression or endogenous envy. As Aron allows, when pondering "the rich Kleinian imagery of the infant's attempts in unconscious phantasy to enter into the mother's body, we may wonder whether the violent, destructive phantasies encountered are due only to innate greed and envy or whether they are not also the result of the frustration of being denied access to the core of their parents. Could these phantasies be an accurate reflection of the child's perceptions of the parents' fears of being intimately penetrated and known?" (p. 83).

If Aron's question is a fair one, might there be similar implications for analysts' work with patients who are religious? Certain religious patients might be especially difficult for some analysts to treat, due not so much to these patients' inherent "unanalyzability" as to their perceptions of the analyst's fears of being intimately known along what is often highly personal terrain—the analyst's own relations to mystery and transcendence.

In the spirit of Aron's reversal, I could also turn around my original questions by countering, How could it *not* make a difference what the analyst's experience was with respect to transcendence? And why should not it matter? Once we shift our analysis from a one- to a two-person psychology, how could anything about either of the participants not matter? Indeed, the wish to not matter, and the guilt about making a difference in the relational field just by the very act of the observer observing, is itself an anachronistic feature of a largely outmoded positivistic ideal for science. Moreover, because this shift to a two-person psychology entails not only a shift from a drive to a relational model, but also from a positivistic to a constructivist epistemology (Hoffman, 1998), our understanding of everything, including notions of transcendence (our own and how we view our patients', theirs, and their perceptions of ours), is necessarily incomplete and perspectivally situated. It thus becomes a misplaced question to ask whether the analyst believes in God, because the question must be asked, Whose God? And which God? There is evidence that "God" is an object that is, or can be, continually constructed and revised throughout life (Sorenson, 1990; Key, 1994). From this it follows that no two persons' Gods are alike, nor is one's God necessarily identical across one's lifetime—and this is true even of the Gods we reject or the Gods in which we don't believe (Rizzuto, 1979).

The question then becomes, Must religious patients only be treated by religious analysts? I think not, any more than holocaust survivors, for example, must only be treated by analysts who are the same. Several years ago a Roper poll, however, reported that more than one-third of the American population believes the holocaust never happened. Although the polling methodology has been questioned, and a subsequent Gallup study found that the number of Americans who think Nazi genocide may be fictional is only one in ten, not one in three (Kifner, 1994), the question for psychoanalysis still remains: What if the analyst were among this ten percent? What difference would it make to the analysand as a holocaust survivor to have an analyst who was technically skilled in empathic listening, but who did not believe the patient? This analogy is especially apropos to religiously committed patients, since, as with holocaust survivors, the relevant experience in question obviously has central significance to the person's psychological organization and representational world. Perhaps if the analyst were a fellow survivor, he or she might be too close to the experience, and be at risk to understand the patient through the analyst's experience rather than the patient's. But to varying degrees, fortunately or unfortunately (depending on your epistemology), is that not what always happens in all forms of empathic knowing? Is direct apprehension of another person's subjective state—unmediated by our own organizing principles of subjectivity—possible or desirable? And besides, at issue in the holocaust illustration is not whether analyst and patient experience could be too proximal, but rather if it ever could be too distal, and what impact the analyst's private disagreement with what the patient counts as real might have on the treatment, even if cloaked in technical neutrality or skilled empathic listening.

Take childhood sexual abuse as another example. Once again, we may ask the question, Would it make any difference if the therapist did not believe the patient? This change in illustrations complicates matters because there are, in fact, some therapists who manufacture false memories of abuse in their clientele, whereas most all therapists would acknowledge the horrible historicity of the holocaust and would view it as tantamount to an obscenity to pretend the atrocity never happened. The historicity of divine intervention in human affairs is more ambiguous than evidence for the incidence of genocide or incest. Even so, the point here is that divination of notions such as "reality orientation" or "mental health" are necessarily perspectival and value-laden enterprises in which the contribution of moral and political judgment is typically and subtly disowned by proponents.

Martin Frommer (1994) made a similar argument about the role of technical considerations when analyzing homosexual men. Point for point, the tensions Frommer outlined for psychoanalytic perspectives toward homosexuality are the same for religion: a history of pathologizing the orientation, with little if any attention to helping patients develop a positive sense of this aspect of their identity; earlier techniques that tried to encourage patients' renunciation of their commitments and convictions; and more modern approaches that seek to avoid taking sides on the issue and instead seek a pattern of neutral inquiry. As much as the more modern approaches are an advance and an improvement, Frommer is suspicious of analytic claims to "neutrality," a term that psychoanalyst and professor of German Axel Hoffer (1985) has argued should more faithfully be translated as "indifference." Frommer (1994) explains the basis for his suspicions:

> One might think that a depathologized view of homosexuality would naturally result in a neutral stance, but it is a mistake to assume that the analyst operates from a position of neutrality regarding the patient's homosexuality merely because he or she adopts a technically neutral stance toward it.
>
> Recent concepts of intersubjectivity that have reshaped traditional thinking about transference and countertransference suggest that whether or not the analyst behaves as if he were neutral, the patient is nonetheless influenced by the subjectivity of all the analyst's feelings, whether or not they enter treatment through overt verbal communication [p. 217].

Because indifference about sexual orientation in one's own personal life is an unlikely state of subjectivity, Frommer argues for the advantage of homosexual analysts being better suited to treat homosexual patients, by virtue both of being more directly empathic via similar experience themselves, and by being a source for positive role modeling for the struggling analysand.

While I am open to Frommer's arguments regarding psychoanalysis and homosexuality in general, and find many parallels with regard to religious patients in particular, I find myself less enthusiastic to recommend analyst-patient matching on the basis of religion as an unequivocally good thing. My reluctance is not based on an endorsement of "neutrality," and has more to do with what, at core, may be the therapeutic action of psychoanalysis. Freud's answer to this question, on more than one occasion, was that in psychoanalysis "the cure is effected by love" (McGuire, 1974, pp. 12-13), or again, "our cures are cures of love" (Nunberg and Federn, 1962, p. 101)—and by this he meant transference love. The differences between this type of love and its romantic and infantile precursors for Freud were negligible, a point made especially well by Joan Riviere's translation of Freud's essay "On Transference Love" (Freud, 1915).

It is true that the love consists of new editions of old traces and that it repeats infantile reactions. But this is the essential character of every love. . . . The transference-love has perhaps a degree less of freedom than the love which appears in ordinary life and is called normal; it displays its dependence on the infantile pattern more clearly, is less adaptable and capable of modification, *but that is all and that is nothing essential* [p. 167; emphasis added].

For Freud, transference was an error, "a *false connection*" (Breuer and Freud, 1893–1895, p. 302), and there are those analysts today who remain faithful to Freud's epistemology.

The great importance of the transference in psychoanalysis lies in its unique epistemological role. When a patient reports past or present experiences with a spouse, sibling, or parent, the analyst, who is not omniscient, can only defer to the patient's long experience with people the analyst has perhaps never even met. When the patient's experience of the analyst himself is at issue, the analyst is in a position to make an independent assessment, since he has himself had the opportunity to observe first hand all the events that have gone into forming the patient's experience of him. Or rather, he has observed all the relevant events external to the patient. This enables him to infer with a relatively high degree of certainty the contribution that internal events have made to the patient's overall experience of the analyst. The sense of conviction about these internal events that both analyst and patient may thus arrive at is unparalleled in any other type of interpretation [Caper, 1988, pp. 62–63].

For Freud, as for contemporary analysts who follow Freud's positivism, the claim to authoritative certainty was the axis on which successful analyses turned. The value of transference love was that it provided the necessary motivation for the patient to submit to Freud's interpretative explanations—"when it is lacking, the patient does not make the effort or does not listen when we submit our translation to him" (McGuire, 1974, p. 12).

Other contemporary analysts are less sanguine about the prospect of finding refuge in certitude. Jay Greenberg (1991), for example, argued that, even when patient and analyst alike share the conviction that an episode in treatment should be labeled as transference, this may serve a defensive function to protect both participants from uncomfortable observations patients make about their doctors. About her critical appraisal of her analyst, for example, a patient declared, "If I didn't know it was all projection, I couldn't have said a word of it" (p. 52). Stephen Mitchell (1993) likewise noted how an appeal for compliance and deference on the part of the patient toward the doctor, while congenial to Freud and his era, strikes contemporary sensibilities as strangely discordant and anachronistic. And from the various perspectives of intersubjectivity theory (Stolorow, Brandchaft, and Atwood, 1987; Stolorow and Atwood, 1992) and dialectical constructivism (Hoffman, 1998), still other modern psychoanalytic theorists have questioned the value of any person's claim to epistemic hegemony.

André Haynal (1993), psychoanalyst and main editor of the Freud–Ferenczi correspondence, has noted that, if for Freud love meant transference love, for Sándor Ferenczi it meant *counter*transference love, much as Leopold Szondi, a student of Ferenczi from Zurich, "often spoke of the therapist as a 'soul donor'—an analogy with 'blood donor'" (p. 202). If this characterization of Ferenczi's view is fair, then there are potentially profound and fertile connections between the early Hungarian theorists in psychoanalysis (including Ferenczi and his student Michael Balint) and later Hungarian theorists in epistemology and philosophy of science (such as Michael Polanyi). What Ferenczi was struggling to articulate was an epistemology that required frank and candid human involvement in the human sciences—an inclination that was in many ways ahead of his time and is today decidedly more contemporary than aspects of Freud's positivism.

This brings me full circle to my hesitation about the supposed benefit of analyst-patient matching on the basis of religious (or nonreligious) status. If the question is reframed in contemporary terms of the vitality and centrality of what Ferenczi referred to as countertransference love, then adjudication of "fact" and "fantasy" or "accurate" versus "distorted" reality perceptions becomes misguided and beside the point. In the sense of postcritical epistemology, transference and countertransference become the fundament by which we know anything at all; rather than being embarrassing sources of error, they are the means by which we organize personal meaning and significance. Projection, rather than being a distortion of reality, becomes the precursor for empathy (Grotstein, 1981). And empathy, even with all these ongoing changes in psychoanalytic theory, invokes no epistemological circumvention of hermeneutics. Rather than being an unmediated channel to another's mental state, empathy is always interpretive (Stern, 1994).

In Ferenczi's sense of countertransference love, empathic knowing takes more than just humoring the patient. It requires authentic participation, and the same must surely apply to psychoanalytic explorations of spirituality. What matters more than the particular religious status of either participant is a willingness and openness for authentic personal involvement, which conceivably could include a disjunction of subjectivities between analyst and patient. Ferenczi's complaint in his personal analysis with Freud, after all, was that the latter was too reluctant to take up the negative transference (Ferenczi, 1932). Perhaps even Ferenczi's term "countertransference" is an expression of the language available to him at the time, whereas today we have other options that presume less unidirectionality, as Aron (1996) indicates:

> In my view, referring to the analyst's total responsiveness as counter-transference is a serious mistake because doing so perpetuates the defining of the analyst's experience in terms of the subjectivity of the patient. Thinking of the analyst's experience as "counter" or responsive to the patient's transference encourages the belief that the analyst's experience is reactive rather than subjective, emanating from the center of the analyst's psychic self. . . . It is not that analysts are never responsive to the pressures that the patient put on him or her. Of course, the analyst counterresponds to the impact of the patient's behavior. But the term countertransference obscures the recognition that the analyst is often the initiator of the interactional sequences, and therefore the term countertransference minimizes the impact of the analyst's behavior on the transference [pp. 76–77].

In previous work (Sorenson, 1994b), I found no support for the notion that a particular religious orientation on the part of the analyst was necessarily boon or bane:

> [What seemed to matter was] not the co-religionist status of the participants per se nor the noetic content of specific beliefs, but the manner in which religious issues are approached. Creedal parallelism and doctrinal twinship between patient and therapist was neither a necessary liability, as some theorists have suggested, nor a necessary asset, as others have proposed. Instead, a stance of respectfully curious, sustained empathic inquiry into the subjective meanings of the religious person's world of experience seemed to have the most transformative effect on these patients' subsequent practice as therapists. Picking a therapist of the same religious denomination was no guarantee of securing this most precious quality, any more than was a therapist from a different religious orientation—or nonreligious orientation—a warrant for its absence [p. 341].

If the therapeutic action of psychoanalysis is indeed love—not only in Freud's sense of transference love but also in Ferenczi's sense of counter-transference love—and if even the word countertransference is as Aron (1996) argues "a serious mistake because doing so perpetuates the defining of the analyst's experience in terms of the subjectivity of the patient" (p. 76), how can it be any different when it comes to our patients' experience of our own spirituality? The clinical objection that such exploration has no place in psychoanalytic technique strikes me as tenuous.

A Pedagogical Objection

The third objection to examining empirically the patient's experience of the analyst's spirituality is pedagogical. It is well known by now that psychoanalysis is one of the few intellectual disciplines in the twentieth century to develop outside the environment of the university. Also well known is that in North America, contrary to Freud's wishes and consonant with his fears, so-called lay analysts, such as clinical psychologists—arguably the ones with the best university training for empirical research—have historically been denied full access to psychoanalytic education. The result is a psychoanalytic pedagogy that systematically excludes, and even devalues, research. Allan Compton (1994) develops precisely this point with prose that is at once eloquent and stark:

> The structure of psychoanalytic education has mitigated strongly against the development of research. The "tripartite model" of psychoanalytic education—seminars, supervised case work, and training analysis—is built upon the idea that psychoanalysis in its essence is a method of scientific investigation—that is, the erroneous idea that work in the context of discovery on single cases only is sufficient for scientific advance. Nowhere is the absence of the dimension of research more strikingly clear than in the comparison to that of a graduate department in a university, where the keystone is research.
>
> The tripartite model of psychoanalytic education is, in addition, hierarchical rather than three legged: classes are less important than supervision, which is less important than the training analysis. Institutes function mainly as referral clubs and devices to support financially those who have attained training analyst status, a forum where masters can attract apprentices, not as centers of graduate education. Training analyst status is the career goal; and the rewards of that status are an enhancement of one's practice. This is very clearly a self-perpetuating situation [pp. 16–17].

Compton's argument is that the structure of institutes, the structure of curriculum, and the structure of psychoanalytic practice all stand in opposition to psychoanalytic research. When institutes are typically structured to serve the faculty, rather than the other way around, for example, research programs are seen to "impinge on the hegemony of the faculty-training analysts, and consequently tend to be short-lived" (p. 18). And the typical psychoanalytic curriculum, while it emphasizes diagnosis and clinical technique, virtually ignores the contributions of research to both these areas. Most challenging of all Compton's critiques, in my view, is how the structure of psychoanalytic practice has profound financial ramifications for the prospect of psychoanalytic research:

> The structure of psychoanalytic practice also discourages research. All money generated by psychoanalytic practice goes into the pocket of the practitioner—not unlike the results of other forms of professional service. But, because of the free-standing, university-unaffiliated status of almost all psychoanalytic training programs, there is no tradition of a career track in empirical research in psychoanalysis. Academic departments in universities tend to be unfriendly towards members of their faculties who "waste time" with psychoanalysis, rather than "real research." Psychoanalytic institutes tend to see academicians as "not real analysts." Grant awarding bodies are readily put off by the loose science and grand claims of psychoanalysts [pp. 18-19].

As an analyst in private practice who also teaches both at an APA-approved doctoral program in clinical psychology and at psychoanalytic institutes, Compton's assertions ring true to me. The APA Division 12 (Clinical) Task Force for the Promotion and Dissemination of Psychological Procedures, for example, has as its mission "to formally identify treatments with demonstrated efficacy and to disseminate these empirically validated treatments to practitioners," and to date has identified dozens of such approaches (Sanderson, 1995, p. 4). Although the movement has backpedaled slightly and now speaks of empirically *supported* treatments (rather than empirically validated), needless to say, psychoanalysis is still not on this list. My sense is that psychology is moving toward a future that increasingly recognizes only those treatment modalities with empirically proven efficacy. If this proves so, and if current models prevail in institute training, the day may come when psychoanalytic approaches to clinical practice—irrespective of other considerations regarding third-party reimbursement and managed care—will not be able to be a part of any psychology graduate school doctoral program that seeks APA approval. That is, quite apart from questions of whether practitioners will find patients who would receive any insurance compensation for psychoanalysis, students in psychology (and presumably other mental health professions) could not even be taught psychoanalysis in university graduate schools. Given the previously mentioned separation between psychoanalytic institutes and university graduate schools, this might seem to pose no real loss. To those of us who believe the future of psychoanalysis depends in part on vigorous participation in the world of ideas that is university life, however, forfeiture of this opportunity could well result in a corrosive marginalization of psychoanalysis in North America.[2]

There are similar tensions within institute life. During a term as Director of Doctoral Programs at a psychoanalytic institute, for example, my task was to coordinate curricular and staff resources for candidates who seek a Ph.D. in psychoanalysis, which the state has accredited the institute to award. I found some reluctance on the part of prospective faculty to be associated with courses having to do with research. Some analysts are reluctant to be exclusively pegged as "researchers"—a position they feel has diminished status—thereby limiting their access to potential referrals for candidate-analysands' training analyses or supervision of control cases. Others have no interest in, or are intimidated by, the world of research. By at least one measure, the pattern of analysts' dearth of interest in psychoanalytic research seems to apply beyond my local institutes to the national level, too: I once counted the number of APA Division 39 Section I members (Psychologist-Psychoanalyst Practitioners) who also

---

[2]I view the work of Lester Luborsky and his colleagues (Luborsky et al., 1999) on "allegiance effects" to be a significant challenge to the empirically supported treatments (EST) movement. In a metaanalysis of 29 studies of treatment comparisons, Luborsky et al. found that comparative study outcomes correlated .85 with the investigator's own theoretical orientation, thereby explaining 69% of the variance (in practical terms, all the variance there is)! Cognitive behavioral researchers made cognitive behavioral therapy look good. Existential researchers made existential therapy look good. Psychoanalytic researchers made psychoanalysis look good, and so on. It is not that Luborsky and his colleagues allege fraud or conscious deceit, but rather that investigators from a given clinical orientation know which therapists to pick and which measures to use to cast their preferred modality in the best light. I anticipate that critics of Luborsky will try and fault him for indulging in an allegiance effect of his own as a researcher, to the extent that he has been sympathetic to the impact of social influence in research for decades (see Luborsky, Singer, and Luborsky, 1975). If the findings of Luborsky et al. (1999) hold up to further scrutiny, however, it presents a methodological confound that threatens to render all extant comparative-competitive psychotherapy outcome studies, and thus the entire EST movement, moot.

chose to join Section VI (Psychoanalytic Research), and found that the number was less than 15%. This was so even though the sections have roughly the same number of members, and the tuition to join Section VI is extremely modest.

The upshot of all this is that, compared to the number of service hours performed annually by all practitioners, very little research is done in psychoanalysis. As further evidence of this, perhaps the most indicting sentence for psychoanalysts in the 864-page fourth edition of Bergin and Garfield's (1994) *Handbook of Psychotherapy and Behavior Change* is the following, taken from a chapter that summarizes psychodynamic approaches: "When all the published articles on transference are considered, the ratio of theoretical to empirical articles is roughly 500 to one" (Henry et al., 1994, p. 479)! When it comes to research, analysts seem inclined to engage in all-or-nothing thinking. Either it is what we are doing all day long in our offices just by seeing patients (Brenner, 1982, p. 5) or it is no more valuable than interesting clinical vignettes because every moment is unique (Hoffman, 1995, p. 110).

When it comes to the viability of the analyst's taking a position with regard to issues of transcendence, the philosophical objection is, "it's impossible," the clinical objection is, "it's unhelpful," and the pedagogical objection is, "it's unnecessary." Contemporary epistemologies suggest it is none of these. Instead, it may be indeed possible, helpful, and necessary—particularly for patients who consider themselves religious, and perhaps for all patients regardless of their conventional religious involvement—to work with analysts who welcome their patients' exploration of the analyst's spirituality. This possibility I tested empirically.

Method

I teach doctoral seminars on psychoanalysis and psychotherapy at an APA-approved clinical psychology program, which has as part of its specific charter to examine points of commonality and tension between Christianity and the behavioral sciences. In the course of my teaching, I thought to ask students to write autobiographical accounts of (a) their own developmental representations of God that arose from their family of origin, (b) their experience with how religious issues were addressed in their own personal therapy as the patient, and (c) their ways of working as therapists with religious issues in other persons who sought treatment. I viewed the assignments as personal rather than the standard academic fare, so I offered students the option of writing on different topics of their choosing for full course credit if they so elected. Because I also wanted to avoid as much as I could any interpersonal circumstance that pulled for a confessional tone of mandatory or compulsive self-disclosure on students' parts, out of regard for their privacy I suggested that if there were something particularly personal or sensitive that they would prefer I not know, they could exercise their right by not including it in their papers. Most students elected to write these essays, and their efforts struck me as both honest and courageous.

As I read the different assignments across a semester, I had the unintended experience of imagining that I could match the essays by author despite the months that separated the assignments, and even if all identifying and stylistic information were thoroughly removed or controlled. *How students worked on religious issues in their own therapy as the patient seemed to shape both how they came to experience their developmentally evolving conceptions of God, and how they themselves worked as therapists when interpreting religious issues in others as their patients.* If, for example, persons had a representation of God as a distant and cold figure, they seemed to be much less comfortable hearing about religious issues from their clients. This made sense intuitively. Even more striking, however, was that when it came to how student therapists worked with their clients' religious issues in treatment, even more powerful a determinant than the students' God concepts was the students' experience of how religious issues were handled in their own therapy as the patient. If the students' God concepts influenced how they worked with their own patients' religious issues in treatment, these God concepts seemed themselves to be a product of how, for these students, their therapist worked with them.

In an earlier study, I found that expert judges could in fact make the same sort of matches as I did, but I could not infer any causal relations from the research design, which merely counted the frequency of successful versus unsuccessful matches via a Chi-square contingency analysis (Sorenson, 1994b). The present research is a replication of the previous study, only this time with a sample size five times larger, using structural equation modeling. With this, I could specifically test a model of causality that my previous study only suggested. The model I proposed is also a test of the contemporary theory of narrative psychology (Spence, 1982, 1987; Sarbin 1986; Howard, 1991), which argues that retrospective self-report by patients in clinical work can be a co-created construction in the present as much as an archeological unearthing from the past.

What I Measured

I rated therapist essays according to adjectives from Gorsuch's (1968) higher-order factor of a "Companionable/Benign Deity" (in which God is experienced as comforting, warm, real, powerful, approachable, and gracious), and an orthogonal, first-order factor Gorsuch labeled "Wrathfulness" (which depicted God as avenging, blunt, critical, cruel, jealous, and damning). Because therapists wrote about not only their current God concepts during ongoing therapy, but also their retrospective accounts of their notions of God prior to therapy, I made an assessment of each.[3]

I rated the therapists' experience of how religious issues were handled in their own therapies with them as the patient, plus how they worked as the therapist with religious issues in others. For the first scale, I scored the students' experience of their therapist depending on whether students said the therapist: (1) made interpretations that conveyed a sense of the transcendent as "real" (as opposed to interpreting references to transcendence in terms of human tradition only, or as transference only); (2) approached issues of transcendence in an open and comfortable fashion

---

[3]Because a conservative subject-to-variable ratio for multivariate statistical methods is approximately 10 to 1, and my sample was 60 subjects, I wanted to select a total of six scales that were as representative as possible of the three domains: God concept, experience in personal therapy, and clinical practice. For parsimonious assessment of God concepts, one possibility was Osgood, Suci, and Tannenbaum's (1957) classic Semantic Differential, which seeks to account for all human construction of meaning along just three dimensions: evaluation (for example, good versus bad); potency (strong versus weak); and activity (active versus passive). While reviewing the literature on assessment of God concepts, Carrie Doehring (1993) noted, however, that two weaknesses of the Semantic Differential are that it forces judgments to be bipolar and dichotomous (good or bad, but never both), and that some of the core adjective pairs, when applied to representations of God, seem peculiar (such as "sharp versus dull") (p. 33).

A more comprehensive and useful instrument according to Doehring's review was Richard Gorsuch's (1968) Adjective Ratings of God Scale, which involved a factor analysis of 100 adjectives, including ones from the Semantic Differential. Gorsuch found eight oblique primary factors, five of which were represented by just two second-order factors, which in turn loaded on a single third-order factor, which assessed a benign-companionable Deity. An orthogonal first-order factor measured persons' conceptions of God along a dimension of Wrathfulness. A subsequent study confirmed many of Gorsuch's original findings, including the third-order and Wrathfulness factors (Schaefer and Gorsuch, 1992). For the present research, students' essays were scored dichotomously as credit/no-credit (1 or 0) for the two Gorsuch God adjectives I used, with scales ranging from 0 to 2 for God-Representation-Before-Therapy (1 point for Benign Deity, and 1 point for Wrathfulness), and the same for God-Representation-After-Therapy.

Ten percent of the protocols were selected at random and scored independently by a second rater, which yielded good inter-rater reliability for both scales (.82 and .87, respectively).

(as opposed to an approach that was more conflicted, less open or comfortable, and inhibited exploration); and (3) made interpretive connections regarding the patient's representational experience of God, parents, and the analyst, and pursued these at the therapist's own initiative, in which the therapist was respectfully curious, broached the topic, and made a detailed inquiry into the patient's world of experience (as opposed to remaining passively receptive if the patient wanted to broach the topic, but viewing analysis of this material as especially precarious—something requiring extraordinary sensitivity).

For a second scale, I also rated students' experience of their therapist depending on whether students said the therapist: (1) viewed the patient's experience of the sacred as something positive and as a potential resource for strength and healing (as opposed to viewing it negatively and emphasizing only its pathological functions); (2) viewed religion as a natural topic of exploration in psychotherapy (as opposed to viewing it as a foreign or peripheral topic that had no legitimate place in psychoanalytic inquiry); and (3) showed personal openness to mystery, and to mutual exploration of the patient's experience of the analyst's spirituality (as opposed to having antipathy toward spirituality, or an orientation toward transcendence which the patient found aversive).

Next I rated the students' work as therapists in clinical practice themselves, using the same scales as above.[4]

Latent Variables

Until fairly recently in the history of psychology, it was not possible to compare multivariate models with measures of statistical significance. Solutions to multiple regression, canonical correlation, or factor analysis, unlike their univariate counterparts, offered no basis by which to compare results from different samples. With multivariate research, the best that anyone could do was to perform exploratory analyses endlessly, and hope that the factors that surfaced were similar to those of previous studies. This wish was rarely fulfilled, however, because all exploratory analyses capitalize on chance associations in a given data set, and thus conflate spurious sources of variance with the model being generated. A

---

[4]The three items were scored dichotomously, as with the God Concept assessment, thus yielding a possible range of scores from 0 to 3 for each scale. Inter-rater reliability for each scale was satisfactory when measuring students' experience of their therapists' spirituality, as well as the students' work as a therapist for their own clients (.80, .76, .84, and .79, respectively).

further limitation is that repeated, exploratory multivariate studies were usually atheoretical, functioning primarily via computer algorithms rather than a particular scientific hypothesis or theory. This approach obviously impedes both development of better theories in science and the utility of scientific findings for clinical theory and practice.

Karl Jörskog (Jörskog, 1969; Jörskog and Sorbom, 1979) pioneered the development of causal modeling with latent variables. This strategy has increasingly entered the mainstream of contemporary psychological research, providing the benefit of multivariate hypothesis testing, without assuming the absence of error in hypothesized models, and without requiring contrasting control groups in order to establish the efficacy of a given intervention (Bentler, 1980). These developments are especially useful for clinical research, in which no-treatment control groups are often not practical (if not potentially unethical), and in which the clinical variables in question neither operate in isolation nor are necessarily synonymous with paper-and-pencil measurements.

Figure 5 shows the initial causal model that was submitted for analysis in this study:

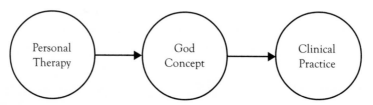

FIGURE 5. A model that did not fit the data: Personal therapy shapes clinicians' God concepts, which shape how clinicians handle spirituality in clinical practice.

An Empirical Test of Narrative Truth

Because the latent factor for God concept, which includes retrospectively narrative elements on God representations prior to therapy, is placed in the causal sequence after the influence of the experience in personal therapy, the above model provides a possible test empirically of the debate on whether clinical truths are found or made. Freud favored the former. For all his dedication to the power of the unconscious in coloring all human perception, Freud's epistemology was what contemporary philosophers of science would call "Naïve Realism," and one of his favorite metaphors was the psychoanalyst as archeologist (Freud, 1937).

But just as the archeologist builds up the walls of the building from the foundations that have remained standing, determines the number and position of the columns from depressions in the floor and reconstructs the mural decorations and paintings from the remains found in the debris, so does the analyst proceed when he draws his inferences from the fragments of memories, from the associations and from the behavior of the subject of the analysis [p. 259].

Donald Spence (1982) argues that the archeological metaphor is misleading, and that analysts' interpretations are usually unwitting narratives that would benefit from empirical process and outcome studies to determine the historical truth of what really happened, although others call for a hermeneuticism untethered to external "verification" (see Bruner, 1993). Another author who articulates with consistency and clarity a thoroughgoing constructivist epistemology that truth is as much constructed as discovered is Donnel Stern (1994). He reminds us that "to assume that the patient's experience is already 'there' makes it difficult to appreciate how fully the analyst and the patient participate moment-to-moment in the construction of one another's experience, how they co-create everything that takes place in the analysis—not only the transference-countertransference, but even the patient's memories and reports of concurrent events outside the treatment" (p. 443).

I think a position somewhere between historical truth and narrative truth—one that clearly rejects positivism but stops short of social constructivism—is that of intersubjectivity theory developed by Robert Stolorow and his colleagues (Stolorow, Brandchaft, and Atwood, 1987), who stress that

the reality that crystallizes in the course of psychoanalytic treatment is an intersubjective reality. This reality is not "discovered" or "recovered," as implied in Freud's (1913a) archeological metaphor for the analytic process. Nor, however, would it be entirely accurate to say that it is "created" or "constructed," as some authors have claimed (Hartmann, 1939; Spence, 1982; Schafer, 1990). Rather, subjective reality becomes articulated through a process of empathic resonance. The patient comes to analysis with a system of developmentally preformed meanings and organizing principles, but the patterning and thematizing of his subjective life is prereflectively unconscious (Atwood and Stolorow, 1984, ch. 1). This unconscious organizing activity is lifted into awareness through an intersubjective dialogue to which the analyst contributes his empathic understanding. To say that subjective reality is articulated, rather than discovered or created, not only acknowledges the contribution of the analyst's empathic attunement and interpretations in bringing these prereflective structures of experience into awareness. It also takes into account the shaping of this reality by the analyst's organizing activity, because it is the analyst's psychological structures that delimit and circumscribe his capacity for specific empathic resonance. Thus analytic reality is "old" in the sense that it existed before as an unarticulated potential but it is also "new" in the sense that, prior to its entrance into an empathic dialogue, it had never been experienced in the particular articulated form that comes into being through the analytic process [pp. 7-8].

From the perspective of contemporary interpersonal psychoanalysis, I understand Paul Wachtel's (1977) "woolly mammoths" analogy as getting at a point similar to Stolorow's intersubjectivity theory. Wachtel writes about how impressed Freud was by the seeming freshness of repressed memories, as though these were kept in an amnestic deep freeze from the Jurassic era. "Freud's description of the persisting influence of the past is reminiscent of the tales of woolly mammoths found frozen in the Arctic ice, so perfectly preserved after thousands of years that their meat could be eaten by anyone with a taste for such regressive fare" (p. 28). For Freud, the mystery was how early beliefs could persist despite the myriad disconfirmations throughout subsequent life. For Wachtel, early beliefs persist not *despite* subsequent life experiences but *because* of them: "the early pattern persists, not in spite of changing conditions but because the person's pattern of experiencing and interacting with others tends continually to recreate the old conditions again and again" (pp. 552-553). Wachtel concludes: "Rather than having been locked in, in the past, by an intrapsychic structuring, the pattern seems from this perspective to be continually being formed, but generally in a way that keeps it quite consistent through the years. It may appear inappropriate because it is not well correlated with the adult's 'average expectable environment,' but it is quite a bit more closely attuned to the person's idiosyncratically skewed version of that environment" (p. 53).

Results

At precisely the point of theoretical controversy mentioned above regarding historical truth versus narrative truth, the model I had initially pro-

FIGURE 6. A model that fits the data: Personal therapy shapes God concepts after therapy, which shape how clinicians handle spirituality in their clinical practice.

posed did not fit the data; amendment of this one offending component, however, resulted in a model that fit the data extremely well. That is, if subjects' retrospective accounts of developmental God representations were forced to be causal products of individuals' experience in personal therapy, the multivariate model failed to converge.[5] When data on the God concepts *before* therapy were dropped as causal products of therapy, leaving only the Wrathfulness-After-Therapy and Benign-Deity-After-Therapy, the resulting model fit the data extremely well.[6] Figure 6 depicts this model.

Two questions ensue: (1) Where then in the model to put the pre-therapy God concept? and (2) Is this outcome a disconfirmation of the narrative theory of historical construction? Regarding the first question, I tried placing the pre-therapy God concepts causally prior to therapist behavior, because a common assumption is that analysts' options are determined by the nature of the religious patient's God representation. For example, if the patient's God representation prior to treatment were too punitive or rigid, many clinicians would say this greatly limits and affects the analyst. Data from the present study, however, do not support this hypothesis. Placing as a latent variable subjects' "God-Concept-Before-Psychotherapy" causally prior to these persons' experience with religious issues as the patient in their own personal therapy produced another model that could not be solved through repeated iterations. Figure 7 depicts the model that had to be rejected as a poor fit with the data.

---

[5]As many as 60 iterative attempts failed to yield a solution. Examination of standardized residuals, which reveal points of potential model misspecification, showed that the failure of convergence involved the God concept items Wrathfulness-Before-Therapy and Benign-Deity-Before-Therapy.

[6]χ^2 = 3.304, 7df, p = .856, Bentler-Bonett Normed Fit Index = 0.960.

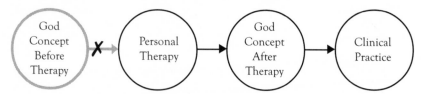

FIGURE 7. Another model that did not fit the data: Clinicians' God concepts before therapy shape how their therapists work, which in turn shapes clinicians' God concepts after therapy and how clinicians handle spirituality in their clinical practice.

Students' God concepts prior to experience in personal psycho-therapy were generally unrelated to anything else in the model, including (1) how their therapist worked with religious issues in them as the pa-tient, (2) how these persons as mental health practitioners worked with religious issues in others, and even to (3) how their God concepts emerged during or subsequent to therapy.[7] By contrast, God concepts that arose during or subsequent to therapy not only shaped how therapists worked with religious issues in others, *but also were themselves a function of how the therapists' analysts addressed issues of transcendence in the students' own thera-pies.* Whether this therefore entails refutation of narrative psychology, which was my second question, I take up in the following section.

Discussion

The notion that these data contradict narrative clinical theory is some-thing I address first, followed by two vignettes that illustrate the results clinically. I conclude with what I think are implications for analysis of transcendent experience in psychoanalytic process.

An Orthogonal Narrative?

Do the present study's outcomes constitute a refutation of narrative psy-chology? What are the alternatives? One possibility is that subjects did, in fact, create retrospective God stories that just didn't happen to fit per-sons' current narrative constructions of God, but this is a weak argu-

---

[7]The one exception was Wrathfulness with and without therapy, .327, which means about 10% of the variance is accounted for and 90% is indeterminate. Consistent with Gorsuch's previous studies, Wrathfulness was orthogonal to notions of a Benign Deity, whether for God representations with therapy ($r = 0.086$, $p > .05$) or without ($r = .027$, $p > .05$).

ment. It is not just that they created comedies or tragedies (White, 1973; Gergen and Gergen, 1983); it is not that God was once bad and then became good, once harsh and now friendly, or the reverse. If this outcome were the case, then there would have been significant negative correlations, when in fact there was none. Moreover, if the subjects were indeed creating revisionist history, it was apparently in a fashion that was largely stochastic, an outcome which, to the best of my knowledge, hermeneutic theory would not predict. Even so, we cannot say that pre-therapy God concepts are brute facts in history either, because these conceptions did not fit a causal model in which they determined the therapist's behavior in personal therapy. The biggest point from the present research is this: *it was difficult to predict how a religious patient's God concept would turn out, given its pre-therapy status; much more determinative was how the therapist acted in-session and the attitudes he or she conveyed toward spirituality and issues of transcendence. Moreover, how the therapist handled issues of spirituality in the consulting room had a bigger impact on the patient's spirituality than did even the patient's parents in his or her family of origin.* The present research also failed to provide evidence for the necessary superiority of religious matching between patient and analyst. To conclude from the present data that religious patients should only see religious analysts is unwarranted—indeed, many who did have such matches experienced alienation from their God, and many who did not had opposite outcomes. I doubt that the outcomes from the present study "refute" narrative psychology. The whole notion of the so-called decisive experiment is part of the larger saga of positivism in scientific lore; in real life, progress in science rarely works that way (Kuhn, 1962). I likewise make no claims that this study "proves" anything definitively for psychoanalysis merely because my presentation of an unconventional topic for psychoanalytic inquiry is articulated in the methodological terms of conventional science.

Indeed there are those who would argue that psychoanalysis, as a clinical practice, is a convention of language in its own right, one which neither permits nor requires experimental "correspondence" (Spezzano, 1993a). Even if we grant this position, I believe results of studies such as the present one nonetheless add an interesting voice to the conversation, and it is myopic to disregard their contribution merely because they are scientific in the conventional sense.

Some analysts might also take issue with the legitimacy of asking questions about patients' religious experience. The old view was that the analyst should never make inquiries, and should instead let patients bring up whatever they want, for fear of otherwise "contaminating" the transference with the analyst's agenda. To this I reply that if it were anything else we valued—a significant developmental relationship, for example, or the possibility of childhood sexual abuse, or a potential transference manifestation—we'd find a way at some point, tactfully and sensitively, to ask. To not value exploration of something the patient views as central is not a neutral intervention.

Two Clinical Illustrations

One implication of the present chapter is how much influence we have as analysts on our patients' experience of God. This is probably an odd finding for most psychoanalysts, who typically have no special training in theology or religious studies, who have no particular interest in the topic, and who tend to be less theistic or religious than the public we serve. The results of this chapter's research are either encouraging or sobering— encouraging, because there is evidence that our patients' spiritualities are not locked into previously dysfunctional or abusive family patterns; sobering, because how patients change seems to have to have a lot do with how we treat them. Therapists who treat a patient's sense of transcendence as "real" and not transference only; who are respectfully curious of a patient's spirituality and make a detailed inquiry into the patient's world of meaning; who welcome religion as a natural topic of exploration in psychotherapy, and view it as a potential resource for personal transformation; and who do all this with an attitude of openness and a lack of foreclosure to spirituality themselves—these clinical behaviors and attitudes are associated with patients whose own spirituality deepens and matures. Therapists who viewed the topic as fraught with special peril and avoided it whenever possible; who emphasized only its pathological expressions and nothing else; or who viewed spirituality as a peripheral topic that had no legitimate place in psychoanalytic inquiry—data from the present research indicate these therapist behaviors cause a patient's experience of spirituality to be quarantined and dissociated. Moreover, what seems to matter is the analyst's attitude and style in approaching the topic, and not whether, in terms of their respective spiritualities, analyst and patient are identical twins.

Ms. X, a student from the first study, was a Protestant Christian in her late 20s who could not remember a time in her life when she did not believe in God. There was not a lot of stability in her household growing up, and her single mother moved frequently and had a steady succession of boyfriends. Ms. X had assumed this was how everyone lived, and she said it was not until much later in life that she realized "living from crisis to crisis was dysfunctional." She began therapy with an older white male who was in his 60s and Jewish. She got the sense that his religious identity was important to him, but more so for a grounded sense of identity than for religious beliefs and practices. She wrote:

> My religious concerns were discussed very early in therapy and this probably had a lot to do with my choice of a therapist. At first I told him how important my Christian belief system was to me. Then I tried to undermine it because I was afraid of offending him.
>
> He confronted this issue and challenged me to develop an understanding of this fear. He also expressed a vivid interest from the start in discussing religious beliefs and their meaning in my life.
>
> Not only was my therapist comfortable and interested in exploring religious material, he felt it was essential to who I was as a person. Indeed, he told me that if I felt uneasy discussing my Christianity with him, I had better find a different therapist since this has everything to do with my personal growth and maturity.

Not surprisingly, given this chapter's research, Ms. X feels close to her God and is comfortable dealing with religious issues as they arise in the lives of the people who see her as their own therapist.

Mr. Y also grew up with a God with whom he felt an emotionally engaged relationship and from whom he experienced friendly interest. In beginning personal therapy, he knew his therapist by reputation to be a Christian, and chose him partly for that reason. Mr. Y wanted to know that there was, in his words, "a common thread and commitment to a similar God present in our relationship." He also hoped to not have to discuss his own representations of God: "I wanted someone where there would be little chance of being challenged in my belief system." His therapist went along with Mr. Y's unspoken directive, and faith issues were never addressed by either his therapist or himself in treatment. In terms of Mr. Y's experience of his therapist's spirituality, Mr. Y summarized, "As far as my therapist is concerned, I probably know more about his theoretical orientation than I do about his religious orientation."

About his present God concept, Mr. Y reports, "Currently I am fairly disengaged with God emotionally." He is not affiliated with a religious denomination, nor does he attend church on a regular basis. In Mr. Y's own clinical practice, he sees parallels with his view of God and his own therapy: "As with my own therapy, religious issues have not been a significant concern of many of my clients thus far." In his experience, all the clinical populations with whom he has worked so far have not yet been ready or able to explore dynamic formulations of God representations. Mr. Y is very honest and insightful, and the parallel with his own circumstances troubles him:

> Of course, this brings up questions in my own mind. Does my own lack of exploration of spiritual issues in therapy translate into the lack of it in my work with clients? Does my own ambivalence about the subject impact the way in which I listen to and interpret possible religious struggles or questions? Do I actually keep the client's religious issues at bay because of a process that is occurring in me? These are not only difficult questions to answer, but, now that I see them in relationship to my own effectiveness at truly addressing client issues, it concerns me.
>
> I would, of course, like to say I am willing to discuss any issue that a client may bring up. However, quite honestly, this exploration has made it apparent to me that I have a long way to go in understanding who I am, not only personally, but professionally.

The Faint, Sweet Smell of Apologetics—But Whose?

From these two brief vignettes the question arises, Aren't the changes in God concepts largely introjection of the therapy experience? To this I answer, Yes, of course, but—and this is the point—what exactly is introjected depends on what the analyst does and how he or she does it. Moreover, for patients who happen to be religious and who are themselves clinicians, their experience of the analyst's spirituality not only has a big effect on these patients' God concepts, but also impacts their subsequent clinical work with all the other religious patients who see these therapists across their professional careers. The scale of influence is multiplicative.

Nonetheless, some psychoanalysts will question the possibility of useful interdisciplinary dialogue between psychoanalysis and religion on the basis of either positivism and a commitment to classical psychoanalytic theory (Rice, 1994), or the claim that all such conversation is contaminated by "the faint, sweet smell of apologetics that hangs over the writings" (Beit-Hallahmi, 1992, p. 121). All ad hominem arguments entail omnidirectional olfaction, however, and prove little: they can always be used with equal effect to detect the apologetical aroma of the critic's commitments as well. For example, if one's motivation for imagining fruitful dialogue between psychoanalysis and religion were dismissed as an expression of ideology, then reluctance to adopt newer psychoanalytic epistemologies would be presumably no less motivated by *other* ideological commitments. Besides, as I argued in chapter 2, ideology per se is no culprit; openness presupposes prejudice (Gadamer, 1975).

What, then, might be the proper import of this chapter? While only 5 percent of the American public does not believe in God or a higher power (Gallup Organization, 1985), one survey found as many as 56 percent of mental health practitioners to be agnostic or atheistic (American Psychiatric Association, 1975). In terms of not emotional equivalence but statistical incidence, analysands who are religious may find themselves facing odds equivalent to those of holocaust survivors who encounter the obscene claim that Nazi genocide is fiction. If we analysts tend to be less religious (or at least less conventionally religious) than the typical person who seeks our services, how we behave with regard to patients' experience of transcendence—welcoming not only analysis of our patients' spirituality, but also analysis of our patients' experience of our own spirituality—can often be, for these patients, something like a divine gift.

Chapter 5

The Analyst's Experience
Of the Patient's Religion

Clinical Considerations

Anne's initial consultation disturbed me. It was not the painful details of her history, which she told unblinkingly and in matter-of-fact tones. It was not even the discrepancy between what she had to say and how she said it, at least not directly. It was that I found her ability to express herself to be breathtakingly competent—something between beautiful and awe-inspiring, really. It was not even that I felt some sort of conflict between my feeling drawn to her courageous ability to narrate her experience, while at the same time also repulsed by the horror of what she had to say. It was worse. What disturbed me most was that I found myself in awe of her ability to describe her own experience—and nothing more. I could tell that I did not care about her at all as a person. Not one whit. All that mattered to me was her amazing ability at self-narration, and I did not like knowing this to be true of myself. It did not fit with the version of myself I preferred to recognize as someone caring and interested in people.

I thought of a television documentary I had seen recently on gang violence. In one scene, the camera zoomed in on a gang member, seated in-studio, who was being questioned by an off-camera interviewer about a time that he had shot another young man in the stomach with a shotgun. The gang member gazed off camera and got a far-away look in his eye as he recalled that where his victim's midsection had previously been, there was now simply nothing, a gaping absence. He spoke in tones of

104

awe and reverence about how in that moment he had developed "new respect for the shotgun." As I had watched the television screen, the gangster's awe horrified me. He was in awe of the power of the shotgun, and yet completely oblivious to the human being he had just murdered. My mind shifted back to Anne. Here I was in this consultation, only now *I* was the gangster. I was in awe of the shotgun, her capacity to speak, and although I was not clear who between us had pulled the trigger, I could tell I was indifferent to whether she was alive or dead. Much as I preferred to be the documentary interviewer off-camera, away from the spotlight, somehow with Anne I was quickly and effortlessly becoming the very sort of person I despised.

In that initial consultation I learned that Anne was in her late twenties and a Ph.D. candidate at a nearby, prestigious institute of science. She had no close friends and had never married. She had recently been hospitalized for depression and, while not actively suicidal, had periods during which she did not feel that she wanted to keep on living. She was the firstborn of her parents, who were both biochemists in a distant city and who suffered from life-long bouts of depression themselves. Anne saw her mother as someone who felt unsuited and uncomfortable in her own skin as a female and mother, and who did better relating to males. When two younger sons were subsequently born to Anne's parents, Anne characterized her mother as having shifted her interests to Anne's brothers, and having withdrawn from Anne as her daughter altogether. In the years thereafter throughout her childhood, Anne said she spent long periods of time in the basement alone interacting with her favorite stuffed animal, which was a worm. Father was comparatively livelier than mother and more fun to be around, but, as a compulsive gambler who had been treated for years for manic-depressive illness, Anne said his humor was often at other's expense and bordered on cruelty.

I wondered about all that time in the basement with the worm and what it represented. A phallus? An under-formed self? An identificatory process to make contact with mother's inner world, not so much because Anne necessarily wanted the same thing her mother wanted, but because she simply wanted her mother, wanted her mother's attention, and was trying to figure out who her mother was and what animated her? Was Anne's time with the worm pathetic and pathological—a regressive illusion that kept her from exploring contact with real others? Or was it a profound gesture of hope, a way of keeping a nascent if under-formed self alive, so that even if the existing conditions were not favorable for life, she would be ready if more hospitable circumstances might open in the future? I really did not know, but all these possibilities seemed plausible to me, and none seemed mutually exclusive.

As Anne and I continued to meet together, we began to meet more often, and eventually were meeting four times a week in an analysis. Across my accumulating time with Anne, I learned that she had a knack, if it can be called that, for alienating or enraging others in almost any social circumstance: from housemates with whom she lived, to colleagues with whom she collaborated, to professors under whom she studied or by whom she was employed—in short, just about anybody. One session she even relayed how she had called the receptionist at her physician's office for an appointment, and within less than a minute the woman was yelling at Anne over the phone. Throughout her life, it was as though Anne were wearing the sort of "Kick Me" sign that mischievous grade school kids sometimes tape on the back of an unknowing classmate. Not unrelatedly, Anne's characterizations of others struck me as something like two-dimensional cardboard figures, and, from time to time, as opportunity and tact permitted, I said so to her. Anne tended to view others as lacking any sort of psychological interior or motivational state other than a relentless hostility toward her, a sheer malevolence that was best subdued by Anne's threatening to smack them, to punch them in the face, which was the only way they would learn that they could not get away with mistreating her. She actually did not get into many physical fights and, more typically, was perplexed as to why others seemed to single her out for conspicuous mistreatment when she was just minding her own business.

The one circumstance where Anne acknowledged more activity on her part was when she would encounter a certain sort of woman a few years older than herself who suggested promise for maternal interest or showed some evidence of kindness toward Anne. She then would direct all of her energies toward this woman, would want time with her as often as possible and, by Anne's account, would phone the woman as many as 20 or 30 times a day. Even if she felt the woman's disgust or revulsion, Anne needed her and, like a drowning swimmer, was generally unconcerned with the woman's own subjectivity or Anne's effect on her. Apart from any prompting or suggestion from me, Anne said she wanted to crawl up inside the woman's abdominal cavity and just stay there in a manner I took to be like a fetus or a parasite. Eventually the woman would extricate herself from Anne, which would precipitate a huge depression in Anne, both in the sense of loss and of her own unworthiness of love. Then after a few months, Anne would find a new woman, and the cycle would begin again.

I knew from my time with Anne that she was also a Christian, and her relationship with God, whenever she mentioned it, seemed much different than these other relationships. It was much more mature than it should have been if it were consistent with her other objects with whom she related. How could this be? In the history of psychoanalytic theory there are two contrasting answers to this question.

God as a Corresponding Object

One of the most influential books in psychoanalysis during the second half of the twentieth century was Margaret Mahler's volume, *The Psychological Birth of the Human Infant* (Mahler, Pine, and Bergman, 1975). Mahler and her collaborators offered a creative synthesis of ego psychology and object relations theory to make sense of infant observational research. Although their theory is legitimately complex, and aspects of it, like any theory, have been challenged (e.g., Stern, 1985), one of its main points is this: human infants and toddlers go through a predictable developmental process of *psychological* birth—a coming into existence as psychological beings—only this "birth" isn't simply a single day, but instead proceeds across a period of months and years after the date of biological birth. If human gestation takes approximately nine months, according to Mahlerian theory the process of psychological birth takes a lot longer, a minimum of two to three years.

What Mahler did for psychoanalytically informed infant observational research, Ana-Maria Rizzuto did for psychoanalytically informed clinical considerations of religious experience. Her 1979 book, *The Birth of the Living God*, applied a Mahlerian sensibility to humans' constructions of God as a psychological object. Just as Mahler had shown that psychological birth is a complex process that is crucially mediated by intersubjective involvement with others extending over a period of years, Rizzuto argued that our construction of any God in which we believe (or, for that matter, any God in which we disbelieve) comes into being through similarly mediated relational experience. Richard Lawrence, a Roman Catholic priest and clinical psychologist, appreciated the insights of Rizzuto when doing parish counseling and clinical work. He noticed that persons' "God in the gut" was often quite different than their "God in the head"; in times of crisis or anxiety, the God to whom people turned for solace, or against whom they railed, often bore little resemblance to catechetical answers to which they gave intellectual assent. For his dissertation, Lawrence created the God Image Inventory (GII), a 156-item instrument that has been normed on a national sample and operationalizes those psychoanalytic dimensions of faith that Rizzuto's work suggested (Lawrence, 1991, 1997; see also Hall and Sorenson, 1999).

The work of Rizzuto and Lawrence builds on object relations theory, and object relations theory, to the extent that it emphasizes character structure and an individual's pervasive way of being in his or her world, tends towards a *correspondence* theory of religion psychoanalytically. In this view, how persons unconsciously organize their relations with significant others in life is also likely to correspond to how they unconsciously organize their construction of a God in whom they believe (or disbelieve). There is empirical evidence from an object relations perspective that supports such a proposed correspondence (Tisdale et al., 1993; Brokaw and Edwards, 1994; Hahn, 1994; Hall et al., 1998). From the related perspective of psychoanalytic attachment theory, Kirkpatrick (1999) summarized more than a decade of recent research that found that adults with secure attachments were likely to envision God as loving and accessible. By contrast, adults who were classified as having an avoidant attachment style were most likely to describe themselves as agnostics or atheists. Good examples of psychoanalytic interpretations that presume a correspondence between a person's level of object relations in general and his or her experience of God in particular can be found in the interpretive reports for the GII (Gattis, Sorenson, and Lawrence, 2001). Patients with a sense of God's being there for them are expected to have had mothers or significant care-givers who were also there for them; patients who suspect that God does not love them as much as they feel that they deserve presumably acquired this God image from a parent who was not perceived as giving the love that was merited; patients with a God who offers providence but not an experience of closeness are seen as arising from a parent who gave the child everything under the sun but was never around and never listened. Rizzuto's second book (1998) is another example of a correspondence view of God insofar as she argues that Freud's early developmental experience failed to instill the substrate necessary to sustain a God worthy of Freud's trust.

God as a Compensatory Object

If God as a corresponding object is basically consistent with the person's other object relations, God as a *compensatory* object is just the opposite:

something always longed for but never experienced with others. This view has fallen on hard times in contemporary psychoanalysis, both empirically and theoretically. Empirically, it has received mixed or ambiguous support at best (Granqvist, 1998; Kirkpatrick, 1999). Theoretically, ongoing change in psychoanalysis has shifted away from viewing reality and illusion as mutually exclusive categories, and instead sees the two as now more mutually enhancing (as discussed in chapter 2). Whereas Freud saw religion as a pathological flight from reality, Heinz Kohut (1985) articulated more contemporary epistemologies when he argued that religion is poor as science but outstanding as psychology.

> That was Freud's mistake and Freud's correctness. [Religion] is poor science. But if it's good, it may be outstanding psychology. In its best and central part, religion puts into words an awareness of what is in people. When you talk about paradise, the idea is that there is something greater than the individual life. Although some ideas become debased and vulgarized and popularized in terms of very specific concrete images, like hymn-singing angels, I think in the eyes of a deep searcher for religious truths these things fall by the wayside [p. 264].

Gordon Allport (1950) emphasized something similar, years earlier, when he wondered why psychotics often express their experience in religious language. Rather than viewing religion as synonymous with psychosis, Allport reasoned that people suffering with wrenching experience that is excruciatingly close to the core of their being gravitate toward religious imagery and religious metaphor because these do justice to the ache psychotics feel in themselves. In Kohut's more recent terminology, religious language works for people in great distress because it can be outstanding psychology.

Allport was also curious about how religion could serve such disparate purposes in people's lives. Some people's religiousness made them more unselfish, altruistic, and inclusively humanitarian whereas others became more ethnocentric, exclusionary, and provincial. For some, religion fostered high self-esteem, feelings of agency and competence, an opposition to prejudice, and a sense of a loving and forgiving God; for others, religion was associated with bigotry, racism and misogyny, coupled with low self-esteem and a stern, punitive God. Allport realized, as have all psychologists of religion before and since, that religion is a multidimensional entity, and not something simply reducible to wholesale psychopathology or developmental immaturity. He distinguished between what he termed Intrinsic and Extrinsic religious orientations: Intrinsics *live* their religion for purposes of personal and societal transformation; Extrinsics *use* their religion for purposes of personal convenience and social gain (Allport, 1950; Allport and Ross, 1967). Daniel Batson extended another dimension that he thought was present but underemphasized in Allport's psychology of religion: a Quest orientation. According to this dimension, some people's religious orientation facilitates not only a readiness to face existential questions without reducing life's complexities, but also an openness to self-criticism and a positive valuation of doubt (Batson and Raynor-Prince, 1983; Batson and Schoenrade, 1991a, 1991b; Batson, Schoenrade, and Ventis, 1993). More recently, James Jones (2002) has argued on explicitly psychoanalytic grounds that religion generates noble and ignoble human cultural achievements due to the paradoxical effects of idealization. At its best idealization offers self cohesion and exemplars of personal and societal goals, while at its worst idealization fosters a kind of splitting that demonizes outsiders and rationalizes cruelty.

Interacting with Anne

So where was Anne in this? How did her religious faith fit these two traditional typologies for the psychoanalytic psychology of religion? There were a few occasions when she seemed to think of God along the lines of her other relationships, consistent with the correspondence theory of religion. Once, for example, she paged me and when I called her back I learned that she was in distress because she was going for a job interview and couldn't find her car keys. She launched into a cursing torrent of vindictives toward God for being a cosmic sadist who delighted in keeping her from getting things she hoped for. These moments were unusual, however, and, as I mentioned earlier, I experienced Anne's faith more typically as a conspicuous asset—if anything, shockingly so, given the other relationships in her life. I suppose her faith might be liable to charges of compensatory functions, but it didn't have restrictive or evasive qualities, in my view. If anything, Anne's religious commitments made her more open to life—to others and herself—and created space for self-reflection and self-scrutiny, something more like Allport's Intrinsic religious orientation, or Batson's Quest.

One day when we were well into her analysis, Anne came in for her session, reclined as usual on the couch right next to me, and began an hour that didn't seem conspicuously different from many others that we had shared by now. Not too long into the hour I found my voice shaking and myself gripped in the midst of an experience I did not understand and did not know what to do with. I interrupted her and, with obvious distress in my voice, hissed: "Anne, I have an overwhelming urge to hit you right now." I gulped and added, "I'm not going to, but I want you to know that I really want to." That was all I said. There was a pause between us, and I wondered what I had just done. Although this exact moment had never happened to me before, nor has it since, there are all kinds of moments clinically when I feel "off the map," not in the sense that I go looking for them as a reckless or brave explorer of new worlds, but simply that they just manage to show up. In fact, in ordinary daily clinical work, it is as though the edge of the map seems to come to me more than I go looking for it, and even when I prefer to stay safely within the confines of what I think I already know and understand, I consistently find that the edges next to what I do not know are a lot closer than I think. Usually I reflect on my experience and do not share it with the patient, but this was not one of those times. I felt pulled into something where I did not have a choice. Or maybe I should say the barest choice I felt I had was to tell her, rather than just to do it.

Anne paused a moment longer and then said in a quiet voice that once when she was young her mother had slapped her. My mind jumped ahead to parallels with me, and wondered if my "slap" just now was a similar trauma for Anne. That was not what she said. She added that as much as the blow had stung her, it was a moment when she felt close to her mother, when she felt she really knew her and had made contact with an authentic part of her. She said so often she felt completely neglected by her mother, especially since the births of her brothers, and when her mother hit her, Anne could tell for sure that she existed in her mother's mind, if only for that moment.

How are we to understand what happened between Anne and me? Traditional psychoanalytic formulations tend to be fairly linear: either the experience was primarily generated by Anne or it had its origins in me. If it came from Anne, it is transference. If it came from me, it is countertransference. Transferential renderings would see Anne's orienting to me as she had toward her parents. Along these lines, Anne unconsciously organized me as though I were her mother, someone in whose mind Anne could not tell if she existed unless I hit her, or her father, someone episodically less depressed than mom but whose liveliness bordered on cruelty. Countertransferential renderings would see it the other way around: my experience of Anne stemmed from unfinished business from my own family of origin that, were I sufficiently or adequately analyzed myself, would fade to the point of insignificance or else be neatly circumscribed by self-knowledge.

For nearly a century, many analysts have been suspicious of the transference/countertransference dichotomy as something that is unhelpful because it tries to bifurcate a matrix, a system, that is irreducibly interactive and coconstituting. One of the earliest analysts to write about this was Sándor Ferenczi (1932), who once confessed, "I have finally come to realize that it is an unavoidable task for the analyst: although he may behave as he will . . . the time will come when he will have to repeat with his own hands the act of murder previously perpetuated against the patient" (p. 52). By "murder" Ferenczi meant to traumatize psychologically, a murder of the soul, not the body. "In contrast to the original murder, however," continued Ferenczi, "[the analyst] is not allowed to deny his guilt; analytic guilt consists of the doctor not being able to offer full maternal care, goodness, self-sacrifice; and consequently he again exposes the people under his care, who just barely managed to save themselves before, to the same danger, by not providing adequate help" (pp. 52–53). As Ferenczi saw it, the only recourse for remedy was for the analyst to admit his own fallibility and vulnerability to the patient, in the faith that "there is nevertheless a difference between our honesty and the hypocritical silence of parents" (p. 53).

With Anne, I certainly was not silent about my own murderous wishes—or at least I should say I sure was not now—but I wondered about my reluctance to acknowledge the part of me that, from the opening consultation, was in awe of the power of the shotgun. True, Anne likely enraged others and me in order to make an authentic connection, not just with us but, vicariously and ultimately, with her mother, and she did so in the one way that she knew from experience had indeed worked. Still I wondered, How much had Anne been trying to get me to confront an aspect of myself that I wanted to ignore, in addition to whatever happened with her mother? I thought of Harold Searles' (1979) notion of the patient as therapist to her analyst. For Searles, all people have an innate desire to heal those to whom they are close, and patients are ill because, and to the extent that, their previous ministrations to early caregivers were spurned. What is pathogenic in this view is not so much the parents' vulnerability or limitation per se, but rather their refusal to be helped with this by their children.

Margaret Crastnopol (1997, 1999, 2001) has written a series of persuasive articles that show how in any analysand-analyst dyad there are irreducibly idiosyncratic features of the two people's personalities that contribute decisively to therapeutic process and outcome—including ethnicity and culture, socio-economic status, physical appearance, and of course family dynamics—and these features are not really accounted for by knowing the clinician's professed theoretical orientation. In my own childhood, I was always tall for my age, reasonably athletic, and did well enough in school that I didn't have occasion to get into fistfights; I was neither bully nor bullied. I certainly felt moments of helplessness in my childhood and could be competitive or aggressive, but I tended to sublimate these through my culture's sanctioned outlets of achievement, whether academic or athletic. Because physical hitting was not modeled in my family of origin or valued by the cultures in which I was socialized, I think Anne was pushing me to acknowledge and explore a disavowed and underdeveloped dimension of myself so that I could be of use to her. As Bass (2001) and Davies (2002) have recently argued, it takes one to know one, and our patients' and our own inner worlds commingle because empathy is a form of projection.

If for Winnicott (1971) the object's survival of ruthless hate was essential in object usage as opposed to object relating, I read him as generally articulating this in terms of the analyst surviving the patient's hatred of the analyst. I think of Winnicott's patient, Margaret Little, who in a fit of rage destroyed an expensive vase in Winnicott's consulting room. When Little returned for analysis the following day, she noticed that the vase was whole again and in its ordinary spot. Little said nothing about it at the time, and it wasn't until later that she asked Winnicott about the incident. Only then did Winnicott tell her that the vase, which he had replaced immediately, had meant a great deal to him and her destruction of it had hurt him. According to Winnicott's theory, it was important for the vase to rematerialize unscathed, and for Winnicott not to retaliate. (For their respective accounts of the analysis, see Little [1990, pp. 41–71] and Winnicott [1975, pp. 289–294].)

I see Ferenczi as having stressed a complementary point. For Ferenczi, no less vital is patients surviving *their analysts' murder of them*, and this murder isn't simply an excusable by-product that comes from serving as a container for the patients' bad objects. I am not sure what exactly Anne said that precipitated my wanting to hit her, but it had to do with what felt to me like a systematic negation of my own subjectivity—something I had experienced many other times before with Anne, although it did not produce the result it did this time. This time was different. What was different? In hindsight I suspect I was making a bid for recognition, in Jessica Benjamin's (1992) sense of the word, and I had some sense that Anne was ready for this in a way that had not been possible before. I also suspect, however, that Anne had been working on me, and I had not been ready to face what she had been trying to help me with until then either. Beyond this, the two of us as a couple needed time to find our footing, to get our bearings for a while, before we had the basis to try and work our way out of places in which Anne got stuck. It makes sense to me that for the patient to change and grow, the analysis and the analyst have to grow and change, too.

God as Object X

For me, the problem with *both* corresponding and compensatory formulations of religion is that, however different they appear from each other initially, they end up being too much alike. They both are entrapped in a psychological reductionism that sees all religious commitment as nothing more than a person's past—either a recapitulation of what always happens, or its opposite, something longed for that never happens. What is missing in these sorts of interpretations is an appreciation for the possibility of something genuinely new happening in the present that is relatively unscripted, to some degree even unpredictable, and involves an experiential encounter with alterity, an otherness beyond ourselves that is accepted as "real." When summarizing the contributions to their edited volume on psychoanalysis and religion, for example, Smith and Handelman (1990) found the consensus of contemporary psychoanalytic scholarship to be that "unless a thinker can conceive of God as real or, at a minimum, conceive that another can nondefensively conceive of God as real, he or she is significantly barred from understanding religious texts or religious belief" (p. xi).

To be clear, I am not proposing a territorial demarcation, as though there should be a sign on a fence somewhere that says "Religion Only—Psychoanalysis Keep Out." In my view, all of human experience is fair game for psychoanalytic investigation, including all religious experience, but this begs the question of how we want to formulate psychoanalytic inquiry. If psychoanalysis is a discipline that proceeds via vicarious intro-

spection, empathy, or an openness to making contact with the unconscious or unconscious knowing, it would seem that a certain amount of
epistemological humility is in order. Indeed a case could be made that
psychoanalysis is a discipline that specializes in uncertainty or not-know-
ing, and in any case psychoanalysis deals with the life of the mind. In
their book *Why God Won't Go Away*, neurobiologists Newberg and D'Aquili
(2001) argued that the human brain is structured in a way to create religious experience, and that these structures have been favored by selective
evolutionary processes across the past 200,000 years as enhancing the
survival values of the species by instilling hope and prosocial behavior to
counter the despair of mortality and human finitude.[1] Freud imagined
that religion, as an illusion, had no legitimate future and saw some variant of his own psychoanalytic stoicism as religion's imminent successor.
If Newberg and D'Aquili are right, however, religion isn't going away any
time soon, and we psychoanalysts, to the degree that we are students of
the human mind, must not only come to terms with this, but also be
wary of a restrictive reductionism in many of our psychoanalytic accounts
of religious experience.

Consider the following dream reported by Guntrip (1969) that a
patient relayed while in analysis with him:

> I'm looking for Christ on the seashore. He rose up as if out of the sea
> and I admired his tall and magnificent figure. Then I went with Him
> to a cave and became conscious of ghosts there and fled in stark
> terror. But He stayed and I mustered up courage and went back in
> with Him. Then the cave was a house and as He and I went upstairs,
> He said, "You proved to have greater courage than I had," and I felt I
> detected some weakness in Him [p. 351].

Guntrip interpreted the dream in a way that cast all of the patient's allu-
sions to Christ in terms of the patient's relationship to his mother, his
father, and Guntrip. John McDargh (1993) questioned what we lose by
interpreting the transference so unidirectionally, reasoning that "if the
therapist is beginning to assume salvific significance for the client, it may
also be accurate to observe that the client's God is becoming more therapeutic, that is, more reliably available to the client in his struggle for
freedom from his negative introjects" (p. 176). McDargh continued:

---

[1] For a thoughtful critique of the reputed results of research in brain physiology and its
direct relevance for psychotherapy or psychoanalysis, see Brothers (2001).

> Guntrip's interpretation misses the significance for the client of the
> fact that the figure in the dream is not the therapist, but rather Christ.
> An interpretation that assimilates the client's relationship to Christ
> entirely and without remainder to the transferential client-therapist
> relationship or to other internalized object relations ignores the pos-
> sibility that something new and *sui generis* may be occurring in the
> client's relationship with the divine, something that may well have
> implications for the therapeutic relationship and for the structure of
> all other significant object relations [p. 176].

Moshe Spero (1992) addressed much the same point from the perspective of a psychoanalyst and a religious Jew when he affirmed that "believers seek to view the object of their representations and beliefs as an
existential given, not further reducible to this or that psychological instinct, endopsychic need, or transitional phenomenon" (p. 48). Or again:
"A childhood concept of God, to be sure, is a *childhood* concept. But it is
also *of God*, just as a childhood concept of a father is nonetheless of *a*
father" (p. 83).

I was not sure how I wanted to conceptualize Anne's God object
psychoanalytically, and even entertained calling it "The Uncertainty object." This did not quite capture what I wanted to convey, however, because I believe uncertainty is essential and ubiquitous in *all* knowledge,
not just knowledge that purports to be about God. I thought about extol-
ling the virtues of doubt, but rejected that one, too, because I think radical doubt is as elusive as it is unhelpful; to doubt anything there must be
something else we are using that—at least in that moment—we are *not*
doubting. Even to doubt invokes some sort of faith, just as faith is impossible without its complement, doubt. I also realize some may feel my
continued use of the word "object" is anachronistic. Guntrip objected to
the term "object" in object relations because he thought it was too inanimate or mechanistic, and proposed dropping it in favor of the term "personal relations theory." I don't see it that way. For me, the value of the
term "object" is its very multiplicity and ambiguity: it refers both to internal representations and to external others, and to all the interactions
between. I thought about Winnicott's concept of transitional objects,
which might come close to doing justice to Anne's experience. I wasn't
satisfied with that term, however, not only because it doesn't quite fit
religious believers' experience of God as really *there* in a way that's something more than just a convenient illusion, but also because I believe the
term can be used by analysts with religious commitments to justify reli-

gious belief on the basis of limitations in human knowledge, something philosophers of religion call a "God of the gaps." I considered calling Anne's relationship toward God a new object experience, but was dissatisfied with that, too. In one sense each moment is new, never before repeated, and yet in another sense the opportunity for innovation and change always comes through engagement with what has happened before, what is old and familiar.

I settled on calling Anne's object relations toward her God not simply a compensatory or corresponding object, but instead as object X, out of appreciation for the work of one of my favorite authors, the sociologist of technology Jacques Ellul. Among his many talents and accomplishments (he was a member of the French resistance fighters against the Nazis, an academic who wrote dozens of books, and later in life became the mayor of Bordeaux, where he established social programs to care for troubled adolescents), Ellul was also a lay theologian. In one of his theological books, *The Subversion of Christianity*, Ellul (1986), a Christian, proposed doing away with the word "Christianity" and in its place substituting some arbitrary symbol, such as X, whose meaning we would not immediately think we understood, thus forcing us to be open to new thought and new possibilities for what X meant or could mean. For Ellul, not only was Christianity not an "-ism," a fixed and tightly arranged system, but the human propensity to pretend otherwise is a bastardization of Christianity, or in Ellul's terms, sin.

Although Anne's God occasionally corresponded closely to her archaic objects, as happened when she paged me while looking for her car keys, her God more typically seemed to me this sort of object X. I suppose Anne's God was to some degree a compensatory object insofar as she could contact her God as many times a day as she wished and not feel like she had worn out her welcome, but the way she spoke of her faith, Anne's God also challenged her to face herself, and disturbed or provoked her to grow and to change—none of which is directly comparable to a compensatory or regressive God who would permit her to crawl up inside a divine abdomen and never come out. In fact, in my earlier description of Anne's targeting a desired woman and her yearning to live inside her, I said that I understood this as her wish to become a fetus or parasite. In hindsight it seems the former and not the latter, only the kind of God Anne got was one who went into labor. If Rizzuto extended Mahler's psychological birth of the human infant, thereby enabling, for humans, the birth of the living God, Anne's God completed the circle and gave birth to the living Anne.

Skeptics might think that Anne's God was a transferential extension of her experience with me in the analysis. I suspect this is probably
so, to a point. When I first met Anne, I did not care whether she was
alive or dead. Over a course of years, she became alive to me in my own
mind, she mattered to me, and I enjoyed being with her. But Anne's God
seemed well ahead of me in all these regards and had seemed to enjoy
Anne and to care about her well before Anne and I ever met. I present
my work with her as one example of analyst behaviors and attitudes that
the research in chapter 4 found facilitative for patients' growth and development.

Graduation

Several years into her analysis, Anne was approaching the time when she
was to complete her dissertation, and this task proved as challenging and
problematic as many others in Anne's life. In particular, she was having a
rough time of negotiating interactions with her advisor, who was also her
dissertation Chair. He seemed dismissive and abusive toward Anne in
much the same way that she had known other relationships to be, so
much so that I wondered if she would ever manage to pass her oral defense of her dissertation. The task seemed so daunting and nearly insur-
mountable that one day I volunteered that if she ever managed to pass
her orals, I would throw a party with her in the office during a session.
This was not standard technique for me, but it was not completely out of
character for me either. Truth be told, I find that I do something a little
bit different with every analysand, and this was something that felt right
for me to offer.

Months passed, and as details that Anne relayed from session to
session made it seem like she might actually make it to her orals, I stopped
by a party supply store and bought a couple of those small, conical party
hats with the elastic strings that go under the chin, and some noise-makers that unfurl and honk if filled with exhaled air. I kept them in their
small plastic bags in a basket that was on the floor next to my therapist's
chair in the office. One day Anne came in for her session, plopped down
on the couch, and said quietly, "Well, I passed." Then she paused for a
few moments, and I reached down into the basket to get the party favors.
She heard me wrestling with the plastic bags to open, and I wordlessly
handed her a hat and a noise-maker over her shoulder. We both donned
our hats and tested our noise-makers, and proceeded to have what was an

otherwise typical psychoanalytic session. The only difference was that we kept wearing the hats throughout that hour, and, when the spirit moved either of us, we would interrupt the other with a toot. We would wait long enough until the other had maybe forgotten about the horns and then use them as a surprise attack, or else use them to punctuate the other's point appreciatively. The accoutrements seemed better suited for a raucous and densely populated party. It was odd to blow the little horns or wear the silly hats in such a quiet atmosphere as the analytic consulting room, whose stillness resumed the moment a horn stopped, although the hour was festive in its own way, nonetheless.

She said later that it had been so many months since my offer that she had wondered if I would have remembered. She also began to date men, and eventually decided to take a job in distant city. She wanted to continue to meet with me by phone, which we did for a while at a decreased frequency. In the other city she married someone who sounded to me like a kind man who was good to her. She wanted to pursue marital therapy in order to work out other issues that were surfacing in her marriage, and I helped her find a local marital therapist that she could see in person and was comfortable with. We concluded shortly thereafter with a planned termination over the phone, and I would like to conclude here with a letter I got in the mail from Anne about a year later, but before I do, I would like to circle back to my impression of Anne during the initial consultation.

Some might say my initial experience of Anne is best characterized as idealization, but if so, it is in a very proscribed sense. An idealized figure is typically ascribed esteem that becomes global, even if the esteem originates from just one particular feature. With Anne, this did not apply. My admiration for her breathtaking competence at self-narration did not generalize to esteeming her more broadly as a person. Anne's comments in her letter a year after termination, while no less honest and direct than I had experienced her as being in the initial consultation, offered a stark contrast. I still admired her ability to express herself, only now I also felt moved by her. She was as smart as ever, but to my ears she spoke with a lot more heart. I will never know if she had been this way all along and I had just been deaf to it, or if she became this way as result of her analysis, but as I said earlier, I think the question, "Did Anne change or did you?" is the wrong question. I think we both changed. Being with me, she grew and changed. Being with her, I grew and changed. I suspect my initial disinterest in whether she was alive or dead was something common to others' experience of Anne, too, but I think my esteem for her self-expression was less common. It provided a toehold for me to find interest in Anne, to not simply dismiss her so quickly as others often did, and it bought us more time to generate other sorts of connections between us. I concur with Dale Boesky (1990), who observed, "If the analyst does not get emotionally involved sooner or later in a manner that he had not intended, the analysis will not proceed to a successful conclusion" (p. 573). Neville Symington (1983) has written about such unintended shifts in engagement as the x-factor in treatment, an inner act of freedom on the analyst's part that is genuinely new, a creative act, something not explicable in reductionistic terms as though this shift were merely repetitive, countertransference and nothing more. With Anne, however, this shift felt more like a joint construction between us than something either of us possessed or achieved apart from the other, not unlike her experience of God as an X-factor as well, as her concluding letter suggests:

> It's hard to find words to express my gratitude for a relationship that lasted so long and experienced such a wide range of emotions. I'm glad you had the faith to hang in there with me through the tough times. Few people have stuck it out so long with me. I think that has had a powerful healing influence in my life—just not having to go it alone. I know that I have learned much from you about myself, about people, about relationships. It's difficult to articulate these things. They have just become a part of who I am.
>
> I remember the party we had when I finished my defense—the hats and noise-makers—and it makes me smile. I'm grateful for some good memories in some of the darkest years of my life.
>
> It's such a strange pilgrimage I am on, not at all what I expected. In many ways I have ceased being disappointed with life and begun to be amazed. I do not expect my future to be an easy one. I expect it to be full of joy and sorrow. I expect the Lord to walk with me and care for me through all these things. And just as He was faithful to bring you into my life in the years of need that have passed, so I expect that He will bring others to walk with me through the years of need to come.
>
> Surely goodness and mercy will follow me.

Chapter 6

Psychoanalytic Institutes
As Religious Denominations

Fundamentalism, Progeny,
And Ongoing Reformation

I remember hearing many years ago a story attributed to Joe Zawinul, an accomplished jazz pianist who was one of the early adapters of electronic keyboards in music. He complained of not wanting to be stuck in excessively stereotypic "licks" or improvisational habits that all musicians develop and indeed are recognizable marks of their own musical signatures. Zawinul wanted to be able to find a way to hear new music coming from his fingers, so he altered his electronic keyboard such that the tones, instead of ascending across the keys from left to right, worked the other way around: to the right were increasingly lower notes, and to the left increasingly higher ones. Then he played his modified keyboard as though it were a conventional one, listened for new "licks" he found himself creating, and remembered the ones that he liked, so that he could he could play them again once he restored the keyboard to its original configuration.

In what follows, I propose to use theoretical and empirical studies in the sociology of religion as a guide for thinking about the structure of psychoanalytic education. Like Zawinul's modified keyboard, this sounds different from what we are used to hearing, perhaps even inverted or backward. My hope is that, however strange what I am proposing may sound initially, it not only opens up the possibility for new thought but also, like Zawinul's modifications, is reversible and need not be permanent in order to be worthwhile. The argument I want to develop progresses across three main points. First, I believe psychoanalysis has had an idealized perception of science and university life that has led to excessively polarized and polemical portrayals of psychoanalysis and religion such that analysts have felt perplexed and ashamed by stubbornly "religious" elements in organized psychoanalytic education and institute life. Second, I argue that studies using Kelley's strictness hypothesis for the sociology of religious denominations offer us new ways of understanding the function of psychoanalytic orthodoxy. And third, in light of these new understandings, I describe four intra-institute structures as these exist in experimental form at a relatively new institute that is wrestling with ways to honor psychoanalysis' ongoing reformation. My argument is not about religion so much as it is the sociology of knowledge, using religious denominations as a means for considering the function and future of psychoanalytic education. Throughout all that follows my central interest is in thinking about ways of structuring our associations, within and between institutes, such that these structures can facilitate psychoanalytic education.

Idealization of Science and University Life

Perhaps because of its unique status as the only significant intellectual discipline in the twentieth century to develop outside the context of the university system, psychoanalysis has been able to sustain a peculiar idealization of science and university life. Organized psychoanalysis has had, to paraphrase Freud, university envy. Writing in 1966, Anna Freud surveyed the previous 50 years of psychoanalytic education and lamented how it was that essentially part-time candidates—exhausted and bedraggled from a week of work devoted to tasks often unrelated to psychoanalysis—arrived for institute seminars at the end of the day, the end of the week, or other off-peak hours, to receive instruction from a faculty of part-time volunteers with no necessary interest or aptitude for teaching. She longed for a model of psychoanalytic education that involved full-time students taught by full-time faculty, which she envisioned was the case in university life. Holzman (1976) suggested actually moving psychoanalytic institutes onto university campuses, in which psychoanalysis would exist as an interdisciplinary department within the university. In his portrayal of the university as every institute's ideal, Holzman's enthusiasm has a ring of either innocence or naïveté: "Whereas much of the theory and technique of psychoanalysis is taken as 'received doctrine' within the institute, *nothing* is taken for granted in establishing a theoretical position in the universities" (p. 270, emphasis added).

For many psychoanalysts, the allure of universities as the ideal institutes stems from a particular view of science that, ironically, is no longer widely held in many of these very universities, due to scientific developments within the universities themselves. Anna Freud's (1966) "utopia" for institutes entailed a scientific epistemology that sought to purge all knowledge of projected human subjectivity. She spoke of how, from her earliest memories of hearing books read aloud to her as a toddler, stories that contained elements "which precluded their happening in reality" bored her. "As soon as animals began to talk . . . my attention flagged and disappeared." This sentiment endured throughout the rest of her life, confessing: "To my own surprise, I have not altered much in this respect" (p. 74). A similar epistemological commitment was evident in Otto Kernberg's (1986) model of the university as an ideal for psychoanalytic institutes, contrasting what he called "an atmosphere of indoctrination" with "open scientific exploration" (p. 799).

The problem with these views, as I see it, is that *science* works through indoctrination, too. Normal science, in Kuhn's (1962) classic sense of the term, presupposes and requires indoctrination in order for science to function. What is more, radical breakthroughs in science often occur through explorers projecting their own aesthetic preferences and human wishes onto the field of study. For example, physicist Andrew Strominger, lauded for his recent work connecting two seemingly unrelated topics, black holes and subatomic strings, described his process of inquiry in personally aesthetic and subjective terms. "[Another physicist] would say: If A and B, then C. And he'd set out to prove it. I would say: Gosh, wouldn't C be nice. And then set out to prove it" (Cole, 1997, p. A16). Furthermore, what Strominger offers as support for his preferences, given that strings are 100 billion times smaller than a proton and thus far beyond the scope of all existing technology for measurement, is not the kind of proof arising from direct empirical inspection. In a sense, Strominger was able to connect black holes and string theory because he imagined a world in which, to play with Anna Freud's comment, the animals speak. By this I do not mean to inflict on science an unchecked religious mysticism such as Gary Zukav's (1984) *The Dancing Wu Li Masters*, something the Nobel prize winning physicist Leon Lederman (1993) rightly parodied as "The Dancing Moo-Shu Masters" (pp. 189–198).

Lederman noted that such authors "are apt to conclude rapturously that we are all part of the cosmos and the cosmos is part of us. We are all one! (Though, inexplicably, American Express bills us separately)" (p. 190). I mean, rather, that the kind of positivistic science for which many psychoanalysts pine—one that dichotomizes truth and illusion, myth and science, dogma and data—is no longer tenable in many university settings.

Organized psychoanalysis' idealization of university environments is also strangely discordant with a broad array of contemporary criticism, with titles such as *The Closing of the American Mind: How Higher Education Has Failed Democracy and Impoverished the Souls of Today's Students* (Bloom, 1987), *Profscam: Professors and the Demise of Higher Education* (Sykes, 1988), *Biotechnology: The University-Industrial Complex* (Kenney, 1986), and *The Dictatorship of Virtue* (Bernstein, 1995). Sharon Daloz Parks (1992) of the Harvard Business School and the Kennedy School of Government has noted how "increasingly our institutions are organized such that faculty are expected primarily to produce ideas, knowledge, research grants, research data, theories, lectures, papers, articles, books, programs, patentable (read lucrative) discoveries in technology and biotech" (p. 11). Her description of prestigious university environments is something different from what Anna Freud imagined would have been in store for students of a full-time faculty: "Institutions find themselves in bidding wars for good faculty, and when faced with limited monetary resources, throw in various perks to sweeten the deal, typically reduced time with students, less responsibility for students, less accountability to students" (p. 11).

Lest I be misunderstood on this point, my intention is not to fundamentally disparage university life. Cooper (1996) deemed Anna Freud's utopian institute of 1966 to now be "an urgent necessity rather than a luxury" (p. 151), and Wallerstein (1996) commended it as a valuable if unlikely prospect, and I agree with them. As a university professor and a training analyst myself, I have already noted in chapter 4 my concern for how disastrous a continued separation between clinical psychoanalysis and university settings could prove to be for analysis in the future. My point is rather that it strikes me as a profound irony that what we psychoanalysts yearn for in idealized universities already exists in many seminary settings, even though most of us would reflexively and "vehemently" (Kernberg, 1986, p. 809) reject such a model. When we ask, "Can psychoanalytic institutes change so that they become full-time academies with cross-disciplinary faculty, with provision for research activities, and with an atmosphere that encourages challenge, doubt, and disputation?" (Holzman, 1976, p. 270), we could well be describing currently established standards for theological education. There are far more divinity schools than psychoanalytic institutes that are associated with major universities, and their faculty are full-time, interdisciplinary scholars in linguistics, hermeneutics, cultural anthropology, semiotics, intellectual history, and social science research, among others, for whom doubt is inevitable and disputation essential.

As I mentioned near the conclusion of chapter 2, contemporary theological education tends to take conservative students and turn them into critically thinking liberals, an outcome that I would welcome if it were also typical of the effects of organized psychoanalytic education. Seen in this light, Kernberg's (1993) comment about the danger of reading Freud in only one translation (Strachey's *Standard Edition*) seems a peculiar warning: "There is always the danger, of course, of transforming the reading of Freud into a Bible reading—a religious rather than a scientific enterprise" (pp. 51–52). The Bible has scores of translations in English, with one or more new ones occurring every few years, each the product of teams of as many as 50 to 100 linguistic scholars who engage in highly contested readings. If reading Freud were really analogous to Bible readings, we would have 100 translations in English, and lively, scholarly debate about the meaning of specific words and phrases in appropriate cultural contexts; by comparison, reading Freud in English is almost a pre-religious exercise.

In the spirit of Zawinul's altered keyboard—and, I suppose, at the risk of offending conventional habits of thought—I suggest that psychoanalysis, rather than being excessively religious is, in this sense, not religious enough. Were psychoanalytic education to become more religious in the sense of modeling itself after contemporary theological education, it would more likely take on the characteristics for which we psychoanalysts repeatedly call. And once psychoanalysis and religion are (even temporarily) not forced to be antithetical, this permits exploration for how research on religious groups may be applied to psychoanalytic associations, which is what I propose to do, using Kelley's "strictness" hypothesis.

Kelley's "Strictness" Hypothesis

It is a well-documented fact that in the United States mainline Protestant denominations are dying. Somewhat less clear is precisely why. For two hundred years, Presbyterians, Congregationalists, Methodists, Episcopalians, Lutherans, and other Protestant denominations had grown steadily in membership. Since the mid-1960s, however, all have steadily lost membership—ranging from a fifth to a third—and current levels are at twentieth-century lows (Johnson, Hoge, and Luidens, 1993, p. 13). The Methodist church, as just one example, has lost 1000 members every week for the past 30 years (Tooley, 1995).

Various hypotheses have been proposed to account for the decline, including: (a) shifts toward greater autonomy and a mistrust of institutional authority prevalent in the 1960s; (b) ecclesiastical structures that either excessively accommodated to modernity or did the opposite, and failed the test of "relevance"; and (c) changing demographic trends which produced a more secularized populace. All of these hypotheses have failed to gather empirical support, including (c), the secularization hypothesis, which I suspect would be the most intuitively appealing to many psychoanalysts. The secularization hypothesis is that industrialization, urbanization, and an increasingly educated populace make religious belief difficult to sustain. In a recent review of the literature, however, Hoge (1996a) concluded: "My main message is that the empirical evidence available—and it is quite substantial—provides *no* support for the secularization model" (p. 24, emphasis added).

The one hypothesis that has received empirical support repeatedly was first introduced by Kelley in his 1972 book, *Why Conservative Churches Are Growing*. Kelley's hypothesis was that churches that are strict, whether liberal or conservative, are strong sociologically, much like Williamson's model of fundamentalism (addressed in chapter 1). Strictness in Kelley's typology is defined by *absolutism* (a belief that "we have the truth and all others are in error"), *conformity* (an intolerance of diversity or dissent), and *fanaticism* (a missionary zeal to spread the message of the group to outsiders). Religiously weak groups, by contrast, are marked by what Kelley termed *relativism* (the belief that no one has a monopoly on truth and all insights are partial), *diversity* (an appreciation for individual differences), and *dialogue* (an interest in exchange with outsiders, and a reluctance to try and impose one's beliefs on them) (see Kelley, 1972, p. 84). Although Kelley's hypothesis has generated considerable controversy, his views have been largely sustained empirically by a wide range of investigators (see Roof and McKinney, 1987; Finke and Stark, 1992; Johnson, Hoge, and Luidens, 1993; Hadaway and Marler, 1996; Hoge, 1996b; Iannaccone, 1996a, 1996b; Reeves, 1996).

Kelley acknowledged how his hypothesis paralleled the earlier theoretical work of Peter Berger, who is probably best known to psychoanalysts for being one of the earliest authors to present in English the concept of social constructivism (Berger and Luckmann, 1966). The next year, Berger (1967) extended and applied his work in social constructivism to a sociological theory of religion. For Berger, every human society is a collective enterprise in what he called "world building" (p. 3), in which a socially constructed order, or "nomos," serves as a sacred canopy, a shield against the terror of meaninglessness (p. 22). "Every socially constructed nomos must face the constant possibility of its collapse into anomy. Seen in this perspective of society, every nomos is an area of meaning carved out of a vast mass of meaninglessness, a small clearing of lucidity in a formless, dark, always ominous jungle" (p. 24). Religion, in this context, is "the human enterprise by which a sacred cosmos is established" (p. 26).

> Religion implies the farthest reaches of man's self-externalization, of his infusion of reality with his own meanings. Religion implies that human order is projected into the totality of being. Put differently, religion is the audacious attempt to conceive of the entire universe as being humanly significant [p. 28].

As with Zawinul's keyboard, this is certainly something different from what we are used to hearing as religion's function, although it is strikingly consistent with contemporary formulations of what psychoanalysis, at its best, can offer analysands, as detailed in chapter 2. If for Freud projection was largely a contamination or distortion, a source of error to be minimized in the equation, Berger's inversion offers projection as a necessary and essential aspect of how humans know anything—a means of making contact with otherness in ways that open up possibilities for imagining human significance. Berger (1967) playfully went one step further by developing what he called "an intellectual man-bites-dog feat" in which the reduction of theology to anthropology ends in "the reconstruction of anthropology in a theological mode" (p. 181):

> [T]o say that religion is a human projection does not logically preclude the possibility that the projected meanings may have an ultimate status independent of man. Indeed, if a religious view of the world is posited, the anthropological ground of these projections may itself be the reflection of a reality that *includes* both world and man, so that man's ejaculations of meaning into the universe ultimately point to an all-embracing meaning in which he himself is grounded. . . . Put simply, this would imply that man projects ultimate meanings into reality because that reality is, indeed, ultimately mean-

ingful, and because his own being (the empirical ground of these projections) contains and intends these same ultimate meanings [p. 181].

This possibility he developed further in a subsequent book published two years later (Berger, 1969).

If some might say that knowledge is power, for Berger (1967) it is as much the other way around: power is knowledge in the sense that "the fundamental coerciveness of society lies not in its machineries of social control, but in its power to constitute and to impose itself as reality" (p. 12). For Berger, as for Kelley, fundamentalism has its advantages. Religion traffics above all else in meaning making, and strong religious groups instill and sustain hearty constructions of socially sanctioned meanings. Weak groups fail to impose a socially shared sense of what passes for "reality," and thus fail to retain members or generate progeny. I am proposing that Kelley's strictness hypothesis can be a useful model for understanding psychoanalytic groups and, if true, explains stubbornly cultic elements in psychoanalytic associations.

Fundamentalism and Progeny in Psychoanalysis

Psychoanalysis is often described in religious, if not frankly cultic, terms: "Virtually the entire history of psychoanalysis has been bedeviled by accusations and counteraccusations of 'orthodoxy' and other forms of religious fanaticism" (Eisold, 1994, p. 796); "We are approaching a postapostolic era in psychoanalytic history. In a few years we will no longer have with us colleagues who had direct or indirect contact with the Founding Fathers" (Arlow, 1982, p. 18); "The language of orthodoxy and dissidence, of adherence to Freud or God, of what is pure analysis or gospel and what has been diluted as psychotherapy (rather than psychoanalysis) or become heretical, of initiation ceremonials and rites of passage to join the elect analysts, training analysts, priests or high priests; of journals which do not accept heterodox articles—these are only a few examples of an institutional religious perspective which has its origins in Freud" (Kirsner, 1990, pp. 97–98). Once we have become familiar with Kelley's strictness hypothesis, and also allow ourselves to imagine religious and psychoanalytic groups in a less polarized fashion, new and somewhat startling questions arise. Must psychoanalysis be strict in order to preserve itself? Is pluralism the kiss of death for psychoanalysis? Might the fanaticism long acknowledged within psychoanalytic circles be a boon rather than bane, the means of survival rather than some inexplicable and shamefully "religious" spasm? And were psychoanalysis to succeed in becoming the tolerant, diverse, and pluralistic association that Protestant mainline denominations are, what is to keep it from suffering the same fate of ineluctable decline?

Rather than immediately rejecting the questions I just posed on ideological grounds that religion and psychoanalysis are mutually exclusive—a view which I have argued assumes an idealized and outmoded view of science—I propose treating these questions as empirically testable possibilities, and offer two pieces of evidence, one an historical case study, the other a recent empirical research project, which support Kelley's strictness hypothesis as something applicable to psychoanalysis.

The historical case study involves the British Independents, who, when the group was first formed, were the super-majority of the British psychoanalytic society, with more members than the other subgroups *combined*. Eric Rayner (1991), himself a British Independent, chronicled the history of the group, which sought exclusive membership among neither the Kleinians nor the Anna Freudians: "The majority of the British Society, particularly those who had been its original members, wished to take sides with neither group. They came to be known first as the 'Middle' group and later as the 'Independents'" (p. 2). Their group identity, by Kelley's standards, fits perfectly the definition of a sociologically weak group, with its commitment to doubt and dissent, pluralism, and civil discourse with outsiders.

> Independents come together because they are all committed psychoanalysts in the first place, and then, not because they espouse any particular theory within it, but simply because they have an attitude in common. This is to evaluate and respect ideas for their use and truth value, no matter whence they come. Here the positive use and enjoyment of doubt is essential. Ideological certainty and factionalism are alien to their spirit. Where differences occur the Independents prefer to settle them by discussion and compromise. This attitude is sometimes seen by other analysts as a sloppy eclecticism. It can certainly deteriorate into this, but essentially it requires careful scholarship and intense intellectual discipline. The demands upon an Independent mind are very high [p. 9].

Not surprisingly, given Kelley's strictness hypothesis, the British Independents' numbers have declined while the Kleinians' have increased, compared to their respective proportions initially. Rayner (personal communication, December 1996) relayed the comment of a Contemporary Freudian colleague, who described present-day Independents as "turkeys wandering 'round the woods at random, easily picked off one-at-time by well organized Kleinian hunting parties." I gather that, among the dues-paid-up members of the British Psycho-Analytical Society who are not in retirement and are in active practice in the greater metropolitan area of London, the number of Kleinians and Independents is now roughly equivalent (with the Contemporary Freudians comprising a much smaller third group); also, perhaps even more indicative of future trends, among current institute candidates who are pre-first-year, first- through third-year, or post-seminar fourth- and fifth-year students, the number of those in training with a Kleinian analyst now surpasses the numbers of those in training with an Independent or a Contemporary Freudian *combined*. Granted, candidates can adopt theoretical orientations different than their analysts', and indeed a key part of my argument is in fact to emphasize how this can occur. Even so, among the three elements in psychoanalytic education—coursework, supervision, and one's own experience in analysis—I believe the latter has the greatest influence on how we practice and, if this is so, then it is the Kleinians who are poised to have a greater influence than the Independents in Britain's future.

Their very openness to dialogue and reluctance to affiliate under the banner of any specific ideology make the Independents fall short of being the kind of fundamentalists who readily proselytize and generate intellectual progeny. Gregorio Kohon (1986) portrayed the Independents as analysts who valued creative autonomy so strongly that their membership existed mainly by default.

> In fact at the beginning this was not a group at all; the analysts who found themselves belonging to it had merely refused to belong to either of the sectarian groups that had been formed. This was then, and still continues to be today, the attraction for many analysts. Most of its members refuse to be politically organized, or to have any one leader, or to proselytize [p. 49].

Kohon's conclusion about the Independents as a group was at once ominous and prescient: "*This, in a tough world of political life, might in the end make it disappear*" (p. 49; emphasis added).

The second instance of what I believe is evidence for the applicability of Kelley's strictness hypothesis, not only for British Independents but for a broad array of contemporary analysts in North America, is the empirical research by Hamilton (1996). She conducted one- to two-hour interviews with 65 leading psychoanalysts in London, Los Angeles, New York, and San Francisco, scored the resulting transcripts on 27 different scales using four independent raters, and subjected the data to cluster and factor analyses. She sampled a broad range of theoretical orientations, including classical and contemporary Freudians, ego psychologists, British Independents and Kleinians, American interpersonalists, self psychologists, and intersubjectivists. One of the major findings of Hamilton's study was that the Kleinians and Kohutians, despite the theoretical antagonism between them substantively, were quite similar in how their respective groups were structured functionally. "The results of the cluster analysis confirmed those of the factor analysis in that two groups of analysts, those of a Kleinian/Bionian orientation and those of a Kohutian/self-psychological orientation, appeared to be the most cohesive groups, acknowledging much less influence by any other sources of influence" (p. 15). In a sense, the two groups with growing numbers in Great Britain and the States were the fundamentalists: they interpreted everything from one cohesive theory, cited those from within their own camps often, and generally ignored those outside except as these could serve as object lessons to demonstrate the folly of alternative views.

Hamilton's research was a paean to psychoanalytic pluralism, a view that celebrates the inherent multiplicity of interpretation and laments any premature adjudication of what counts as real or unreal. In a style reminiscent of Rayner's comments about the British Independents, Hamilton averred, "The pluralist must think imaginatively, for to interpret a radically different mind or community is to exercise an effort of imagination so that the interpreter enters into the hopes and fears, loves and hates, fights and desires, of the other individual or culture" (p. 4). Even though Hamilton found that practicing psychoanalysts outside the two most cohesive groups were more pluralistic than they publicly claimed, she concluded that, even in a pluralistic culture, fundamentalism "tends to win out" (p. 25). If not belonging to a tightly cohesive group can create a sense of subtle loneliness and a chronic tentativeness, authenticity nonetheless has its own rewards, as Hamilton confessed upon concluding her study:

A British colleague once described me jokingly as "a mongrel." He commiserated with the sense he thought I might have of not belonging to a particular group. Not being a Kleinian or a Freudian, or a self psychologist/intersubjectivist here in Los Angeles, can create a feeling of not belonging. This is particularly so when, in my clinical work, I face uncertainty over a long period. For instance, if I find a client particularly difficult to understand, and if also that client is particularly hostile or rejecting, I find myself thinking So and So would know exactly what to say. Or, if I were So and So, I would interpret this way. Trouble is that I don't. For the most part, however, the project has helped me to feel freer of an analytic superego, of the feeling that "we," the Independents, Kleinians, or whoever, really know. Nobody *really* knows [p. 317].

Ongoing Reformation

To the degree that Kelley's strictness theory applies, fundamentalism's advantage is its ready ability to generate progeny, to reproduce itself through a process something like ideological cloning. It is much less adroit, however, at courting novelty, and from a perspective of the sociology of knowledge, as I have noted in chapter 2, all orthodoxies are essentially heresies that were successful. From this inherent tension between fidelity and innovation, the question arises: How can psychoanalysis not only preserve itself, but also continue to change and reinvent itself? Or, what makes psychoanalysis psychoanalysis? How much can psychoanalysis change and still be legitimately called analysis? Who decides?

One answer is to look to a quote from Freud on the matter, but this quickly proves problematic not only because he changed his mind as he continued to develop his thinking across his own lifetime, but also because psychoanalysis has continued to develop and change after Freud's death. Even Wallerstein (1990), who sought to broker consensus for what might pass as common ground among current psychoanalytic heterogeneity, conceded, "The structure of psychoanalysis has by far burst the thought boundaries set for it by Freud, boundaries which he had intended to be enduringly maintained by the famous committee he created, of the seven ring holders" (p. 3). Freud's (1914) definition of psychoanalysis as any therapy that works by analysis of transference and resistance, for example, is a less straightforward solution than it first seems because many practicing psychoanalysts today, though they may continue to use the words transference and resistance, mean very different things by them than Freud did. For Freud, transference was an error, "a *false connection*" (Breuer and Freud, 1893–1895, p. 302). For psychoanalysts who endorse a more postcritical epistemology, however, as detailed in chapter 4, adjudicating between fact and fantasy is not the point. Instead, transference and countertransference become the means by which we know anything at all; instead of being embarrassing sources of error, they are the center around which we organize personal meaning and significance.

The notion of resistance has undergone radical revision as well, due to shifting conceptions of the unconscious. If for Freud the unconscious is, among other things, a seething cauldron of putatively asocial drives, many contemporary analysts have become suspicious of any claims for pre-existing, singular universals—grand metanarratives, oedipal or otherwise, that presume binding applicability for all people, irrespective of historical and cultural circumstance. What is more, much of contemporary psychoanalysis is apt to view both classical analysis and the humanistic psychologies that developed in opposition to it as ironically identical in how they imagine the relation between individual and society. If a classical perspective is that society is a compromise we live with in order to keep from killing each other off, and a humanistic perspective is that society corrupts our pristine nature, a point in common is the assumption that society distorts human nature, either because we are much better, or much worse, than we seem. In contrast to this shared assumption, contemporary psychoanalytic epistemologies insist that conceptions of self, human nature, and even "the unconscious," are necessarily social constructions, thus profoundly recasting the possibilities of what exactly "resistance" opposes.

I think a more fruitful approach to understanding both what might define psychoanalysis, as well as allow its ongoing reformation, is to follow the example of Laudan's (1983) analysis of the "demarcation problem" in science. The problem (distinguishing real science from pseudo-science) is trickier than it looks, and Laudan's solution (science is what scientists do) is more sophisticated than it might first appear. When he playfully laments, "Epistemology is an old subject; until about 1920 it was also a great one" (Laudan, 1977, p. 1), he is proposing a functional view of science measured by its ability to solve problems: "*The first and essential acid test for any theory is whether it provides acceptable answers to interesting questions; whether, in other words, it provides satisfactory solutions to important problems*" (p. 13). From this view, science pursues research programs so long as they pose possible answers to interesting questions. When the questions change, so does the research. This explanation fits

Hamilton's (1996) findings that analysts who changed theoretical orientations—from Klein to self psychology, for example—"tend not to 'add on' new beliefs, but rather to go through a sort of 'conversion' experience from the old to the new model" (p. 67). Psychoanalysts do this not because they have become suddenly or shamefully "religious," but because, as Kuhn (1962) argued in the climax of his famous treatise on the incommensurability of paradigms in science, this is something scientific knowledge in groups requires—what Kuhn called a "conversion" (p. 150) or "a conversion experience" (p. 151). According to Laudan's deceptively simple proposal, psychoanalysis is defined by what psychoanalysts do, and its definition changes as psychoanalysts do new things.

How such change manages to occur is something that depends, in part, on the relationship we can imagine between new ideas and tradition. Harold Bloom (1973) proposed that creative persons must misread their predecessors in order to make imaginative space for their own new thought, but I think this depends on having a relationship with mentors who are threatened by subsequent innovation. Bertrand Russell took on Ludwig Wittgenstein as his protégé, the intellectual heir apparent who was to carry forth Russell's analytic philosophy into the next generation: "He is the young man one looks for" (Monk, 1990, p. 41). And yet Russell was also open to receiving Wittgenstein's subsequent contribution, even though it dismantled Russell's life work and did so in a way that Russell, arguably one of the best minds in recent centuries, could not fully grasp: "I feel in my bones that he must be right, and that he has seen something that I have missed" (pp. 81–82). The quality of mentoring relationship Russell offered Wittgenstein stands in dramatic contrast to the relationship between Freud and Sándor Ferenczi, as the recently unfolding English translation of the latters' correspondence attests (Brabant, Falzeder, and Giampieri-Deutsch, 1992; Falzeder and Brabant, 1996: Falzeder, Brabant, and Giampieri-Deutsch, 2000). Feldman (1994) has made a case that Freud's psychology inclined him toward Greek myths rather than Biblical narratives precisely because the latter were not preoccupied with patricide:

> Biblical fathers, it would seem, are not made for the Freudian masterplot. Rarely expressing aggression, they seem to avoid conflict rather than arousing (and resolving) it. This does not mean, however, that conflict totally disappears. It is recreated on the "horizontal" level, in the relationship between the brothers, thus highlighting one of the major ways in which the patriarchal stories diverge from Freud's interests: their focus on intragenerational sibling rivalry rather than on filial rebellion [p. 11].

It could be that anxiety over filial rebellion and patricide was more a product of Freud's own psychology than it is a ubiquitous truth that applies to all fathers and all sons (Stolorow and Atwood, 1993).

Apropos of this possibility is Falzeder's (1994) genogram of psychoanalytic filiations, a giant wall map of who-analyzed-whom during the early decades of psychoanalysis. To me, one of the most fascinating features of Falzeder's research is the differing fecundity of various training analysts in terms of the subsequent creativity of their analysands. Some, occasionally even those quite famous, generated descendants who contributed little of anything new to psychoanalysis. Others, who were themselves rather obscure or otherwise unnotable analysts, yielded a whole brood of especially innovative analysands who made profound contributions to the field.

Traditionalism, not tradition, is the enemy of innovation. "Tradition is the living faith of the dead, traditionalism is the dead faith of the living," Yale church historian Jaroslav Pelikan (1984) has reminded us, adding that it is traditionalism that has given tradition such a bad name (p. 65). If psychoanalysis has taught us anything it is that we ignore our roots at our peril, not because the past is fixed or immutable, but because articulation of our history permits both an experience of gratitude and a recognition of the other's subjectivity, which are themselves substantial developmental achievements. As Pelikan averred, "Maturity in relation to our parents consists in going beyond both a belief in their omniscience and a disdain for their weakness, to an understanding and gratitude for their decisive part in that ongoing process in which now we, too, must take our place, as heirs and yet free" (p. 54). For progress and ongoing reformation in psychoanalytic theory, this means doing the work of situating contemporary contributions within a debt of gratitude to those who have preceded us, as Rudnytsky chronicled in an exchange between Winnicott and Balint. Winnicott (1975) often began his papers with the disclaimer: "I shall not first give an historical survey and show the development of my ideas from the theories of others, because my mind does not work that way. What happens is that I gather this and that, here and there, settle down to clinical experience, form my own theories and then, last of all, interest myself in looking to see where I stole what" (p. 145). Rudytsky (1991) cited Balint, who took Winnicott to task for this:

> Perhaps I ought to say here that this has happened several times during our friendship. You emphasized on more than one occasion that "though—(I quote from memory)—Ferenczi and Dr. Balint have said

all these many years ago, here I am not concerned with what they said," or "I have not had time to read that but I shall ask the Honorary Librarian to fill this gap," etc. Of course, in this way you always have the audience laughing and on your side—no-one among us likes to read boring scientific literature and if somebody of your stature admits it in public, he can be certain of success. . . . Your way of expressing your ideas forces one into the position of either saying "this is splendid and entirely new" or of remaining silent [p. 86].

Winnicott's (1967) reply was contrite in a way that I think prefigures Benjamin's (1995) work on recognition: "I've realized more and more as time went on what a tremendous lot I've lost from not properly correlating my work with the work of others. It's not only annoying to other people but it's rude and it has meant that what I've said has been isolated and people have had to do a lot of work to get at it. It happens to be my temperament, and it's a big fault" (p. 573).

Even so, it is not as if a sense of the past can never have a restricting presence, as a personal experience from my own life might illustrate. Several years ago I heard Seiji Ozawa guest-conduct the Los Angeles Philharmonic in a concert that concluded with Brahms' first symphony. I was not familiar with this piece, and, while listening, I closed my eyes and let the music wash over me. I found myself playing a thought experiment: If I did not know this music was by Brahms, who would I think had written it? "It sounds like Beethoven, only not as good," I found myself day-dreaming. I let myself go with a fantasy: What if someone discovered this score locked away in a dusty old attic somewhere—a lost symphony of Beethoven, never heard before—would I believe it? It still did not quite ring true. For me, it was nice enough. It was not bad. But it seemed too derivative, too tame, and lacked Beethoven's emphatic confidence and raw authenticity. Suddenly, however, staccato strings at the opening of the fourth movement jostled me from my daydream. They seemed impish, playful, and made me think of the way cartoon characters can tiptoe from tree to tree in a forest, with each narrow trunk obscuring an impossibly wide body. They also made me think of early contractions in a woman's labor: something was up; something new was coming. Then this absolutely gorgeous melody came from the horn section, passed innocently to the flutes, took on regal proportions with the trombones and, by the time it moved to the full string sections, the piece felt like it had emphatically turned a corner, with the march that followed reminding me of a commencement or a graduation ceremony—a victory processional. I was floored. I staggered home and, in the days that followed, I tried to make sense of what had hit me. As I read more about Brahms, I learned that he had begun his first symphony in about 1855, but had left it unfinished for over 20 years because he did not know how to end it. Even though he had by then developed a considerable reputation as a composer of international prominence, he felt haunted by the looming presence of Beethoven. "You have no idea of how someone like me feels when he constantly hears a giant (Beethoven) marching behind him," Brahms once confessed, adding on another occasion: "In everything that I try, I tread on my predecessors' heels, which troubles me" (Dimpfel, 1983, p. 7). While vacationing in Switzerland he heard an alphorn and wrote back excitedly that he now had gained access to his own voice, his own authentic idiom, and he actually cut portions of the earlier movements to make more room for the triumph of the fourth.

Structuring Psychoanalytic Education

I wonder how we who are psychoanalytic educators can facilitate our candidates' encounter with their own "alphorns." Perhaps one way is by being open enough to let the event register in us, with appreciative recognition, whenever it happens for them. How often are we the predecessors upon whose heels they tread? We would do well to remember Nietzsche's (1908) dictum: "One repays a teacher badly if one always remains nothing but a pupil" (p. 78). Kirsner (1996), one of the most perceptive critics of organized psychoanalysis in North America, complained: "Much analytic education is if anything 'miseducation' since it does not so much 'draw out' students as systematically move them towards conformity with their teachers and analysts." This sentiment concurs with Siegfried Bernfeld's (1962) call for what he termed a "student-centered" psychoanalytic education. Bernfeld objected that institute structures, by being "teacher-centered," were actually pre-psychoanalytic, and inconsistent with principles of psychoanalytic inquiry:

> The idea of a student-centered system is quite alien to our institutes; and, what is even worse, matters of local policies and administration are mainly decided by a national committee, according to the interest of the national professional association, whereas according to psychoanalytic theory and practice it is obvious that nothing should count so heavily as the concrete local relationships [p. 458].

I think many psychoanalysts have an understandable aversion to fundamentalism of any kind, which they equate with conservatism, and conclude—as Bernfeld's comment suggests—that the culprit is group affiliation, at least at national or international levels, and perhaps even at local ones. I certainly find Kelley's second set of attributes (relativism, diversity, dialogue) a lot more appealing than the first (absolutism, conformity, fanaticism), and I am reluctant to sacrifice what I see as the virtues of the one for the progeny of the other. Recall, however, that strict groups in Kelley's sense may be liberal, too, and not just conservative, because strictness refers to a methodology or orientation rather than the substantive content of particular commitments. If fundamentalism begets progeny, what might it be like to have a *liberal* version—one that gave its blessing to subsequent generations' innovations, much like Russell's treatment of Wittgenstein, Nietzsche's dictum about gratitude in education, or the otherwise unnotable analysts in Falzaeder's research who consistently spawned theoretically and clinically creative analysands whose fame superseded their teachers'? Our answers to this would also address my earlier concerns about pluralism necessarily leading to psychoanalysis' demise, since institute structures for a resolutely student-centered education would qualify as a strict group in Kelley's sense, and not simply an association by default, formed by those who were endlessly equivocal and could not bring themselves to take a stand.

I can think of four examples of structures for such a "liberal fundamentalism," and I would like to conclude with a brief description of each. They exist in experimental form at a relatively new institute in Los Angeles, the Institute for Contemporary Psychoanalysis (ICP), and involve intrainstitute relations ("training" analyses, control cases, curriculum, and membership). I must hasten to add that I am keenly aware of the tendency for each of us as analysts to regard our experiences in our own institutes as normative, and to view alternative models as peculiar or wrong-headed (see Sandler, 1990). I describe ICP not because, like Balint's complaint to Winnicott, I fancy its pedagogical structure is "splendid and entirely new," or that it is the only way to offer student-centered education. In my view, it is neither. Instead, it is merely an illustrative example of one group's struggle to institute structures that might generate progeny in a way that prized and insisted on psychoanalysis' ongoing reformation.

Conferral of status as "training analyst" has long been acknowledged as a problematic appointment tinged with political considerations (Kernberg, 1996; Kirsner, 1996). "It is an open secret that the appointment of training analysts," Kernberg (1986) declared, "is politically motivated, that the actual qualifications of the training analyst may be less important than his or her reliability with regard to local politics" (p. 805). Even the term itself has been awkward, as Balint noted in 1948:

> The original name for the analysis was "instructional," a servile translation of the German "Lehr"; this was followed by "didactic" still under Germanic influence; and was eventually changed to "training analysis". Apparently this too, was felt as being too forceful and recently the term "personal analysis" is being introduced. It is a bad term, because every analysis is personal, there is no "impersonal" analysis, but it shows clearly the awakening conscience for which even "training" is too forceful [pp. 171–172].

As Eckstein (1969) rightly clarified, psychoanalytic training and psychoanalytic education are not synonymous, and he wisely preferred the latter. A student-centered psychoanalytic education must empower candidates to make decisions and to assume responsibility for their own learning. To that end, one potentially emancipatory structure in psychoanalytic education is to let candidates decide whom they want as their own analyst, with minimal credentialing activity or other political considerations by institute governance. At ICP, analysts who have more than two years since graduation from any institute or its equivalent, and who apply to ICP and are accepted, are eligible to be the candidate's personal analyst. Students may change analysts at any time, without prejudice.

When candidates are penalized by having to lose credit and start over with a new case if their initial patient drops out of treatment, there is considerable pressure for candidates to select a relatively "safe" patient who is reasonably high functioning, rather than someone who is closer to stretching the limits of the candidate's capacities. This decision occurs even though the more challenging patient might prove to be both a better learning experience for the candidate in intensive supervision, and more representative of the clinical populations the candidate might otherwise see. ICP decided to structure partial credit for control cases that terminate prematurely, and encourages candidates' willingness to treat difficult patients.

Offering few required courses, with most of the curriculum being comprised of electives, encourages candidates to build their own courses or independent studies, and even to recruit their own instructors. ICP allows anyone to propose a class, submits the descriptions to candidates, and offers all classes that reach a minimal quorum of student enroll-

ment. One of its few required courses is for first-year, first-semester candidates, who hear a senior member present one of his or her own cases in
detail, including his or her own moments of clinical choices, regrets, and
uncertainties.

Participation should be sufficiently demanding to satisfy Kelley's
criteria for a sociologically "strong" group. In addition to non-trivial annual dues, in its first decade all ICP members were required to meet
monthly in a peer supervision group, during which they took turns pre-
senting process notes of their own work for critique and evaluation among
colleagues. As a nonreporting institute, members do not present cases in
which candidates are the analysands. In order to minimize cliques or
theoretical insularity, members are assigned to study groups at random,
and every two years the groups are reshuffled. Participation in study groups
is now required for the first two years postgraduation, and is voluntary
thereafter.

The long-term success of ICP at implementing a student-centered
education remains to be seen, although initial results show promise. In
the years since its inception, ICP's membership has grown to over 200
active participants, a sizeable number for any new institute, especially
one located outside New York. The institute is structured via a participatory democracy that evenly represents candidates, recent graduates, and
senior members, and all positions are circumscribed by explicitly defined
term limits in an attempt to prevent any one member, or cadre of members, from monopolizing institute governance or installing themselves
permanently in power. In his biography of sociologist Max Weber, Diggins
(1996) argued that, whereas America's view of democracy and history,
steeped in Jeffersonian liberalism and Deweyan pragmatism, saw democracy everywhere as moving progressively upward, Weber was sympathetic
to the view "that direct democracy was impossible since elites always rise
to the top by virtue of strategic position, superior talent, or whatever it
takes to bend an organization to the will of a closed minority" (p. 85). If
Weber is right, even participatory democracy cannot remain innocent of
irony and of tragedy, because the very activities that promote liberty inexorably lead to institutions that pose a threat to that liberty.

Another ICP distinction that is too young to measure is its emphasis on psychoanalysis' *contemporary* formulations, and here the philosopher Bryan Magee's (1997) cautions are in order. In any creative endeavor,
a tension exists between studying the work of acknowledged masters from
the past and offering one's own contribution in the present. Using the
example of a music academy, Magee warns us that whenever we dichoto-

mize a creative discipline as *either* a subject *or* an activity, the latter tends to be lauded as authentic and an advance, whereas the former is dismissed as antiquated and irrelevant.

> A music academy can conduct itself ultimately in one of two ways. It can base its teaching on the works of great composers, encouraging its students to learn by emulation; in their composition classes they can study such music, and as instrumentalists they can perform it. The advantages of this approach are that they become saturated with great music, getting to know some of it extremely well, deriving their own standards and models from it, and developing their own skills through it. But there will be critics of this approach who protest: "Your academy is a museum, if not an embalming parlour. You play only music by dead people. Your young people are slaves to the dead, and you are ignoring the fact that music is a living, breathing art. An academy of gifted people ought to be among the pioneers of progress, at the cutting edge of musical advance. You ought to be encouraging live composers; and your young instrumentalists ought to be playing the music of their own contemporaries. *Making* music is what this is all about. You and they ought to be breathing the air of practical innovation, the exciting and the new" [p. 423].

The problem with this protest, according to Magee, is that the artists who endorse it end up creating little of lasting value, whether to their contemporaries or even themselves, and become the functional equivalent of journalists who chronicle the intellectual fads of the moment. Worst of all, they will have "lived their lives marinating in the formaldehyde of fourth-rate music, which is not something that anyone who loves music could possibly want to do" (p. 424). If Magee's caveat applies, a psychoanalytic pedagogy preoccupied with contemporary expression may find itself pickling in similar brine.

To summarize, my argument is not that diversity does not exist in psychoanalytic institutes, but rather that there has been an intolerance of diversity. What is more, however repugnant the notion is for most of us as analysts, this very intolerance may have ironically been the means of the intergenerational survival of psychoanalysis, if a sociology for other kinds of groups applies to psychoanalytic ones as well. Over most of the twentieth century, it is precisely toward fundamentalism that most of our psychoanalytic associations gravitated, for reasons that have almost nothing to do with conscious choice. Our usual explanations for why fundamentalism and sectarian schisms occur in psychoanalysis (self-selecting tendencies that favor narcissism in our leaders, the long hours of isolation and uncertainty in our work that pull for a counter-balancing and compensatory fanaticism when we congregate, etc.) I think are true, but the part I want to add has to do with how our institutes' educational systems are structured. We analysts tend not to want to recognize systemic factors that unwittingly institute the very fundamentalistic qualities we so regularly lament—and recognize—in our educational institutions. Kenneth Eisold (1994) wrote about how we as analysts "devalue and fear" (p. 785) those institutions that situate us within larger social contexts, and I think proposals like mine, which presume or argue for such contexts, risk a similar reception.

Joe Zawinul rewired his keyboard only temporarily. Perhaps when it comes to imagining positive and useful similarities between psychoanalytic institutes and religious denominations, we must do the same, and revert to more polarized perceptions. (The next time you hear the word *religious* in psychoanalytic discourse, see if it is not an expression of contempt.) Even so, I hope the possibility of structuring relations within and between institutes so as to generate progeny who cherish psychoanalysis' ongoing reformation is more than a momentary reversal. We may yet remember the sound of something new coming from within us, music we did not even know we knew how to make.

Chapter 7

Psychoanalysis and Religion: Are They In the Same Business?

O bviously not. The history of religion and science is one of chronic warfare, with religion on the losing side due to the steady advances of secularization. Religion is about belief, science is about practice, and psychoanalysis, like any science, therefore has little in common with religion. It is a different business.

Or is it? Scholarship during the past half-century in the history of science, sociology of religion, and philosophy of science now generally regards every one of the objections I just mentioned as false. The history of religion and science is not one of chronic warfare. Religion is not on the losing end of the steady advances of secularization. The bifurcation of belief and practice, whether in religion or science, is viewed as neither possible nor desirable. And the demise of foundationalism in philosophy has recast our conceptions of science in more social and cultural terms, thus blurring previous criteria for distinguishing scientific and religious pursuits. Add to all this the intramural debate within contemporary psychoanalysis about whether analysis already is or is not a science, or could be science—or even whether it ought to be—and whatever the business in which psychoanalysis and religion are now thought to be, they are no longer so obviously different.

In what follows, I highlight the trends of scholarship regarding the *warfare* metaphor in the history of science, the *secularization* hypothesis in the sociology of religion, and the impact of the demise of *foundationalism* in the philosophy of science. To anticipate my conclusion, my one-word answer to my opening question is No. I don't think psychoanalysis and religion are in the same business, although contemporary scholarship suggests that the differences are not what was once thought, and I think these differences, as currently understood, can be enriching for psychoanalysis and religion alike.

Warfare

The relationship between science and religion is much more complicated—and much more interesting—than what the caricature of warfare or conflict simplistically conveys. In a review of the literature, physicist and professor of religion Ian Barbour (1997) summarized, "In recent decades this conflict thesis has been extensively criticized as a selective and oversimplified account. Science and religion were not unified forces opposing each other like armies on a battlefield" (p. 25, italics removed). No one disputes that conflicts occurred, but they were most often within the same person, or within a group of theologians or a group of scientists. Moreover, at issue were conflicting metaphysical commitments to which various scientific positions gave substance. Historians of science John Brooke and Geoffrey Cantor reaffirmed this insight: "[S]trictures against theological dogmatism have repeatedly struck a popular chord. It takes a little more discernment to see that much of the perceived conflict was not between science and theology but between *competing forms of science* in which theologians might have an interest or between *competing forms of theology* in which appeal might be made to the authority of science" (Brooke and Cantor, 1998, p. 18; emphasis added). Even controversies concerning Galileo's argument for a heliocentric cosmology, as one example, or Darwin's theory of evolution, as another, do not fit a metaphor of war. Regarding the circumstances surrounding Galileo, Brooke and Cantor (pp. 106–138) reject the assumption of an inherent conflict between religion and science as a form of proof texting that overlooks a wealth of contrary historical data. And concerning the post-Darwinian controversies, the opening sentence of the first chapter in James Moore's (1979) authoritative historiographic introduction is: "Clever metaphors die hard" (p. 19). Moore deemed the warfare metaphor to be "entirely misleading if not utterly false. There was not a polarisation of 'science' and 'religion' as the idea of opposed armies implies but a large number of learned men, some scientists, some theologians, some indistinguishable, and almost all of them very religious" (p. 99). He concluded: "Nor, finally, was there the kind of antagonism pictured in the discharge of weaponry but rather a much more subdued overall reaction to *The Origin of Species* than is generally supposed and a genuine amiability in the relations of those who are customarily believed to have been in battle" (p. 99). One introduction to the history of science and religion begins with the warning, "To start in the simplest terms, it is necessary to dispell some common myths about a presumed 'split' between theology and science," specifically the "so-called 'warfare' between science and theology/religion" (Welch, 1996, p. 29). Wildman (1996) refers to the story of conflict between science and religion as a legend:

> [It is] a popular tale, told and retold even now in both schools and the media. A few strident intellectuals keep the embers of plausibility glowing beneath the story by urging the rational weakness of religious faith or of church theology. Though actual instances of explicit conflict are rare, there are enough contemporary examples—such as religious creationists, educators, and scientists having it out on daytime television talk shows—to sustain a popular confidence in the story's veracity. . . . The keys to this triumph of science over the pretensions of religion, so the story goes, are its impartial method and the corresponding certainty of its results. What chance did religion have? The dubious assertions of faith, stubbornly based on misinterpretations of beautiful biblical myths and legends, eventually had to bow to the objective and reliable assertions of the natural sciences.
>
> It is quite a story. In many ways, however, it is dissociated from reality. In it, a profound tension within human rationality as this has developed in the West is grossly distorted by cartoonlike caricatures, to the point that the story conveys little useful information about anything that really happened. Instead, like the good legend it is, every ritual retelling of it merely expatiates the underlying tension [p. 48].

The legend stems from two works from the nineteenth century, one by a physician, John Draper (1874), entitled *The History of Conflict between Religion and Science*, and the other by the U.S. Senator and first president of Cornell University, Andrew White (1896), entitled *A History of the Warfare of Science with Theology in Christendom*. Draper admitted his lack of training for tackling his subject, but drew solace in the belief that it would be one of many other scholarly volumes to follow. This did not come to pass. Instead, despite the dearth of corroboration from other scholarship in the ensuing centuries, the Draper and White volumes became wildly popular, enjoying between them more than 80 editions and translations into Polish, Russian, Italian, Swedish, Spanish, French, German, and Japanese. Historians of science David Lindberg and Ronald Numbers (1986) noted that in the early years "White's *Warfare* apparently did not sell as briskly as Draper's *Conflict*, but in the end it proved more influential, partly, it seems, because Draper's strident anti-Catholicism soon dated his work and because White's impressive documentation gave the appearance of sound scholarship" (p. 3). Lindberg (1986) reported that Draper's book was last reprinted in 1970 and that White's is still in print.

A psychoanalytic explanation for the enduring popularity of the Draper-White warfare metaphor is that it is a form of wish fulfillment based on splitting—a wish for something to idealize and something else to devalue, in this case science and religion, respectively. Science is equated with common-sense rationality, and religion with credulity and the suppression of scientific investigation. For at least three reasons, however, it is not that simple. First, a case can be made that modern science developed in the countries it did because of cultures that were especially congenial to science, and one aspect of these cultures was the community's shared theological commitments. Sociologist Robert Merton (1970) argued that the culture of Puritanism in seventeenth-century England provided a context that facilitated the rise of modern science. According to Merton, medieval thinkers had little use for physical matter due to influences of asceticism and monasticism, whereas Puritan theology encouraged and esteemed professions that engaged in rational and empirical scrutiny of Creation, which was seen as the genuinely free act of a Creator and thus known inductively rather than through deductive speculation. Historian Reijer Hooykaas (1972) made a similar case for the role of Western monotheism, which, by positing a rational and nonpantheistic God who was distinct from Creation, legitimized rational inquiry and intervention into what were deemed natural, rather than supernatural, phenomena. If the rise of science is credited in part to theologically supportive cultures, then the relationship between religion and science is more interesting than the simplistic and wholesale opposition of one to the other.

Second, it is no longer clear that the role science plays in modern life is completely on the side of commonsense rationality, as a humorous vignette by communications theorist Neil Postman (1993) illustrates. Postman has described how he would perform a social experiment on colleagues at work by asking them if they had seen the day's *New York Times*, and if not, he would continue:

> "You ought to check out Section C today," I say. "There's a fascinating article about a study done at the University of Minnesota." "Really? What's it about?" is the usual reply. The choices at this point are almost endless, but there are two that produce rich results. The first: "Well, they did this study to find out what foods are best for losing weight, and it turns out that the normal diet supplemented by chocolate eclairs eaten three times a day is the best approach. It seems that there's some special nutrient in the eclairs—encomial dyoxin—that actually uses up calories at an incredible rate."
>
> The second changes the theme and, from the start, the university: "The neurophysiologists at Johns Hopkins have uncovered a connection between jogging and reduced intelligence. They tested more than twelve hundred people over a period of five years, and found that as the number of hours people jogged increased there was a statistically significant decrease in their intelligence. They don't know exactly why, but there it is" [pp. 56–57].

Postman debriefed us with his results:

> My role in the experiment, of course, is to report something quite ridiculous—one might say, beyond belief. If I play my role with a sense of decorum and collegial intimacy, I can achieve results worth reporting: about two-thirds of the victims will believe or at least not wholly disbelieve what I have told them. Sometimes they say, "Really? Is that possible?" Sometimes they do a double-take and reply, "Where'd you say that study was done?" And sometimes they say, "You know, I've heard something like that." I should add that for reasons that are probably worth exploring I get the clearest cases of credulity when I use the University of Minnesota and Johns Hopkins as my sources of authority; Stanford and MIT give only fair results [p. 57].

Postman mentioned George Bernard Shaw's quip that the average person today is about as credulous as the average person in the Middle Ages, adding that all that has changed is what we take as our authority. "In the Middle Ages, people believed in the authority of their religion, no matter what. Today, we believe in the authority of our science, no matter what"

(p. 58). To the degree this is true, it is not quite right to think of science as something that simply sweeps away credulity and replaces it with commonsense rationality, since the numbing and bewildering array of scientific pronouncements can ironically produce in us the sort of mystification and bracketing of critical inquiry for which science was once thought to be the antidote.

Third, this mystification is a function of not just the sheer volume of scientific findings but their content as well. As one example, an international team of scientists wanted to determine the shape of the universe. Because of the time it takes for light to travel, the more distant the point in space that astronomers examined, the farther back in time they peered. The scientists used an instrument sensitive enough to detect heat from a coffee maker as far away as the moon. The device was suspended from a balloon 5000 miles above Antarctica, where it looked back in time to measure 10- to 15-billion-year-old photons, or light particles, that were present when the universe was newly formed. Prescientific people thought the world was flat, and that if sailors went too far, they would sail off the edge of the earth. Einstein taught us that space is comprised of four dimensions—the usual three we experience, plus time. Ironically, according to scientists' recent analyses of extragalactic radiation, it now seems that although the earth is not flat, the entire universe is. Saying so sounds like one of Postman's tricks, but it is true: our galaxy of the Milky Way, taken together with all other galaxies throughout the universe, is distributed in a pattern that is very nearly flat in three dimensions, which means the entire universe is laid out, in two-dimensional terms, like a sheet of cardboard (McFarling, 2000).

Another example of science's mind-bogglingly surreal findings is M-theory in physics, where M stands for Magic, Matrix, Membrane, Mother, or Mystery. Despite its bizarre premises—physicist John Schwarz introduced the theory to other physicists at a conference in a skit in which he was then hauled off stage by two men in white coats—M-theory in recent years has begun to hold the promise of achieving the Holy Grail in modern physics: the unification of quantum mechanics and the general theory of relativity. Physicist Sidney Coleman marveled, "It's as if some guys had set out to design a better can opener and wound up with an interstellar space ship" (Cole, 1999a, p. A22). If true, M-theory holds startling implications for space and time, which physicist Edward Witten warned may be doomed (Cole, 1999b, p. A1). Physicist David Gross (in Cole, 1999a) acknowledged, "When we talk about space and time, we think there is something there, and we live in it" (p. A22). Instead, the prospect that space and time are illusions is very disturbing. Science writer K. C. Cole (1999b) offered the following possibility: "Hypothetically, if there is no clear difference between now and the instant after, how can we say whether the gunshot caused death—or death caused the gunshot?" (p. A22). Another physicist, Gary Horowitz, added, "We normally think of causality as a basic property. Something effects something else. But when you're getting rid of space and time . . . are we sure that causality is going to be preserved?" (Cole, 1999b, p. A22). M-theory posits that everything in the universe is comprised of a symphony of incredibly tiny strings that are vibrating in 11 dimensions—our usual three, plus time, plus 7 other dimensions we cannot experience directly. "According to this new scenario, the everyday, three-dimensional universe we live in is trapped on a thin membrane—something like the world inhabited by characters playing out their lives within the confines of a movie screen," explained Cole (1999c). "Unknown to these shallow, two-dimensional players, a larger universe spreads into numerous extra dimensions, like theaters in a multiplex" (p. B2).

These possibilities indicate a more complicated, and more interesting, relationship between science and religion than one of simple warfare in which science is necessarily inimical to religious faith. Professors of science and religious studies Mary Gerhart and Allan Russell (1996) have noted that the universe is not only stranger than we imagine, but stranger than we *can* imagine. Because of this, science facilitates more expansive human imagination: "If we contemplate the differences between what is believable today and what was believable five hundred years ago, we can see that the work of science is what makes it possible to believe more. What science proposes for us to believe today is far *less* credible than what religion required of us in the past" (p. 128).

Secularization

What the warfare metaphor was in the history of science and religion, the secularization hypothesis was in the sociology of religion. Briefly put, the secularization hypothesis assumed that modernization necessarily causes a reduction in religious belief and practice, individually and collectively. Max Weber (1922) used the evocative phrase "the disenchantment of the world" to describe what he saw as an irreversible and inescapable process, growing out of the Enlightenment, that replaced the enchanted worlds of colorful folklore and religious mythology with rational and wholly naturalistic explanation. Sociologists of religion hypothesized that increasing urbanization, individualism, and education would make the power and salience of religion less plausible to modern people—and what little religious affiliation remained would become increasingly marginalized and privatized. This certainly seemed to be the case in Europe, where the secularization hypothesis originated: as European countries generally became more modernized, they also became profoundly secularized.

A problem with the secularization hypothesis, however, was that it slowly shifted from something that *might* be true to something that *must* be true. Incrementally "the thesis rather than the data began to dominate the agenda," declared British sociologist Grace Davie (1999). "The 'fit' became axiomatic, theoretically necessary rather than empirically founded—so much so that Europe's religious life was considered a prototype of global religiosity: what Europe did today, everyone else would do tomorrow" (p. 76). When the United States, arguably the most modernized country in the world, was nevertheless acknowledged as also being vibrantly religious, it was initially dismissed as an exception to the rule, and talk of "American exceptionalism" arose in the sociology of religion. Such talk was short lived, however, as it became apparent that countries in Central and South America, Africa, and parts of Asia did not fit the hypothesis either. Instead, it was Europe that was increasingly seen as the exception because secularization only really applied there—and, even then, not uniformly. Levels of religious belief and practice are much higher in Ireland than in Scandinavia, for example, and Central and Eastern Europe have quite different patterns than Western Europe. Poland, for example, has much higher levels of religious belief and practice than does France (see Davie, 1999).

In a recently published volume of international scholarship on the sociology of religion entitled *The Desecularization of the World*, Berger (1999) summarized the prevailing consensus among sociologists: "The world today is massively religious, is *anything but* the secularized world that had been predicted (whether joyfully or despondently) by so many analysts of modernity" (p. 9). Berger explained himself further, and admitted that he has come to alter his views, even though he once was a proponent of beliefs that are no longer tenable, given worldwide data on religious life.

My point is that the assumption that we live in a secularized world is false. The world today, with some exceptions to which I will come presently, is as furiously religious as it ever was, and in some places more so than ever. This means that a whole body of literature by historians and social scientists loosely labeled "secularization theory" is essentially mistaken. In my early work, I contributed to this literature. . . . (As I like to tell my students, one advantage of being a social scientist, as against being, say, a philosopher or a theologian, is that you can have as much fun when your theories are falsified as when they are verified!) [p. 2].

Richard John Neuhaus (2000), a social commentator on religion and public life, remarked, "Were the legendary man or woman from Mars to show up and ask what is the single most important thing now happening on Planet Earth, many possible answers might come to mind. Were I put on the spot in that unlikely circumstance, I think I would say that the most important thing now happening on Planet Earth is the *de*secularization of world history" (p. 87).

Despite its general disconfirmation worldwide, there are nonetheless two instances where the secularization hypothesis emphatically applies. The first involves, as already mentioned, certain countries in Europe, for which Scandinavia generally, and Sweden in particular, is the prototype. Sweden is the least religious country not just in Europe but the world, and as Sweden has become modernized it has become highly secularized, to the point where fewer than one in seven Swedes believes in God (Davie, 1999). The other group for whom the secularization hypothesis applies is a relatively thin cross-section of the world population that consists of Western-educated intellectuals, whom Berger termed elective Swedes. An elective Swede "can move all over the world in the locales shaped by this stratum—universities, media centers, literary conferences, and so on—and be reasonably assured that he will not be assailed by religious voices. Such an individual might well think that this is what the whole world is like. He would be much mistaken" (Berger, 1992, p. 32). "Picture a secular intellectual from Western Europe socializing with colleagues at the faculty club of the University of Texas," suggested Berger. "He may think he is back home. But then picture him trying to drive through the traffic jam on Sunday morning in downtown Austin—or, heaven help him, turning on his car radio! What happens then is a severe jolt of what anthropologists call culture shock" (Berger, 1999, p. 11).

Given the lack of empirical support for the secularization hypothesis, sociologists have worked to develop new theories to explain the data. One such effort is the work of José Casanova (1994), who argued that the flaw was in a theory of secularization that conflates three distinct elements: the differentiation of church and state, the decline of religious beliefs or practices, and the privatization of faith. For Casanova, the first element occurs in all modernization, but the second and third do not at all follow automatically or necessarily. Another approach has been developed by the French sociologist of religion, Danièle Hervieu-Léger (2000), who argues that modern societies—and particularly Europe—are amnesic societies that are less religious not because they are hyperrational but because they lack the resources to sustain cultural memory that is the center of religious life. "This is a rather different situation from one which assumes, uncritically, that modern societies have found satisfactory alternatives to the traditional forms of religion so crucial in their historical formulation," observed Davie (2000). "Manifestly, they have not (p. ix; see also Davie, 1996). For Hervieu-Léger, religion exists as more than just a reactionary response to change or uncertainty because religious forms are continually called forth by the disillusionment inherent in modernity's successes, even as modernity simultaneously corrodes and presupposes those values historically sustained by religious commitment.

Much like Ellul (1964), who proposed that technology is not a neutral means of getting things done so much as an entity with a life of its own that eventually structures our thought, Hervieu-Léger (2000) defined religion less in substantive or functional terms than in its capacity to link an individual within a community of shared memory, something which technology generally opposes. In this sense, it is not that technology has disproved religious faith but that it has tacitly shifted how we imagine. Historian of technology Lewis Mumford (1934) showed how the invention of glass changed human perception by putting the world in a frame. It encouraged analysis by letting us concentrate on one perspective, using straight edges and right angles that occluded the rest of the scene's context. I think the prevalence of glass also fostered a sense of subjective interiority because it offered the experience of being inside and looking out at the world. And from the other vantage point of an outsider looking in, it made a virtue of transparency, which supposedly offered undistorted access to a pre-existing and static self inside. Today, the rapidity of electronic media literally lets images disappear without a trace, thereby encouraging us to imagine ourselves as protean, unconstrained by any inherent structure other than what we ourselves choose. "In modernity," explained Hervieu-Léger (2000), "being religious is not so much knowing oneself begotten as willing oneself to be" (p. 167).

Individualism is not precisely a threat to tradition because individualism is itself a product of certain communal beliefs and practices. I understand this to be the point of philosophical ethicist Alasdair MacIntyre (1997), who questioned how any approach to a topic could ever really be "untraditional": however novel some approach proposes to be, its very proposal as being untraditional invariably follows well-worn conventions for proposals of its genre. Gadamer (1975) affirmed something similar when he said that "history does not belong to us; we belong to it. Long before we understand ourselves through the process of self-examination, we understand ourselves in a self-evident way in the family, society and state in which we live. The focus of subjectivity is a distorting mirror. The self-awareness of the individual is only a flickering in the closed circuits of historical life" (p. 276).

These words would sound strange to psychoanalysts if we took them to mean that Gadamer opposed the value of individual differences and human subjectivity, or thought that familial self-knowledge was innocently self-evident. I think, however, that Gadamer meant nothing of the sort; what he opposed was the notion that we have unmediated access to knowledge through subjectivity—whether others' or our own. For Gadamer, the only way we can know anything is through interpretation, and all interpretation takes place within the horizon of sociocultural traditions.

Because the sociocultural traditions of psychoanalysis made atheism a presumptive standard of mental health (as addressed in chapters 2 and 3), the secularization hypothesis has special relevance for the question of psychoanalysis and religion being in the same business. As mentioned in chapter 1, Berger joked that if India is the most religious country in the world and Sweden is the least, the United States is a country of Indians ruled by Swedes. For psychoanalysis in America the circumstances are similar: the population of prospective analysands is predominately Indian, and the typical analyst is a Swede. Psychoanalysis developed out of the same historical and cultural milieu that gave rise to the secularization hypothesis, and I think it is vulnerable to the same ethnocentrism that led European sociologists to imagine that all the rest of the world would inevitably mirror Europe. Deutsch (1932) described her analysis of an obsessive compulsive Roman Catholic educator who had just become a novice in a convent at the beginning of her treatment. By the point of termination three years later, although the analysand felt "completely satisfied" (p. 189) with the analysis, Deutsch characterized the outcome as less than an unqualified success because the patient decided to stay within her religious order as a nun. Fenichel (1941) likewise declared: "It has been said that religious people in analysis remain uninfluenced in their religious philosophies since analysis itself is supposed to be philosophically neutral. I consider this not to be correct." Fenichel, who was known for his devotion to atheism as well as analysis (see Menninger, 1958, p. 94; Leavy, 1982, p. 138), was apparently more successful at bringing about conversions than Deutsch was with the nun. Reflecting on his experience with his own patients, Fenichel concluded: "Repeatedly I have seen that with the analysis of the sexual anxieties and with maturing of the personality, the attachment to religion has ended" (p. 89). Freud (1915) told the joke about the minister who was summoned by anxious relatives to extract a deathbed conversion from an atheistic and unrepentant insurance salesman. The meeting occurred, and the longer the two continued to consult behind the hospital room's closed door, the more the concerned family members waiting outside took hope. When the door finally opened, however, the salesman "had not been converted," wrote Freud, "but the pastor went away insured" (p. 165). The humor in this anecdote turns on the surprise realization that proselytizing is not proprietary to theists.

Lest these instances be dismissed as anachronisms that no longer apply in contemporary psychoanalytic practice, Cohen's (1986; 1994) creative and path-breaking qualitative research found similar outcomes for religious patients analyzed in more recent decades. The most poignant observation in Cohen's entire study was that patients with histories of religious commitment repeatedly became tormented souls through analysis, developing a split between a public God that they deemed psychologically presentable and a private God to whom they ran for sustenance. After having just been diagnosed with a serious disease, one of the subjects confessed that the God he railed at while walking home was not his "'faceless, genderless Great Chain of Being,' but the old Jesus of 'this I know for the Bible tells me so'" (Cohen, 1994, p. 314). Contrary to Deutsch and Fenichel, and consistent with Freud's joke about secular evangelists, I view the sort of split that Cohen identified as less the inevitable byproduct of successful psychoanalytic inquiry than an iatrogenic malignancy caused by the failure of such inquiry. Such splitting is the result not of the presence of psychoanalysis but rather its absence, a conclusion also supported by quantitative analyses of how analysts treated being religious in psychoanalytic journals. As presented in chapter 3, an analysis of the nearly 7000 occurrences of the word religious in psychoanalytic journals between 1920 and 1994 found that analysts disproportionately pathologized being religious, although this practice decreased dramatically once Freud died. During Freud's lifetime, the number of pathological portrayals of being religious surpassed more integrative appraisals by a ratio of 9 to 1; after Freud's death this dropped to a ratio of 3 to 1.

There's an old saying that self analysis is fine; it is the countertransference that is the problem. In Freud's case, as Breger (2000) argued, the founder of psychoanalysis had a history of early traumas and failed attachments that tragically never had the benefit of psychoanalytic treatment and were thus consigned to habitual repetition throughout Freud's long life. Breger made a case that Freud had propensities to locate a figure to idealize. All would go well so long as the figure did not disappoint Freud, permitted or even welcomed his idealization, and was someone with whom he had little face-to-face interaction—preferably someone who lived in another city or with whom he could correspond through letters. Once the figure failed to meet his idealization, Freud broke off the relationship and sought a replacement, a pattern Freud repeated later in life from the vantage point of a figure who required idealization and dismissed subordinates who were disloyal or boring. Freud's "childhood identification with hypermasculine heroes, his view of himself as a 'conquistador,' and his identity as the commander of a psychoanalytic army can all be seen as . . . reactions to the threat of his weak and helpless position as a child, a threat that he himself associated with 'femininity' and 'passivity'" (p. 205). Freud had a habit of turning his fear of loss into a competitive father-son struggle, which left Freud with developmental blind spots in the midst of his many other profound insights about human psychology: "He could not see how tremendously important he was as a hero to his younger colleagues since, after the Fliess affair, he had disowned his own struggles to find an ideal father; nor could he see how damaged they were when he rejected them" (p. 271). Breger concluded, "Lacking an awareness of these motives, he described himself as the primal father, menaced by rebellious sons, holding the group together with his strength and power" (p. 271), eventually feeling "so disappointed, betrayed, and let down by friends and followers that in his late years, he turned to more trustworthy companions: pet dogs" (p. 355).

Breger's portrayal is consistent with that of Rizzuto (1998), who linked

Freud's history of attachments to having a God who merits faith. In Rizzuto's view, "early attachment, if positive, creates the psychic conditions of trust that later facilitate religious belief in God. Conversely, profound disturbances in emotional attachment between mother and child interfere with the capacity to entrust oneself to others and the later formation of an ego-syntonic God representation deserving belief" (p. 235). For Freud, "God was made to pay in displacement for the failure of all his primary objects: his mother, his nurse, and his father" (p. 269). Rizzuto concluded: "His personal God had no reliability. It did not deserve belief. Strong unbelief was the only protection against the intense pain of unsatisfied infantile, adolescent, and adult longings. Freud's life experiences did not provide him with the psychic conditions for belief in God" (pp. 269–270).

Psychoanalysis is like religion or spirituality insofar as it is an attempt to transcend nihilism. One proponent of nihilism is the evolutionary biologist Richard Dawkins (1998) who, in his introduction to a recent publication, reported that an international editor could not sleep for three nights and a school girl was reduced to tears because they were persuaded after reading Dawkins that life has no meaning. For Dawkins, all of life is mindless genetic competition: mosquitoes exist to replicate mosquito DNA, dung beetles exist to replicate dung beetle DNA, in a universe whose primary orientation to human life is one of indifference:

> Fling your arms wide in an expansive gesture to span all of evolution from its origin at your left fingertip to today at your right fingertip. All across your midline to well past your right shoulder, life consists of nothing but bacteria. Many-celled, invertebrate life flowers somewhere around your right elbow. The dinosaurs originate in the middle of your right palm, and go extinct around your last finger joint. The whole history of Homo sapiens and our predecessor Homo erectus is contained in the thickness of one nail clipping. As for recorded history; as for the Sumerians, the Babylonians, the Jewish patriarchs, the dynasties of Pharaohs, the legions of Rome, the Christian Fathers, the Laws of the Medes and Persians which never change; as for Troy and the Greeks, Helen and Achilles and Agamemnon dead; as for Napoleon and Hitler, the Beatles and Bill Clinton, they and everyone that knew them are blown away in the dust of one light stroke of a nail file [pp. 12–13].

Weber's disenchantment of the world achieves finality in Dawkins' (1998) vision: "The adult world may seem a cold and empty place, with no fairies and no Father Christmas, no Toyland or Narnia, no Happy Hunting Ground where mourned pets go, and no angels—guardian or garden variety. . . . Yes, Teddy and Dolly turn out not to be really alive" (p. 142).

In psychoanalysis, a perceptive and articulate advocate for the implications of nihilism is Hoffman (1998), who argued that "life itself can be viewed as a seduction that is followed by disillusionment, abandonment, and death—in other words, as a cruel deception" (p. xxxviii). "We weren't consulted about being conceived and born, first physically and then psychologically, into a life that leads to our own deaths and the deaths of every person to whom we become attached," observed Hoffman (p. 14). Given that we face a universe that "ultimately, brutally disregards our needs and wishes, ravages us with illness and old age, abuses us, forces on our bodies the most grotesque kinds of physical deterioration, [and] kills us in unspeakably horrifying and unexpected ways" (p. 14), reasoned Hoffman, "[t]here is a sense in which catastrophic anxiety, utter debilitating terror, is always rational and the absence of it is always irrational" (p. 240). As Hoffman explained, "[T]o invest in and enjoy life means, in some measure, to avoid thinking about death; it means drawing the blinds, it means huddling up against a protective wall, against the back of an analyst's couch. Of course, there is an irony here because the irrational becomes rational when we recognize that avoidance is our most sensible course" (p. 240). Psychoanalysis is one of the ways we distract ourselves from "a haunting sense of our ultimate insignificance in order to make living possible," much as we trick our children into becoming invested in living by offering them loving attachments before they have developed the critical capacities that expose life's absurdity, thereby locking in a sense of worth that permits them to withstand the assault of a cruel and ultimately indifferent universe (p. 240). In a review of Hoffman's work, Sass (1999) suggested:

> To the extent that psychoanalysis orients the patient toward the past, holding out hope that insight will dissipate or at least seriously mitigate the sources of unhappiness in life, one might say that it is a huge—and very welcome and salutary—distraction from the real existential issues of living and dying. Indeed, we might say that psychoanalysis is at one important level a particularly potent form of illusion, almost a kind of fairy tale for adults—one laced with enough of the negative to give us the feeling that we are heroically confronting the most difficult issues when, in fact, we are studiously avoiding them [p. 906].

If this is so, what distinguishes Freud's critique of religion as a regressive illusion in the face of the crushingly superior forces of nature, when psychoanalysis does the same thing? Psychoanalysis may work better for one person and religion for another but, either way, the two are in this sense not in such different businesses at all.

Foundationalism

Philosopher Nancey Murphy (1990, 1997) has noted how the beginning and ending of the modern period—which in philosophy lasted from roughly 1650 until 1950—punctuate two turning points in epistemology. The first, which inaugurated modernity in the mid-seventeenth century, entailed a rejection of medieval notions of authority, whether feudal or ecclesiastical, in favor of a foundationalism that sought to reconstruct knowledge so as to establish a secure foundation from which to know everything else. The second turn, which occurred in the middle of the twentieth century and is still in process, involves a rejection of modernity's foundationalism in favor of a more holist epistemology. The two epistemological shifts that occasioned modernity and its eventual demise both center around an assessment of the role of foundationalism, which Murphy (1997) describes as follows:

> Foundationalism is a theory about knowledge. More specifically, it is a theory about how claims to know can be justified. When we seek to justify belief, we do so by relating it to (basing it on, deriving it from) other beliefs. If these other beliefs are called into question, then they, too, must be justified. Foundationalists insist that this chain of justifications must stop somewhere; it must not be circular, nor must it constitute an infinite regress. Thus, the regress must end in a "foundation" of beliefs that cannot themselves be called into question.
>
> The plausibility of the foundationalist theory of knowledge comes from a metaphor: knowledge as a building. Upper stories are built upon lower stories, but the whole structure collapses if it has no solid foundation. This metaphor has so thoroughly imbued our thinking that we can scarcely talk about knowledge without hints of it: good arguments are well grounded and solidly constructed; suspicions are unfounded or baseless; disciplines that explore presuppositions are called foundational [p. 9].

Foundationalism fell into increasing disrepute across the twentieth century. Its last prominent proponents may well have been the logical positivists, who by the 1920s were seeking to isolate belief from practice insofar as they dismissed as "cognitively meaningless" all belief not subject to the practice of empirical confirmation. When this strategy proved unsatisfactory (as reviewed in chapter 4, the positivists' verification principle was itself deemed not amenable to empirical confirmation and thus, by its own criteria, cognitively meaningless!), neopositivists such as Karl Popper and Carl Hempel managed to extend the viability of positivism several decades more through amendment or revision. Popper stood the positivists' original principle of verification on its head by instead emphasizing the possibility of falsification. Hempel formulated the hypothetico-deductive model for science, a variant of positivism that, despite its relatively anachronistic status according to current standards, I suspect many of us as psychoanalysts nonetheless continue to find foundationally self-evident in terms of how to understand our own clinical work. According to the hypothetico-deductive method, observations come first, from these hypotheses are generated, and those which pass further empirical scrutiny become theories. The trouble is that such a view of science and, for that matter, psychoanalytic clinical practice, is no longer congruent with contemporary philosophies of science.

Since about the middle of the twentieth century, what has increasingly replaced the modern period's foundationalism is a postmodern holism in epistemology, which Murphy (1997) summarizes as follows:

> Just as modern epistemology was dominated by an image, that of a building needing to be supported, so postmodern epistemology is dominated by a picture: W. V. O. Quine's [1951, 1978] image of knowledge as a web or a net. There are no sharp distinctions among the kinds of beliefs in the web, and so there is not a distinction between basic (foundational) beliefs and nonbasic beliefs. Beliefs only differ in their "distance" from experience, which provides the "boundary conditions" for knowledge. The requirement for consistency transmits experiential control throughout the web [p. 27].

This conceptual shift has had profound implications for the philosophy of science, and a point in common among such diverse thinkers as Stephen Toulmin (1961), Thomas Kuhn (1962), Imre Lakatos (1970), Paul Feyerabend (1975), and Larry Laudan (1977) is that they all reject foundationalism in favor of a holist view of science. They also criticize modernist depictions emphasizing the "logic of science" as being arm-chair, idealized portrayals that fail to do justice to how knowledge works in groups. For all these contemporary philosophers of science, no hard and fast distinctions between belief and practice are possible—or for that matter desirable—because all scientific inquiry exists within a web or a network of socially sanctioned knowledge, for which no one element is necessarily certain or irreplaceable, although some elements are more central and matter more than others.

How much analysts see psychoanalysis and religion as being in the same business depends on how much analysts agree with modernity's second turning point in epistemology and find this shift persuasive and compelling. To the degree that analysts are familiar and comfortable with this second turn, I think they will also likely see more similarities and points for fruitful dialogue; to the degree that they are unfamiliar or uncomfortable with the second turn, I think they will be much more likely to view psychoanalysis and religion in terms of the first turn, which sees rational inquiry and indoctrination as mutually exclusive alterna-tives. What is more, without the option of the second turn, the prospect of foundationalism's failure incites existential panic, which is why phi-losopher Richard Bernstein (1983) described René Descartes' (ca. 1654) *Meditations* as a journey of the soul. Descartes sought certitude: "Archimedes, in order that he might draw the terrestrial globe out of its place and transport it elsewhere, demanded only that one point should be fixed and immovable; in the same way I shall have the right to con-ceive high hopes if I am happy enough to discover one thing which is certain and indubitable" (p. 149). The threat of the loss of certitude for Descartes was something like a descent into madness, the existential ter-ror of having suddenly fallen into very deep water in which he cannot touch the bottom and cannot stay afloat (p. 149). According to Bernstein (1983), that Descartes found solace in imagining a benevolent God who would not play tricks on or deceive his creatures has existential and per-sonal overtones.

> Reading the *Meditations* as a journey of the soul helps us to appreci-ate that Descartes' search for a foundation or Archimedian point is more than a device to solve metaphysical and epistemological prob-lems. It is the quest for some fixed point, some stable rock upon which we can secure our lives against the vicissitudes that constantly

threaten us. The specter that hovers in the background of this journey is not just radical epistemological skepticism but the dread of madness and chaos where nothing is fixed, where we can neither touch bottom nor support ourselves on the surface [p. 18].

It is philosophy's second turn in the modern period that has informed the more constructivist and holist epistemologies of relational psychoanalysis and, without this second turn, it can seem as though the only alternative to foundationalism is chaos, a kind of dread Bernstein termed "Cartesian anxiety." Many psychoanalysts might likewise assume that religious life presupposes or requires some form of foundationalism, although in many venues this is not the case, and indeed has not been for many years. Writing in 1976, philosophical theologian Nicholas Wolterstorff declared: "[W]ithin the community of those working in philosophy of knowledge and philosophy of science foundationalism has suffered a series of deadly blows in the last 25 years. To many of those acquainted with the history of this development it now looks all but dead. So it looks to me" (p. 33). Ronald Thiemann (1985) has addressed the limitations of any theological system in serving as a basis for a foundationalist epistemology. And George Lindbeck (1984) is one of several authors who have developed nonfoundationalist theories of religious language that offer a cultural-linguistic alternative to the foundationalism of either representationalism on the one hand (words stand for things), or expressivism on the other (words stand for feelings):

Hammers and saws, ordinals and numerals, winks and signs of the cross, words and sentences are made comprehensible by indicating how they fit into systems of communication or purposeful action, not by reference to outside factors. One does not succeed in identifying the 8:02 to New York by describing the history of manufacture of trains or even by a complete inventory of the cars, passengers, and conductors that constituted and traveled on it on a given day. None of the cars, passengers, and crew might be the same the next day, and yet the train would be self-identically the 8:02 to New York. Its meaning, its very reality, is its function within a particular transportation system. Much of the same can be said of winks and signs of the cross: they are quite distinct from nonmeaningful but physically identical eye twitches and hand motions, and their reality as meaningful signs is wholly constituted in any individual occurrence by their intratextuality, by their place, so to speak, in a story [p. 114; for a good example of intratextuality in theological method, see Hays, 1989].

As addressed in chapter 6, much of what occurs in contemporary theology and religious studies is more sophisticated than what psychoanalysts usually imagine theological scholarship to be, and makes facile demarcation between psychoanalysis and religion difficult, if not untenable.

The question of the relationship between psychoanalysis and religion becomes even more complicated once we consider not just the relations between science and religion, but also psychoanalysis and science. Some analysts say psychoanalysis is a science like any other positivistic practice, with analysts empirically collecting raw data and comparing these against hypotheses (Brenner, 1982). Others say psychoanalysis is not a science but should be (Spence, 1994). Still others say psychoanalysis *should* be a science but cannot be (Grünbaum, 1984). And then there are others yet who say psychoanalysis *can't* be a science but does not need to be (Hoffman, 1995). The differences between psychoanalysis and religion become less absolute once we acknowledge that analytic theories, like all clinical psychologies, contain philosophical anthropologies and implicit religio-ethical systems about what constitutes a life well lived (Browning, 1987), and that, according to contemporary philosophy of science, theologies progress in much the same way that scientific theories do (Murphy, 1990). Kirsner (2000), who recently completed a 10-year study of four institutes and 150 analysts affiliated with the American Psychoanalytic Association, noted that Freud's antipathy toward religion may not have been so much because he viewed it as being essentially wrong-headed but because it occupied much of the same turf that Freud wanted for psychoanalysis. From this perspective, psychoanalysis has historically treated religion adversarially because it viewed religion as a competitor that is in much the same business as its own, a formulation that fits Anna Freud's recollection of the psychoanalytic movement from its earliest days:

> It's a good thing there weren't phones then: they'd have been ringing all day and night! My father was pleased, but he was thoughtful enough—he had enough distance from his own ideas—to realize that, as he used to put it, "something larger was going on." He meant by that—he meant people were looking to psychoanalysis for something they weren't getting elsewhere. They weren't only interested in understanding the mind; they wanted answers to all the riddles of existence.
>
> At first, you know, he thought that was a sophisticated form of "resistance"—an attempt to distract us, to divert us, from "depth analysis," from psychoanalytic investigation proper, you could say, into the "murky reaches of philosophical speculation"—that was a phrase I

recall Karl Abraham using once in a conversation. But gradually we all began to see that there was something missing in the lives of people, and that the "problem" wasn't necessarily psychological—do you see what I mean? My father indicated his understanding when he used the word *Weltanschauung* in connection with psychoanalysis. He wasn't being presumptuous, as some of his critics asserted. He was acknowledging that for a lot of people psychoanalysis becomes not only a "treatment," as the doctors would say, but something much bigger and more lasting—it's there for the person long after he or she has stopped being an analysand, and become someone who has been analyzed. As a matter of fact, when he wrote *Analysis, Terminable and Interminable*, the same kind of considerations had occurred to him: for some people, analysis seems to go on and on, and if it may be that something has gone "wrong" to explain that, it also may be that what has happened has been working out quite well for the person in question and for the analyst, too. In earlier times they would have been called "wise friends" of one another [Coles, 1999, pp. 112–113].[1]

I understand Ms. Freud to be saying that, from the earliest days of the psychoanalytic movement, people came to psychoanalysis seeking something far beyond the remediation of psychological disease—something more like a supraordinate philosophy of life or reason for living—and that for many people, in her father's view, psychoanalysis legitimately filled that need. I suppose one could object that in psychoanalysis this meaning is not preformed or imposed by others externally and instead unfolds through the experience of the one seeking help, especially as he or she interacts with the analyst as guide or co-constructor of narrative meanings, but I understand this ideal to be much the same for mature expressions of the major world religions as well, including Buddhism, Judaism, Christianity, and Islam, among others.

Practice Meets Practice

One way to determine whether psychoanalysis and religion are in the same business is to pay attention to their practices. In the final hour of what was a mutually planned termination after many years of working

---

[1] I have excised the editorial clarifications Coles (1999) inserted for readers unfamiliar with psychoanalysis and have presented only Ms. Freud's verbatim comments from Coles's tape-recorded interview.

together, a patient volunteered an event that was for her a turning point in her analysis. She recalled a particular moment some years earlier when, having arrived a few minutes earlier than usual for her appointment, she ran into me exiting the building while she was just entering. I smiled at her, said Hi, and explained that I was stepping around the corner to grab a cup of coffee and that I would be back in time for our session.

She told me that what was meaningful for her in that encounter was that she experienced my love (this was her phrase), something she said was unremarkable in that she knew it regularly *within* the analysis. What was different here was that she experienced it *outside* the confines of the analytic hour, in a moment that was sudden enough to be unguarded and not a part of my professional self, thereby authenticating what she experienced inside the hour as "real." I found myself bemused and wondering, Did all my analytic training, all my supposedly profound interpretations, the hundreds of hours she spent, and her six-figure investment come down to this—a coffee cup cure?

We psychoanalysts have a long history of deep-seated misgivings and anxieties about love that stems from more than just our appreciation for the multileveled and inevitably conflictual aspects in all human experience, something from which love is not exempt. I think less often appreciated is how our legacy as analysts necessarily arises from a particular cosmology, a myth of origins that structures a profession's identity. Any discipline fears the view it formed in opposition against, and for psychoanalysis this was hypnotism. The bane of psychoanalysis became suggestion, and any hint of therapeutic change linked to the analyst's influence became *verboten.*

This was concretized in the legend of Anna O., a story held out as a kind of object lesson which has functioned rather like a medieval morality play for successive generations of psychoanalysts to contemplate. The story, first told by Freud decades after the fact and later embellished by Freud's hagiographer Ernest Jones, dichotomously casts Freud as champ and Breuer as chump. The received view, according to this narrative tradition, is that Breuer stumbled across transference love but failed to recognize it as such. By treating it as "real" he fled from the scene in an hysterical panic, conceived a child with his wife on a hastily planned second honeymoon, and discontinued all further psychoanalytic exploration. The moral of the tale is clear enough. Do not be a Breuer. Do not be a chump. Only psychoanalytic fools confuse transference for love—or, more accurately, fail to realize that transference is all love ever is anyway.

The only problem with this reading is that it is not true. Ellenberger (1970) has shown that the 1882 registry of Viennese citizenry proves Breuer's last child, Dora, was born on March 11, well before Breuer's June termination with Anna O., whose real name was Bertha Pappenheim. Although the location had been disguised, after considerable sleuthing Ellenberger also managed to identify the sanitarium at which she had been hospitalized and visited it. To his surprise, there he found the chart of Breuer's treatment of Pappenheim, still archived in medical records. With directions and encouragement from Ellenberger, Hirschmüller (1989), in the course of doing his dissertation on Breuer, searched the sanitarium and found even more hospital records indicating, contrary to Jones, that Breuer continued his clinical investigations well after 1882.

Freud imagined that love was the therapeutic action of psychoanalysis—and by "love" he meant *transference* love, which induced the patient's willingness to submit to Freud's interpretations. As I have argued in chapter 4, it is no less useful to playfully imagine the therapeutic action of analysis as being indeed "love"—only now in the sense of *counter*transference love, much as Szondi spoke of the therapist as "soul donor," analogous to "blood donor." Social psychologists Shalom Schwartz of Jerusalem and Sipke Huismans of Amsterdam (Schwartz and Huismans, 1995) studied Jews in Israel, Catholics in Spain, Calvinists in the Netherlands, the Orthodox in Greece, and Lutherans and Catholics in West Germany and concluded that some form of soul donorship is juxtaposed as an alternative to materialism in all religions:

> Religions encourage people to seek meaning beyond everyday existence, linking themselves to a "ground of being" through belief and worship. Most foster attitudes of awe, respect and humility, by emphasizing the place of the human being in a vast, unfathomable universe, and exhort people to pursue causes greater than their personal desires. The opposed orientation, self-indulgent materialism, seeks happiness in the pursuit and consumption of material goods [p. 91].

If psychoanalysis is indeed a cure through love, whether defined via transference, countertransference, or anything else, it ends up having something in common with the business of the major world religions.

From the other direction, there is much about contemplative religious practice that is quite similar to psychoanalytic practice. Episcopal priest and friend of psychoanalysis Alan Jones (1985) once described the contemplative practice of spiritual direction with lines from W. H. Auden's poem "For the Time Being":

> For the garden is the only place there is,
> > but you will not find it
> Until you have looked for it everywhere
> > and found nowhere that is not a desert.

On face value, this is a puzzling message. How is it possible to say that the garden is "the only place there is"? If we think about what portion gardens occupy of the earth's crust, the answer is most certainly infinitesimal. Gardens are not ubiquitous precisely because they are so much work. They require planning, and seeding, and soil amendment, and pruning, and watering, and weeding, and fairly consistent attention. How could something that's "the only place there is" be so hard to find? And in what sense can a garden and a desert possibly be considered synonymous? In the spiritual tradition of both the West and the Middle East, for example, the garden is a place of abundant provision for human growth and development, a paradise for human sustenance, whether material or aesthetic, whereas the desert is a place known for spiritual testing or tribulation because of its barrenness and desolation.

One interpretation of Auden's message is that life can be deeply rewarding and fulfilling, but the opportunities for reward and fulfillment are usually in ways other than what we had in mind—indeed it is our very fullness with misleading prerequisites for happiness that thwarts a more mature emptying and willingness to face all of human experience, especially moments of suffering or anxiety, with grace and courage. Spiritual direction in this sense is not about the pursuit of peak experiences or inoculation against loss so much as it is the discipline of paying attention, particularly to how the divine is already present in the quiet or routine moments of ordinary life, an attitude not altogether different from free association in psychoanalysis.

We thus can revisit the initial question: Are psychoanalysis and religion in the same business? Once we recognize that religion and science are not reducible to mutually exclusive, warring factions; once we recognize that religion is not at all in steady and persistent decline through worldwide patterns of secularization; once we recognize that science is an inherently social enterprise, so much so that theology fits the new criteria for science much better than psychoanalysis ever did the old principles of positivism; then just how psychoanalysis and religion are each in a completely different business is a lot less obvious. This means, as presented in chapter 1, that psychoanalysis is right to mind spirituality in the sense of being bothered by it, attending to it, and even exercising stewardship over it. Psychoanalytic theory has continued to evolve and change over the past century, often in profound ways that have very different implications for the analysis of religious experience, as detailed in chapter 2. Our challenge is to keep up with these changes and to make our practice have congruence and integrity with our evolving theory, whether in our psychoanalytic publications, our clinical technique, or our case presentations, as laid out in chapters 3, 4, and 5, respectively. Religion and spirituality, ironically seen as the antithesis of psychoanalysis three-quarters of a century ago, now have something to offer the structure of contemporary analytic education and the purpose and function of analysis, as presented in the penultimate and ultimate chapters, respectively.

I think psychoanalysis is especially good at taking things apart and at patiently exploring hidden layers of motivation. I think it also has much to offer the sociology of religion, which has been overly linear in its Weberian model of the world's disenchantment. That is, contemporary psychoanalytic perspectives tell us that disenchantment is not an altogether bad thing. It is a normal and essential ebb in the flow of a process that is emotional maturity. Persons who never become disenchanted do so via denial, hysteria, or a manic defense; those who do become disenchanted but never manage to recover from it are no less fiercely idealistic, no less trying to protect a cherished object's goodness, except that they are using the other side of the same split that now requires bitterness, cynicism, and even despair. More advanced than either static polarity alone is an ongoing process of dynamic integration: an enchantment that can suffer disenchantment but then survive it with enough faith intact to permit falling in love with the object anew—even though this renewed love provides no guaranty of immunity from suffering, and it, too, will one day come to its own grief, and so on. Philosopher Paul Ricoeur (1970) suggested that if psychoanalysis is a hermeneutics of suspicion, it would benefit from dialectical interplay with its hermeneutical counterpart, a hermeneutics of faith—not the faith of an unexamined life, but a postcritical faith that generates what Ricoeur called a "second naïveté" (p. 28). This makes for a dialogical hermeneutic of unmasking and demystification alongside another hermeneutic that recollects or restores meaning (in the root sense of religion: *religare*, to gather together).

FIGURE 8. Mrs. Hammond! I'd know you anywhere from little Billy's portrait of you! ©The *New Yorker* Collection 1988 Ed Frascino from cartoonbank. com. All rights reserved.

Figure 8 is a cartoon from the *New Yorker* that shows an elementary school teacher seated at her desk, greeting a parent just entering the room for a parent-teacher conference. The humor in the cartoon turns on the surprise realization that the mother entering the classroom doorway really *does* look like little Billy's depiction of her. When psychoanalysis encounters spirituality, the challenge is to do so with the openness of little Billy's teacher, for whom finally experiencing Mrs. Hammond's appearance is less an epiphany than an expected and welcomed arrival. When it comes to spirituality, psychoanalysis' job is to recognize Mrs. Hammond and to welcome her into the consulting room because our little Billys' portraits of her are Auden's desert and, like my patient's coffee-cup cure, a garden.

References

Allport, G. W. (1950), *The Individual and His Religion*. New York: Macmillan.

Allport, G. W. & Ross, J. M. (1967), Personal religious orientation and prejudice. *J. Personality & Social Psychol.*, 5:432–443.

American Psychiatric Association (1975), *Psychiatrists' Viewpoints on Religion and Their Services to Religious Institutions and the Ministry: A Report of a Survey Conducted by the Task Force on Religion and Psychiatry.* Washington, DC.

Anderson, W. T. (1990), *Reality Isn't What It Used to Be.* San Francisco: HarperCollins.

Appignanesi, L. & Forrester, J. (1992), *Freud's Women.* New York: Basic Books.

Arlow, J. (1982), Psychoanalytic education. *The Annual of Psychoanalysis*, 10:5–20. New York: International Universities Press.

Aron, L. (1996), *A Meeting of Minds: Mutuality in Psychoanalysis.* Hillsdale, NJ: The Analytic Press.

Associated Press (1990), "Hello" and "Bonjour" as tunnelers meet. *Los Angeles Times*, December 2, p. A5.

Atwood, G. & Stolorow, R. (1984), *Structures of Subjectivity: Explorations in Psychoanalytic Phenomenology.* Hillsdale, NJ: The Analytic Press.

Balint, M. (1948), On the psycho-analytic training system. *Internat. J. Psycho-Anal.*, 29:163–173.

Balint, M. (1968), *The Basic Fault.* New York: Brunner/Mazel.

Barbour, I. G. (1997), *Religion and Science.* San Francisco: HarperSanFrancisco.

Bass, A. (2001), It takes one to know one; or, whose unconscious is it anyway? *Psychoanal. Dial.*, 11:683–702.

Batson, C. D. & Raynor-Prince, L. (1983), Religious orientation and complexity of thought about existential concerns. *J. Sci. Study Religion*, 22:38–50.

Batson, C. D. & Schoenrade, P. A. (1991a), Measuring religion as quest: 1. Validity concerns. *J. Sci. Study Religion*, 30:416–429.

Batson, C. D. & Schoenrade, P. A. (1991b), Measuring religion as quest: 2. Reliability concerns. *J. Sci. Study Religion*, 30:430–447.

Batson, C. D., Schoenrade, P. A. & Ventis, W. L. (1993), *Religion and the Individual: A Social-Psychological Perspective.* New York: Oxford University Press.

Bediako, K. (1995), *Christianity in Africa: The Renewal of Non-Western Religion.* Maryknoll, NY: Orbis Books.

Beit-Hallahmi, B. (1992), Between psychology and religion. In: *Object Relations Theory and Religion*, ed. M. Finn & J. Gartner. Westport, CT: Praeger, pp. 119–128.

Benjamin, J. (1992), Recognition and destruction: An outline of intersubjectivity. In: *Relational Perspectives in Psychoanalysis*, ed. N. J. Skolnick & S. C. Warshaw. Hillsdale, NJ: The Analytic Press, pp. 43–60.

Benjamin, J. (1995), *Like Subjects, Love Objects*. New Haven, CT: Yale University Press.

Benson, C. H. (2000), Religion as a variable of cultural diversity: A lexical analysis of psychoanalytic journals from 1920 to 1994. Unpublished doctoral dissertation. DAI, 61, 07B:3831. La Mirada, CA: Rosemead School of Psychology.

Bentler, P. (1980), Multivariate analysis with latent variables: Causal modeling. *Ann. Rev. Psychol.*, 31:419–456.

Berger, P. L. (1967), *The Sacred Canopy*. Garden City, NY: Doubleday.

Berger, P. L. (1969), *A Rumor of Angels*. Garden City, NY: Anchor Books.

Berger, P. L. (1992), *A Far Glory*. New York: Macmillan.

Berger, P. L. (1999), *The Desecularization of the World*. Grand Rapids, MI: Eerdmans.

Berger, P. L. & Luckmann, T. (1966), *The Social Construction of Reality*. Garden City, NY: Doubleday.

Bergin, A. E. (1980), Psychotherapy and religious values. *Amer. Psychol.*, 48:95–105.

Bergin, A. E. & Garfield, S. (1994), *Handbook of Psychotherapy and Behavior Change*, 4th ed. New York: Wiley.

Bergin, A. E. & Jensen, J. P. (1990), Religiosity of psychotherapists: A national survey. *Psychotherapy*, 27:3–7.

Bergmann, M. S. (1993), Reflections on the history of psychoanalysis. *J. Amer. Psychoanal. Assn.*, 41:929–955.

Bernfeld, S. (1962), On psychoanalytic training. *Psychoanal. Quart.*, 31:453–482.

Bernstein, R. (1983), *Beyond Objectivism and Relativism*. Philadelphia: University of Pennsylvania Press.

Bernstein, R. (1995), *The Dictatorship of Virtue*. New York: Vintage Books.

Bettelheim, B. (1977), *The Uses of Enchantment*. New York. Knopf.

Bettelheim, B. (1982), *Freud and Man's Soul*. New York: Vintage Books.

Bion, W. R. (1970), *Attention and Interpretation*. London: Tavistock.

Bloom, A. (1987), *The Closing of the American Mind*. New York: Simon & Schuster.

Bloom, H. (1973), *The Anxiety of Influence*. New York: Oxford University Press.

Boesky, D. (1990), The psychoanalytic process and its components. *Psychoanal. Quart.*, 59:550–584.

Boisen, A. (1936), *The Exploration of the Inner World*. Chicago: Willett, Clark.

Borris, H. (1994), About time. *Contemp. Psychoanal.*, 30:301–322.

Bowlby, J. (1940), The influence of early environment in the development of neurosis and neurotic character. *Internat. J. Psycho-Anal.*, 21:154–178.

Brabant, E., Falzeder, E. & Giampieri-Deutsch, P. (1992), *The Correspondence of Sigmund Freud and Sándor Ferenczi, Vol. 1, 1908–1914* (trans P. Hoffer). Cambridge, MA: Belknap Press.

Breger, L. (2000), *Freud*. New York: John Wiley & Sons.

Brenner, C. (1982), *The Mind in Conflict*. New York: International Universities Press.

Breuer, J. & Freud, S. (1893–1895), Studies on hysteria. *Standard Edition*, 2:1–309. London: Hogarth Press, 1955.

Brill, A. A. (1922), Tobacco and the individual. *Internat. J. Psycho-Anal.*, 3:430–444.

Brokaw, B. F. & Edwards, K. J. (1994), The relationship of God image to level of object relations development. *J. Psychol. & Theol.*, 22:352–371.

Bromberg, P. M. (1998), *Standing in the Spaces: Essays on Clinical Process, Trauma, and Dissociation.* Hillsdale, NJ: The Analytic Press.

Brooke, J. H. & Cantor, G. (1998), *Reconstructing Nature.* New York: Oxford University Press.

Brothers, L. (2001), *Mistaken Identity.* Albany: State University of New York Press.

Browning, D. S. (1987), *Religious Thought and the Modern Psychologies.* Philadelphia: Fortress Press.

Bruner, J. (1993), Loyal opposition and the clarity of dissent: Commentary on Donald P. Spence's "The hermeneutic turn." *Psychoanal. Dial.,* 3:11–19.

Cahill, T. (1998), *The Gift of the Jews.* New York: Nan A. Talese.

Cahill, T. (1999), *Desire of the Everlasting Hills.* New York: Nan A. Talese.

Caper, R. (1988), *Immaterial Facts.* New York: Aronson.

Capps, D. & Jacobs, J. (1997), *Religion, Society, and Psychoanalysis: Readings in Contemporary Theory.* Boulder, CO: Westview Press.

Cardinal, M. (1983), *The Words to Say It,* trans. P. Goodheart. Cambridge, MA: Van Vactor & Goodheart.

Casanova, J. (1994), *Public Religions in the Modern World.* Chicago: University of Chicago Press.

Cohen, E. P. (1986), An exploratory study of religiously committed psychoanalytically oriented clinicians. Unpublished doctoral dissertation. DAI, 47, 09B:3949. New York: City University of New York.

Cohen, P. (1994), An interesting contradiction: A study of religiously committed, psychoanalytically oriented clinicians. *J. Psychol. & Theol.,* 22:304–318.

Cole, K. C. (1997), A career boldly tied by strings. *Los Angeles Times,* February 4, pp. A1, A16.

Cole, K. C. (1999a), "M" theory stands for magic, matrix, membrane, mother or mystery. *Los Angeles Times,* November 16, p. A22.

Cole, K. C. (1999b), Time, space obsolete in new view of universe. *Los Angeles Times,* November 16, p. A1, A22.

Cole, K. C. (1999c), Unseen dimensions hold theory aloft. *Los Angeles Times,* November 18, p. B2.

Coles, R. (1999), *The Secular Mind.* Princeton, NJ: Princeton University Press.

Compton, A. (1994), Research: The missing dimension. Presented at the spring meeting of APA Division 39 (Psychoanalysis), Washington, DC, April 16.

Cooper, A. (1996), Psychoanalysis: The past decade. *Psychoanal. Inq.,* 11:107–122.

Crastnopol, M. (1997), Incognito or not? The patient's subjective experience of the analyst's private life. *Psychoanal. Dial.,* 7:257–280.

Crastnopol, M. (1999), The analyst's personality: Winnicott analyzing Guntrip as a case in point. *Contemp. Psychoanal.,* 35:271–300.

Crastnopol, M. (2001), Convergence and divergence in the characters of analyst and patient: Fairbairn treating Guntrip. *Psychoanal. Psychol.,* 18:120–136.

Cushman, P. (1995), *Constructing the Self, Constructing America.* Boston, MA: Addison-Wesley.

Daloz Parks, S. (1992), *The University as a Mentoring Environment.* Indianapolis: Indiana Office for Campus Ministries.

Davie, G. (1996), Religion and modernity: The work of Danièle Hervieu-Léger. In: *Postmodernity, Sociology and Religion,* ed. K. Flanagan & P. C. Jupp. New York: St. Martin's Press, pp. 101–117.

Davie, G. (1999), Europe: The exception that proves the rule? In: *The Desecularization of the World*, ed. P. L. Berger. Grand Rapids, MI: Eerdmans, pp. 65-83.

Davie, G. (2000), Foreword. In: *Religion as a Chain of Memory*, ed. D. Hervieu-Léger (trans. S. Lee). Cambridge, UK: Polity Press, pp. viii-x.

Davies, J. M. (2002), Whose bad objects are these anyway? Repetition and our elusive love affair with evil. Presented at the first biannual meeting of the International Association for Relational Psychoanalysis and Psychotherapy, New York City, January 19.

Davis, G. (1994), The trials of Janet and Jeffrey. *The Nation*, October 28:643-646.

Dawkins, R. (1998), *Unweaving the Rainbow*. New York: Houghton Mifflin.

De Mello Franco, O. (1998), Religious experience and psychoanalysis: From man-as-god to man-with-god. *Internat. J. Psycho-Anal.*, 79:113-131.

Descartes. R. (1969), Meditations. In: *Philosophical Works of Descartes, Vol. 1* (trans. E. S. Haldane & G. R. T. Ross). Cambridge, UK: Cambridge University Press, 1969.

Deutsch, H. (1932), Obsessional ceremonial and obsessional acts. In: *Psychoanalysis of the Neuroses*, trans. W. D. Robson-Scott. London: Hogarth Press, pp. 175-197.

Diggins, J. P. (1996), *Max Weber*. New York: Basic Books.

Dimpfel, R. (1983), *Text for Brahms Symphony No. 1 in C minor, Op. 68.* RCA Victor, CD No. 60086-2-RG, pp. 6-8, trans. A. Smith.

Doehring, C. (1993), *Internal Desecration.* Lanham, MD: University Press of America.

Dorpat, T. L. (1975), Internalization of the patient-analyst relationship in patients with narcissistic disorders: A reply to the discussion by Lygia Amaral. *Internat. J. Psycho-Anal.*, 56:237-238.

Draper, J. W. (1874), *The History of Conflict Between Religion and Science.* New York: D. Appleton.

Eagle, M. (1984), *Recent Developments in Psychoanalysis.* New York: McGraw-Hill.

Eck, D. (2001), *A New Religious America.* San Francisco: HarperSanFrancisco.

Eckstein, R. (1969), Concerning the teaching and learning of psychoanalysis. *J. Amer. Psychoanal. Assn.*, 17:312-332.

Eigen, M. (1981), The area of faith in Winnicott, Lacan and Bion. *Internat. J. Psycho-Anal.*, 62:413-433.

Eigen, M. (1998), *The Psychoanalytic Mystic.* New York: Free Association Books.

Eisold, K. (1994), The intolerance of diversity in psychoanalytic institutes. *Internat. J. Psychoanal.*, 75:785-800.

Ellenberger, H. F. (1970), *The Discovery of the Unconscious.* New York: Basic Books.

Ellul, J. (1964), *The Technological Society*, trans. J. Wilkinson. New York: Knopf.

Ellul, J. (1986), *The Subversion of Christianity.* Grand Rapids, MI: Eerdmans.

Epstein, M. (1995), *Thoughts Without a Thinker.* New York: Basic Books.

Erikson, E. H. (1962), *Young Man Luther.* New York: Norton.

Evans, W. N. (1949), The passing of the gentleman: A psychoanalytic commentary on the cultural ideal of the English. *Psychoanal. Quart.*, 18:19-43.

Fairbairn, W. R. D. (1952), *Psychoanalytic Studies of the Personality.* London: Routledge & Kegan Paul.

Falzeder, E. (1994), The threads of psychoanalytic filiations. Presented at the Institute of Contemporary Psychoanalysis, Los Angeles, CA, November 12.

Falzeder, E. & Brabant, E. (1996), *The Correspondence of Sigmund Freud and Sándor Ferenczi, Vol. 2, 1914-1919* (trans. P. Hoffer). Cambridge, MA: Belknap Press.

Falzeder, E., Brabant, E. & Giampieri-Deutsch, P. (2000), *The Correspondence of Sigmund*

Freud and Sándor Ferenczi, Vol. 3, 1920-1933 (trans. P. Hoffer). Cambridge, MA: Belknap Press.

Feldman, Y. (1994), "And Rebecca loved Jacob," but Freud did not. In: *Freud and Forbidden Knowledge*, ed. P. Rudnytsky & E. Spitz. New Haven, CT: Yale University Press.

Fenichel, O. (1932), Outline of clinical psychoanalysis. *Psychoanal. Quart.*, 1:545-652.

Fenichel, O. (1941), *Problems of Psychoanalytic Technique* (trans. D. Brunswick). New York: Psychoanalytic Quarterly.

Ferenczi, S. (1932), *The Clinical Diary of Sándor Ferenczi*, ed. J. Dupont (trans. M. Balint & N. Z. Jackson). Cambridge, MA: Harvard University Press.

Fetherston, D. (1997), *The Chunnel*. New York: Times Books.

Feyerabend, P. (1975), *Against Method*. London: New Left Books.

Finke, R. & Stark, R. (1992), *The Churching of America*. New Brunswick, NJ: Rutgers University Press.

Finn, M. & Gartner, J., eds. (1992), *Object Relations Theory and Religion*. Westport, CT: Praeger.

Freud, A. (1929), Report of the Eleventh International Psycho-Analytical Congress. *Bull. Internat. Psycho-Anal. Assn.*, 10:489-510.

Freud, A. (1966), The ideal psychoanalytic institute: A utopia. In: *Problems of Psychoanalytic Training, Diagnosis, and Technique of Therapy, Vol. 7*. New York: International Universities Press, pp. 73-93.

Freud, S. (1913a), The claims of psychoanalysis to scientific interest. *Standard Edition*, 13:165-190. London: Hogarth Press, 1955.

Freud, S. (1913b), On beginning the treatment. *Standard Edition*, 12:123-144. London: Hogarth Press, 1958.

Freud, S. (1914), On the history of the psychoanalytic movement. *Standard Edition*, 14:7-55. London: Hogarth Press, 1957.

Freud, S. (1915), Observations on transference-love: Further recommendations in the technique of psychoanalysis, III. *Standard Edition*, 12:157-171. London: Hogarth Press, 1958.

Freud, S. (1923), Psychoanalysis. *Standard Edition*, 18:235-254. London: Hogarth Press, 1955.

Freud, S. (1927), The future of an illusion. *Standard Edition*, 21:3-56. London: Hogarth Press, 1961.

Freud, S. (1937), Constructions in analysis. *Standard Edition*, 23:255-269. London: Hogarth Press, 1964.

Fromm, E. (1970), *The Crisis of Psychoanalysis*. New York: Holt, Rinehart, Winston.

Frommer, M. (1994), Homosexuality and psychoanalysis: Technical considerations revisited. *Psychoanal. Dial.*, 4:215-233.

Fuller, R. C. (2001), *Spiritual, But Not Religious*. New York: Oxford University Press.

Gadamer, H-G. (1975), *Truth and Method, 2nd ed.*, trans. J. Weinsheimer & D. G. Marshall. New York: Continuum.

Gallup Organization (1985), *Religion in America: Gallup Report 236*. Princeton, NJ.

Gallup, G., Jr. (1994), *The Gallup Poll. Public Opinion 1993*. Wilmington, DE: Scholarly Resources.

Gallup, G., Jr. & Lindsay, D. M. (1999), *Surveying the Religious Landscape: Trends in U.S. Beliefs*. Harrisburg, PA: Moorehouse Publishing.

Gartner, J., Larson, D. B. & Allen, G. D. (1991), Religious commitment and mental health: A review of the empirical literature. *J. Psychol. & Theol.*, 19:6-25.

Gattis, J., Sorenson, R. L. & Lawrence, R. (2001), A free, web-based scoring program for the Lawrence God Image Inventory. Presented at the Annual Convention of the American Psychological Association, San Francisco, CA, August 24.

Geha, R. E. (1993), Transferred fictions. *Psychoanal. Dial.*, 3:209–243.

Gergen, K. J. & Gergen, M. (1983), Narratives of the self. In: *Studies in Social Identity*, ed. T. R. Sarbin & K. E. Scheibe. New York: Praeger.

Gerhart, M. & Russell, A. M. (1996), Mathematics, empirical science, and religion. In: *Religion and Science*, ed. W. M. Richardson & W. J. Wildman. New York: Routledge, pp. 121–129.

Gerkin, C. V. (1984), *The Living Human Document*. Nashville: Abingdon Press.

Ghent, E. (1990), Masochism, submission, surrender. *Contemp. Psychoanal.*, 26:108–136.

Glock, C. Y. & Stark, R. (1965), *Religion and Society in Tension*. Chicago: Rand McNally.

Goldberg, A. (1985), *Progress in Self Psychology, Vol. 1*. Hillsdale, NJ: The Analytic Press.

Gorsuch, R. (1968), The conception of God as seen in adjective ratings. *J. Sci. Study Religion*, 7:56–64.

Granqvist, P. (1998), Religiousness and perceived childhood attachment: On the question of compensation or correspondence. *J. Sci. Study Religion*, 37:350–367.

Greenacre, P. (1960), Considerations regarding the parent-infant relationship. *Internat. J. Psycho-Anal.*, 41: 571–584.

Greenberg, J. (1991), Countertransference and reality. *Psychoanal. Dial.*, 1:52–73.

Griffith, J. L. & Griffith, M. E. (2002), *Encountering the Sacred in Psychotherapy*. New York: Guilford.

Grotstein, J. (1981), *Splitting and Projective Identification*. New York: Aronson.

Grünbaum, A. (1984), *The Foundations of Psychoanalysis*. Berkeley: University of California Press.

Guntrip, H. (1969), *Schizoid Phenomena, Object Relations, and the Self*. New York: International Universities Press.

Guntrip, H. (1971), *Psychoanalytic Theory, Therapy, and the Self*. New York: Basic Books.

Hadaway, C. K. & Marler, P. L. (1996), Response to Iannaccone: Is there a method to this madness? *J. Sci. Study Religion*, 35:217–222.

Hahn, D. C. (1994), God as a mirroring and idealizing selfobject function: Its influence on self-cohesion and mood. An empirical study. Unpublished doctoral dissertation. DAI, 55, 07B:3015, San Diego: California School of Professional Psychology.

Halevi, Y. K. (2002), *At the Entrance to the Garden of Eden*. New York: Perennial.

Hall, R. (1993), Critical and postcritical objectivity. *Personalist Forum*, 9:67–80.

Hall, T. W. & Sorenson, R. L. (1999), God image inventory (Lawrence, 1991). In: *Measures of Religiosity*, ed. P. C. Hill & R. W. Hood, Jr. Birmingham, AL: Religious Education Press, pp. 399–401.

Hall, T. W., Brokaw, B. F., Edwards, K. J. & Pike, P. L. (1998), An empirical exploration of psychoanalysis and religion: Spiritual maturity and object relations development. *J. Sci. Study Religion*, 37:303–313.

Hamilton, V. (1996), *The Analyst's Preconscious*. Hillsdale, NJ: The Analytic Press.

Hamilton, V. (1982), *Narcissus and Oedipus*. London: Karnac.

Harlow, H. (1986), *From Learning to Love: The Selected Papers of H. F. Harlow*, ed. C. M. Harlow. New York: Praeger.

Hartmann, H. (1939), *Ego Psychology and the Problem of Adaptation*. New York: International Universities Press, 1958.

Haynal, A. (1993), *Psychoanalysis and the Sciences.* Berkeley, CA: University of California Press.

Hays, R. B. (1989), *Echoes of Scripture in the Letters of Paul.* New Haven, CT: Yale University Press.

Henry, W., Strupp, H., Schacht, T. & Gaston, L. (1994), Psychodynamic approaches. In: *Handbook of Psychotherapy and Behavior Change,* 4th ed., ed. A. Bergin & S. Garfield. New York: Wiley, pp. 467–508.

Hervieu-Léger, D. (2000), *Religion as a Chain of Memory,* trans. S. Lee. Cambridge, UK: Polity Press.

Hill, P. C. & Hood, R. W, Jr., eds. (1999), *Measures of Religiosity.* Birmingham, AL: Religious Educators Press.

Hirschmüller, A. (1989), *The Life and Work of Joseph Breuer.* New York: New York University Press.

Hoffer, A. (1985), Toward a definition of psychoanalytic neutrality. *J. Amer. Psychoanal. Assn.,* 33:771–795.

Hoffman, I. Z. (1991), Discussion: Toward a social-constructivist view of the psychoanalytic situation. *Psychoanal. Dial.,* 1:74–105.

Hoffman, I. Z. (1995), Review Essay. *Psychoanal. Dial.,* 5:93–112

Hoffman, I. Z. (1998), *Ritual and Spontaneity in the Psychoanalytic Process: A Dialectical-Constructivist View.* Hillsdale, NJ: The Analytic Press.

Hoge, D. R. (1996a), Religion in America: The demographics of belief and affiliation. In: *Religion and the Clinical Practice of Psychology,* ed. E. P. Shafranske. Washington, DC: APA Books, pp. 21–41.

Hoge, D. R. (1996b), Response to Iannaccone: Three important clarifications. *J. Sci. Study Religion,* 35:223–225.

Holzman, P. (1976), The future of psychoanalysis and its institutes. *Psychoanal. Quart.,* 45:250–273.

Hood, R. W., Jr., Hill, P. C. & Williamson, W. P. (in press), *The Psychology of Fundamentalism.* New York: Guilford.

Hooykaas, R. (1972), *Religion and the Rise of Modern Science.* Grand Rapids, MI: Eerdmans.

Hout, M. & Fischer, C. S. (2002), Why more Americans have no religious preference: Politics and generations. *Amer. Sociolog. Rev.,* 67:165–190.

Howard, G. S. (1991), Culture tales: A narrative approach to thinking, cross-cultural psychology. *Amer. Psychol.,* 46:187–197.

Iannaccone, L. R. (1996a), Reassessing church growth: statistical pitfalls and their consequences. *J. Sci. Study Religion,* 35:197–216.

Iannaccone, L. R. (1996b), Rejoinder to Hoge, Hadaway, and Marler: Pitfalls revisited. *J. Sci. Study Religion,* 35:226–228.

James, W. (1902), *The Varieties of Religious Experience.* New York: Collier, 1961.

Jenkins, P. (2002), *The Next Christendom.* New York: Oxford University Press.

Johnson, B., Hoge, D. & Luidens, D. (1993), Mainline churches: The real reason for decline. *First Things,* 31: 13–18.

Jones, A. (1985), *Soul Making.* San Francisco: HarperSanFrancisco.

Jones, E. (1953), *The Life and Work of Sigmund Freud, Vol. 1.* New York: Basic Books .

Jones, J. W. (1991), *Contemporary Psychoanalysis and Religion.* New Haven: Yale University Press.

Jones, J. W. (1996), *Religion and Psychology in Transition.* New Haven: Yale University Press.

Jones, J. W. (2002), *Terror and Transformation*. New York: Routledge.

Jordan, C. (1968), *The Cotton Patch Version of Paul's Epistles*. New York: Association Press.

Jordan, C. (1969), *The Cotton Patch Version of Luke and Acts*. New York: Association Press.

Jörskog, K. (1969), A general approach to confirmatory maximum likelihood factor analysis. *Psychometrika*, 34:183-202.

Jörskog, K. & Sorbom, D. (1979), *Advances in Factor Analysis and Structural Equation Models*. Cambridge, MA: Abt Books.

Jung, C. G. (1963), *Memories, Dreams and Reflections*. New York: Vintage Books.

Kant, I. (1787), *Critique of Pure Reason*, trans. N. K. Smith. London: Macmillan, 1963.

Kelley, D. M. (1972), *Why Conservative Churches Are Growing*. New York: Harper & Row.

Kenney, M. (1986), *Biotechnology: The University-Industrial Complex*. New Haven, CT: Yale University Press.

Kermode, F. (1985), Freud and interpretation. *Internat. Rev. Psycho-Anal.*, 12:3-12.

Kernberg, O. (1986), Institutional problems of psychoanalytic education. *J. Amer. Psychoanal. Assn.*, 34:799-834.

Kernberg, O. (1993), The current status of psychoanalysis. *J. Amer. Psychoanal. Assn.*, 41:45-62.

Kernberg, O. (1996), Thirty methods to destroy the creativity of candidates. *Internat. J. Psychoanal.*, 77:1031-1040.

Key, T. (1994), Impact of inpatient psychiatric treatment on object relations maturity, self-esteem, and God image. Unpublished doctoral dissertation. DAI, 55, 12B:5568. La Mirada, CA: Rosemead School of Psychology.

Kifner, J. (1994), Pollster finds error on Holocaust doubts. *The New York Times*, May 20, p. A12.

King, P. & Steiner, R. (1990), *The Freud/Klein Controversies*. London: Routledge Chapman & Hall.

Kirkpatrick, L. A. (1999), Attachment and religious representations and behavior. In: *Handbook of Attachment*, ed. J. Cassidy & P. Shaver. New York: Guilford Press, pp. 803-822.

Kirsner, D. (1990), Mystics and professionals in the culture of American psychoanalysis. *Free Assoc.*, 20:85-103.

Kirsner, D. (1996), The radical edge. Presented to the San Francisco Psychoanalytic Institute, San Francisco, CA, November 1.

Kirsner, D. (2000), *Unfree Associations*. London: Process Press.

Köbler, R. (1989), *In the Shadow of Karl Barth: Charlotte Von Kirschbaum*. Louisville, KY: Westminster/J. Knox Press.

Koenig, H. (1998), *Handbook of Religion and Mental Health*. San Diego: Academic Press.

Kohon, G. (1986), Notes on the history of the psychoanalytic movement in Great Britain. In: *The British School of Psychoanalysis*, ed. G. Kohon. New Haven, CT: Yale University Press, pp. 24-50.

Kohut, H. (1985), *Self Psychology and the Humanities*. New York: Norton.

Kosmin, B. & Lachman, S. (1993), *One Nation Under God*. New York: Crown.

Kuhn, T. S. (1962), *The Structure of Scientific Revolutions*. Chicago: University of Chicago Press.

Kuhn, T. S. (1963), The function of dogma in scientific research. In: *Scientific Change*, ed. A. C. Crombie. New York: Basic Books, pp. 347-395.

Lakatos, I. (1970), Falsification and the methodology of scientific research programmes. In: *Criticism and the Growth of Knowledge*, ed. I. Lakatos & A. Musgrave. Cambridge, UK: Cambridge University Press, pp. 91–196.

LaMothe, R., Arnold, J. & Crane, J. (1998), The penumbra of religious discourse. *Psychoanal. Psychol.*, 15:63–73.

Laor, N. (1989), Psychoanalytic neutrality toward religious experience. *The Psychoanalytic Study of the Child*, 44:211–230. New Haven, CT: Yale University Press.

Laudan, L. (1977), *Progress and Its Problems*. Berkeley: University of California Press.

Laudan, L. (1983), The demise of the demarcation problem. In: *Physics, Philosophy, and Psychoanalysis*, ed. R. S. Cohen & L. Laudan. Dordrecht, Holland: Reidel Publishing, pp. 111–127.

Lawrence, R. T. (1991), The God Image Inventory: The Development, Validation, and Standardization of a Psychometric Instrument for Research, Pastoral and Clinical Use in Measuring the Image of God. Unpublished doctoral dissertation. DAI, 52, 03A:0952. Washington, DC: The Catholic University of America.

Lawrence, R. T. (1997), Measuring the image of God: The God image inventory and the God image scales. *J. Psychol. & Theol.*, 25:214–226.

Leavy, S. A. (1990), Reality in religion and psychoanalysis. In: *Psychoanalysis and Religion*, ed. J. H. Smith & S. A. Handelman. Baltimore, MD: Johns Hopkins University Press, pp. 95–116.

Leavy, S. A. (1980), *The Psychoanalytic Dialogue*. New Haven, CT: Yale University Press.

Leavy, S. A. (1982), Questioning authority: The contribution of psychoanalysis to religion. *Cross Currents*, 32:129–142.

Leavy, S. A. (1988), *In the Image of God*. New Haven, CT: Yale University Press.

Lederman, L. (1993), *The God Particle*. Boston: Houghton Mifflin.

Lehman, E. C. & Shriver, D. W., Jr. (1968), Academic discipline as predictive of faculty religiosity. *Social Forces*, 47:171–182.

Leuba, J. H. (1950), *The Reformation of the Churches*. Boston: Beacon Press.

Lewis, C. S. (1970), *God in the Dock*, ed. W. Hooper. Grand Rapids, MI: Eerdmans.

Lichtenberg, J. D. (1985), Humanism and the science of psychoanalysis. *Psychoanal. Inq.*, 5:343–367.

Lindbeck, G. A. (1984), *The Nature of Doctrine*. Philadelphia: Westminster Press.

Lindberg, D. C. (1986), Science and the early church. In: *God and Nature*, ed. D. C. Lindberg & R. L. Numbers. Berkeley, CA: University of California Press, pp. 19–43.

Lindberg, D. C. & Numbers, R. L., eds. (1986), *God and Nature*. Berkeley, CA: University of California Press.

Little, M. (1990), *Psychotic Anxieties and Containment: A Personal Record of an Analysis with Winnicott*. Northvale, NJ: Aronson.

Loewald, H. (1978), *Psychoanalysis and the History of the Individual*. New Haven, CT: Yale University Press.

Loewald, H. (1980), *Papers on Psychoanalysis*. New Haven, CT: Yale University Press.

Loewald, H. (1988), *Sublimation*. New Haven, CT: Yale University Press.

Luborsky, L., Singer, B. & Luborsky, L. (1975), Comparative studies of psychotherapies: Is it true that "everyone has won and all must have prizes"? *Arch. Gen. Psychiat.*, 32:995–1008.

Luborsky, L, Diguer, L., Seligman, D. A., Rosenthal, R., Krause, E. D., Johnson, S.,

Halperin, G., Bishop, M., Berman, J. S. & Schweizer, E. (1999), The researcher's own therapy alliances: A 'wild card' in comparisons of treatment efficacy. *Clin. Psychol.: Sci. & Pract.*, 6:95–132.

MacIntyre, A. (1997), *After Virtue*, 2nd ed. South Bend, IN: University of Notre Dame Press.

Magee, B. (1997), *Confessions of a Philosopher.* New York: Random House.

Mahler, M. S., Pine, F. & Bergman, A. (1975), *The Psychological Birth of the Human Infant.* New York: Basic Books.

Marsden, G. A. (1994), *The Soul of the American University.* New York: Oxford University Press.

Marty, M. E. & Appleby, F. S., eds. (1991–1995), *The Fundamentalism Project, Vols. 1–5.* Chicago: The University of Chicago Press.

Masson, J. M. (1990), Anna Freud and I. *Tikkun*, 5:23–25, 98–99.

Masson, J. M., ed. & trans. (1985), *The Complete Letters of Sigmund Freud to Wilhelm Fliess, 1887–1904.* Cambridge, MA: Harvard University Press.

McClendon, W. J. (1990), *Biography as Theology.* Valley Forge, PA: Trinity Press International.

McDargh, J. (1983), *Psychoanalytic Object Relations Theory and the Study of Religion.* Lanham, MD: University Press of America.

McDargh, J. (1993), Concluding clinical postscript: On developing a psychotheological perspective. In: *Exploring Sacred Landscapes*, ed. M. Randour. New York: Columbia University Press, pp. 172–193.

McFarling, U. L. (2000), A flat universe? Discovery solves a baffling puzzle: It is hard to visualize, but the cosmos can be likened to a sheet of cardboard—in three dimensions. *Los Angeles Times*, April 27, p. A1.

McGuire, W., ed. (1974), *The Freud/Jung Letters*, trans. R. Manheim & R. F. C. Hull. Princeton, NJ: Princeton University Press.

Meehl, P. (1973), Why I do not attend case conferences. In: *Psychodiagnosis.* Kingsport, TN: Kingsport Press, pp. 225-323.

Meissner, W. W. (1984), *Psychoanalysis and Religious Experience.* New Haven, CT: Yale University Press.

Meissner, W. W. (1990), The role of transitional conceptualization in religious thought. In: *Psychoanalysis and Religion*, ed. H. Smith & S. A. Handelman. Baltimore: Johns Hopkins University Press, pp. 95–116.

Meissner, W. W. (1992), *Ignatius of Loyola.* New Haven, CT: Yale University Press.

Meng, H. & Freud, E. L., eds. (1963), *Psychoanalysis and Faith.* New York: Basic Books.

Menninger, K. (1958), *Theory of Psychoanalytic Technique.* New York: Basic Books.

Merton, R. (1970), *Science and Technology in 17th Century England.* New York: H. Fertig.

Mitchell, S. A. (1988), *Relational Concepts in Psychoanalysis.* Cambridge, MA: Harvard University Press.

Mitchell, S. A. (1991), Editorial philosophy. *Psychoanal. Dial.*, 1:1-7.

Mitchell, S. A. (1992), Introduction to symposium: "What does the analyst know?" *Psychoanal. Dial.*, 2:279-286.

Mitchell, S. A. (1993), *Hope and Dread in Psychoanalysis.* New York: Basic Books.

Monk, R. (1990), *Ludwig Wittgenstein.* New York: Penguin Books.

Moore, J. R. (1979), *The Post-Darwinian Controversies.* Cambridge, UK: Cambridge University Press.

Moore, T. (2002), *The Soul's Religion*. San Francisco: HarperCollins.

Mumford, L. (1934), *Technics and Civilization*. New York: Harcourt, Brace.

Murphy, N. (1990), *Theology in the Age of Scientific Reasoning*. Ithaca, NY: Cornell University Press.

Murphy, N. (1997), *Anglo-American Postmodernity*. Boulder, CO: Westview Press.

Neuhaus, R. J. (2000), Secularization in theory and fact. *First Things*, 104:86–89.

Newberg, A. & D'Aquili, E. (2001), *Why God Won't Go Away*. New York: Ballantine Books.

Nicholi, A. M. (2002), *The Question of God*. New York: Free Press.

Nietzsche, F. (1954), *Thus Spoke Zarathustra*, trans. W. Kaufmann. New York: Viking Press.

Noam, G. & Wolf, M. (1993), Psychology and spirituality: Forging a new relationship. In: *Exploring Sacred Landscapes*, ed. M. Randour. New York: Columbia University Press, pp. 194–207.

Nunberg, H. & Federn, E., eds. (1962), *Minutes of the Vienna Psychoanalytic Society, Vol. 1, 1906–1908*. New York: International Universities Press.

Ogden, T. (1989), *The Primitive Edge of Experience*. Northvale, NJ: Aronson.

Osgood, C., Suci, G. & Tannenbaum, P. (1957), *The Measurement of Meaning*. Urbana, IL: University of Illinois Press.

Pargament, K. (1997), *The Psychology of Religion and Coping*. New York: Guilford.

Pargament, K. (2002), The bitter and the sweet: An evaluation of the costs and benefits of religiousness. *Psycholog. Inq.*, 13:168–181.

Pelikan, J. (1984), *The Vindication of Tradition*. New Haven, CT: Yale University Press.

Pfister, O. (1993), The illusion of a future: A friendly disagreement with Prof. Sigmund Freud. *Internat. J. Psycho-Anal.*, 74:557–579 (1928).

Polanyi, M. (1958), *Personal Knowledge*. Chicago: University of Chicago Press.

Postman, N. (1993), *Technopoly*. New York: Vintage Books.

Powell, L. H., Shahabi, L. & Thorsen, C. E. (2003), Religion and spirituality: Linkages to physical health. *Amer. Psychol.*, 58:36–52.

Pruyser, P. W. (1974), *Between Belief and Unbelief*. New York: Harper & Row.

Radó, S. (1932), The paths of natural science in the light of psychoanalysis. *Psychoanal. Quart.*, 1:688–700.

Randour, M. L., ed. (1993), *Exploring Sacred Landscapes*. New York: Columbia University Press.

Rayner, E. (1991), *The Independent Mind in British Psychoanalysis*. New York: Aronson.

Redman, C. (1990), An island no more. *Time*, November 12, p. 49.

Reeves. T. C. (1996), *The Empty Church*. New York: Free Press.

Regan, C., Malony, H. N. & Beit-Hallahmi, B. (1980), Psychologists and religion: Professional factors and personal belief. *Rev. Religious Research*, 21:208–217.

Rice, E. (1994), Reply to Randour. *Psychoanal. Books*, 5:481–484.

Richards, P. S. & Bergin, A. E. (2000), *Handbook of Psychotherapy and Religious Diversity*. Washington, DC: APA Books.

Richardson, F. C., Fowers, B. J. & Guignon, C. (1999), *Re-Envisioning Psychology*. San Francisco: Jossey-Bass.

Ricoeur, P. (1970), *Freud and Philosophy*. New Haven, CT: Yale University Press.

Rieff, P. (1959), *Freud: The Mind of the Moralist*. New York: Viking.

Rieff, P. (1966), *The Triumph of the Therapeutic*. New York: Harper & Row.

Ringstrom, P. (2002), Thoughts on September 11th, 2001. In: *Terrorism and War: Unconscious Dynamics of Political Violence*, ed. C. Covington, P. Williams, J. Arundale & J. Knox. London: Karnac, pp. 35-49.

Rizzuto, A. (1979), *The Birth of the Living God*. Chicago: University of Chicago Press.

Rizzuto, A. (1998), *Why Did Freud Reject God?* New Haven, CT: Yale University Press.

Roof, W. C. (1999), *Spiritual Marketplace*. Princeton, NJ: Princeton University Press.

Roof, W. C. & McKinney, W. (1987), *American Mainline Religion*. New Brunswick, NJ: Rutgers University Press.

Ross, N. (1958), Psychoanalysis and religion. *J. Amer. Psychoanal. Assn.*, 6:519-539.

Rubin, J. B. (1996), *Psychotherapy and Buddhism*. New York: Plenum Press.

Rubin, J. B. (1998), *A Psychoanalysis for Our Time*. New York: New York University Press.

Rudnytsky, P. (1991), *The Psychoanalytic Vocation*. New Haven, CT: Yale University Press.

Rycroft, C. (1985), *Psychoanalysis and Beyond*. London: Hogarth Press.

Safran, J., ed. (2003), *Psychoanalysis and Buddhism*. Essex, UK: Wisdom Publications.

Saler, B. (1993), *Conceptualizing Religion*. New York: Basic Books.

Sanderson, W. (1995), Which therapies are proven effective? *APA Monitor*, 26:4.

Sandler, A-M. (1990), Comments on varieties of psychoanalytic training in Europe. In: *Tradition and Innovation in Psychoanalytic Education*, ed. M. Meisels & E. Shapiro. Hillsdale, NJ: Lawrence Erlbaum, pp. 45-58.

Sarbin, T. (1986), *Narrative Psychology*. New York: Praeger.

Sass, L. A. (1993), Psychoanalysis as "conversation" and as "fiction": Commentary on Charles Spezzano's "A Relational Model of Inquiry and Truth" and Richard Geha's "Transferred Fictions." *Psychoanal. Dial.*, 3:245-253.

Sass, L. A. (1999), Review of Hoffman's *Ritual and Spontaneity*. *J. Amer. Psychoanal. Assn.*, 47:899-906.

Schaefer, C. & Gorsuch, R. (1992), Dimensionality of religion: Belief and motivation as predictors of behavior. *J. Psychol. & Christianity*, 11:244-254.

Schafer, R. (1990), Narration in the psychoanalytic dialogue. *Critical Inq.*, 7:29-53.

Schlauch, C. R. (1999), Classical and contemporary psychoanalytic interpretations of the self: Implications for religion and the study of religion. In: *Psychological Perspectives and the Religious Quest*, ed. L. J. Rector & W. Santaniello. Lanham, MD: University Press of America, pp. 105-123.

Schwaber, E. (1986), Reconstruction and perceptual experience: Further thoughts on psychoanalytic listening. *J. Amer. Psychoanal. Assn.*, 34:911-932.

Schwaber, E. (1990), Interpretation and the therapeutic action of psychoanalysis. *Internat. J. Psycho-Anal.*, 71:229-240.

Schwartz, S. H. & Huismans, S. (1995), Value priorities and religiosity in four Western religions. *Soc. Psychol. Quart.*, 58:88-107.

Searles, H. (1979), *Countertransference and Related Subjects*. New York: International Universities Press.

Seeman, T. E., Dubin, L. F. & Seeman, M. (2003), Religiosity/spirituality and health: A critical review of the evidence for biological pathways. *Amer. Psychol.*, 58:53-63.

Selinger, S. (1998), *Charlotte von Kirschbaum and Karl Barth*. University Park, PA: Pennsylvania State University Press.

Sendak, M. (1963), *Where the Wild Things Are*. New York: Harper & Row.

Shafranske, E. P. (1996a), *Religion and the Clinical Practice of Psychology*. Washington, DC: APA Books.

Shafranske, E. P. (1996b), Religious beliefs, affiliations, and practices of clinical psychologists. In: *Religion and the Clinical Practice of Psychology*, ed. E. P. Shafranske. Washington, DC: APA Books, pp. 149–162.

Smith, J. H. & Handelman, S. A. (1990), *Psychoanalysis and Religion*. Baltimore: Johns Hopkins University Press.

Smith, T. W. (2001), *Religious Diversity in America*. Chicago: National Opinion Research Center, University of Chicago.

Smith, W. C. (1963), *The Meaning and End of Religion*. New York: Macmillan.

Sorenson, A. L. (1990), Psychoanalytic perspectives on religion: The illusion has a future. *J. Psychol. & Theol.*, 18:209–217.

Sorenson, R. L. (1994a), Sea changes, interesting complements, and tormented souls. *J. Psychol. & Theol.*, 22:319–321.

Sorenson, R. L. (1994b), Therapists' (and their therapists') God representations in clinical practice. *J. Psychol. & Theol.*, 22:325–344.

Spence, D. P. (1982), *Narrative Truth and Historical Truth*. New York: Norton.

Spence, D. P. (1987), *The Freudian Metaphor*. New York: Norton.

Spence, D. P. (1994), *The Rhetorical Voice of Psychoanalysis: Displacement of Evidence by Theory*. Cambridge, MA: Harvard University Press.

Spero, M. (1992), *Religious Objects as Psychological Structures: A Critical Integration of Object Relations, Psychotherapy and Judaism*. Chicago: University of Chicago Press.

Spezzano, C. (1993a), A relational model of inquiry and truth: The place of psychoanalysis in the human conversation. *Psychoanal. Dial.*, 3:177–208.

Spezzano, C. & Gargiulo, G. J., eds. (1997), *Soul on the Couch*. Hillsdale, NJ: The Analytic Press.

Spitz, E. H. (1988), Picturing the child's inner world of fantasy. *The Psychoanalytic Study of the Child*, 43:433–447. New Haven, CT: Yale University Press.

Stein, R. (2002), Evil as love and liberation. *Psychoanal. Dial.*, 12:393–420.

Steiner, R. (1985), Some thoughts about tradition and change arising from an examination of the British psychoanalytical society's controversial discussions (1943–1944). *Internat. Rev. Psycho-Anal.*, 12:27–71.

Stern, D. B. (1992), Commentary on constructivism in clinical psychoanalysis. *Psychoanal. Dial.*, 2:331–363.

Stern, D. B. (1994), Empathy is interpretation (and whoever said it wasn't?). *Psychoanal. Dial.*, 4:441–471.

Stern, D. B. (1997), *Unformulated Experience*. Hillsdale, NJ: Analytic Press.

Stern, D. N. (1985), *The Interpersonal World of the Infant*. New York: Basic Books.

Stolorow, R. D., Brandchaft, B. & Atwood, G. (1987), *Psychoanalytic Treatment*. Hillsdale, NJ: The Analytic Press.

Stolorow, R. D. & Atwood, G. (1992), *Contexts of Being*. Hillsdale, NJ: The Analytic Press.

Stolorow, R. D. & Atwood, G. (1993), *Faces in a Cloud*. New York: Aronson.

Strenger, C. (1991), Between hermeneutics and science. *Psychological Issues, Monogr. 59*. Madison, CT: International Universities Press.

Sykes, C. (1988), *Profscam: Professors and the Demise of Higher Education*. Washington, DC: Regnery Gateway.

Symington, N. (1983), The analyst's act of freedom as agent of therapeutic change. *Internat. Rev. Psycho-Anal.*, 10:283–291.

Symington, N. (1986), *The Analytic Experience.* New York: St. Martin's Press.

Taylor, C. (2002), *Varieties of Religion Today.* Cambridge: Harvard University Press.

Thiemann, R. (1985), *Revelation and Theology.* Notre Dame: University of Notre Dame Press.

Tillich, P. (1952), *The Courage to Be.* New Haven, CT: Yale University Press.

Tillich, P. (1958), *The Dynamics of Faith.* New York: Harper.

Tisdale, T. C., Brokaw, B. F., Edwards, K. J. & Key, T. L. (1993), Impact of psycho-therapy treatment on level of object relations development, God image, and self-esteem. Presented at the Annual Convention of the American Psychological Association, Toronto, Ontario, August 22.

Tooley, M. (1995), Madness in their methodism. *Heterodoxy,* May 6.

Toulmin, S. (1961), *Foresight and Understanding.* New York: Harper.

Toulmin, S. (1990), *Cosmopolis: The Hidden Agenda of Modernity.* New York: Free Press.

Ulanov, A. & Ulanov, B. (1983), *Cinderella and Her Sisters.* Philadelphia: Westminster Press.

Van Herik, J. (1982), *Freud, Femininity and Faith.* Berkeley: University of California Press.

Vitz, P. C. (1990), The use of stories in moral development: New psychological reasons for an old education method. *Amer. Psychol.,* 45:709–720.

Vitz, P. C. (1992a), Narratives and counseling, part 1: From analysis of the past to stories about it. *J. Psychol. & Theol.,* 20:11–19.

Vitz, P. C. (1992b), Narratives and counseling, part 2: From stories of the past to stories for the future. *J. Psychol. & Theol.,* 20:20–27.

Vitz, P. C. (1993), *Sigmund Freud's Christian Unconscious.* Grand Rapids, MI: Eerdmans.

Volkan, V. (1988), *The Need to Have Enemies and Allies.* New York: Aronson.

Von Glaserfeld, E. (1984), An introduction to radical constructivism. In: *The Invented Reality,* ed. P. Watzlawick. New York: Norton, pp. 17–40.

Wachtel, P. L. (1977), *Psychoanalysis and Behavior Therapy.* New York: Basic Books.

Wachtel, P. L. (1981), Transference, schema, and assimilation: The relevance of Piaget to the psychoanalytic theory of transference. *The Annual of Psychoanalysis, Vol. 8.* New York: International Universities Press, pp. 59–76.

Wachtel, P. L. (1993), *Therapeutic Communication.* New York: Guilford.

Waller, J. (2002), *Becoming Evil.* New York: Oxford University Press.

Wallerstein, R. S. (1988), One psychoanalysis or many? *Internat. J. Psycho-Anal.,* 69: 5–21.

Wallerstein, R. S. (1990), Psychoanalysis: The common ground. *Internat. J. Psycho-Anal.,* 71:3–20.

Wallerstein, R. (1996), Psychoanalytic education and research: A transformative proposal. *Psychoanal. Inq.,* 11:196–226.

Watzlawick, P. (1984), Self-fulfilling prophecies. In: *The Invented Reality,* ed. P. Watzlawick. New York: Norton, pp. 95–116.

Watzlawick, P. (1990), *Münchausen's Pigtail.* New York: Norton.

Weber, M. (1972), *Economy and Society,* ed. G. Roth & C. Wittich. Berkeley: University of California Press, 1978.

Welch, C. (1996), Dispelling some myths about the split between theology and science in the nineteenth century. In: *Religion and Science,* ed. W. M. Richardson & W. J. Wildman. New York: Routledge, pp. 29–40.

White, A. D. (1896), *A History of the Warfare of Science with Theology in Christendom.* New York: D. Appleton.

White, H. (1973), *Metahistory*. Baltimore, MD: Johns Hopkins University Press.

White, L. (1960), *The Unconscious Before Freud*. New York: Basic Books.

Wildman, W. J. (1996), The quest for harmony: An interpretation of contemporary theology and science. In: *Religion and Science*, ed. W. M. Richardson & W. J. Wildman. New York: Routledge, pp. 41–60.

Wile, D. B. (1985), Psychotherapy by precedent: Unexamined legacies from pre-1920 psychoanalysis. *Psychotherapy*, 22:793–802.

Winnicott, D. W. (1971), *Playing and Reality*. London: Tavistock.

Winnicott, D. W. (1975), *Through Paediatrics to Psychoanalysis*. New York: Basic Books.

Winnicott, D. W. (1967), D. W. W. on D. W. W. In: *Psychoanalytic Explorations*, ed. C. Winnicott, R. Shepherd & M. Davis. Cambridge, MA: Harvard University Press, 1989, pp. 569–582.

Wolman, B., ed. (1995), *Psychoanalysis and Catholicism*. Northvale, NJ: Aronson.

Wolterstorff, N. (1976), *Reason Within the Bounds of Religion*. Grand Rapids, MI: Eerdmans.

Worthington, E. L., Jr., Kurusu, T. A., McCullough, M. E. & Sandage, S. J. (1996), Empirical research on religion and psychotherapeutic processes and outcomes: A 10-year review and research prospectus. *Psycholog. Bull.*, 119:448–487.

Wuthnow, R. C. (1998), *After Heaven*. Berkeley: University of California Press.

Zukav, G. (1984), *The Dancing Wu Li Masters*. New York: Bantam Doubleday.

Index